CW01496812

UK Economic and Social Change

1700-2019

Three Centuries of Progress

*Being an investigation of the evidence that reveals the **best known facts** regarding the quantifiable economic and social history of the peoples of the United Kingdom of Great Britain and Northern Ireland (but particularly the English peoples) since the 18th century; including their population, economy, the role of the state, earnings, income inequality, living costs, household expenditure, housing, the retreat of real poverty, the air quality of their environment and their life expectancy.*

Collated, graphically presented with text written by:

J. R. Cooper

A data collation, analysis and presentation conducted from 2017 to 2023; but also founded upon five decades of the study of history, economics and the sociology of life and its political manifestations. Sources are derived from the most respected academic, authoritative and best researched origins. All underpinned by the thorough use of valid mathematical principles and the scientific methodology.

Title font Georgia
Text font Cambria
Chart font Arial

Self published with IngramSpark
Printed by Lightning Source UK Ltd.

Paperback (2023)   ISBN: 978-1-7395094-6-0
Hardback (2023)   ISBN: 978-1-7395094-0-8
Supplementary Volume 1 (2023)   ISBN: 978-1-7395094-1-5
Supplementary Volume 2 (2023)   ISBN: 978-1-7395094-2-2
Supplementary Volume 3 (2023)   ISBN: 978-1-7395094-3-9
Supplementary Volume 4 (2024)   ISBN: 978-1-7395094-4-6
Exploring Climate History (2024)   ISBN: 978-1-7395094-5-3

Dedication

Dedicated to my mother, father, sister and grandmothers.

Thank you for your unconditional love, care, support, guidance and tolerance (of which you needed a great deal).

To my maternal grandmother, who knew great hardship throughout her life, losing her father when she was aged three, losing her third baby in infancy, my grandfather in and out of work throughout the 1930's; with many debilitating consequences to her health and well-being.

To my paternal grandmother, losing her mother when she was six, forced to foster her first son (my father) for the first six years of his life due to extreme hardship in the 1930's; losing her second baby in infancy.

But also dedicated to my maternal great-grandmother, a lady I never met, but who was clearly a very resourceful and strong lady.

She was widowed in 1909, aged 32, with 3 young children (including her youngest, my maternal grandmother) and pregnant with her fourth child.

With only the Poor Law to turn to, instead she picked stones from local farmer's fields for coppers (old farthings, halfpennies and pennies) and took in washing.

She has described herself in the 1911 census as "Charwoman".

She had been forced to give her fourth child into the permanent care of her parents at her birth, yet still mistakenly listed her in her 1911 census return, before crossing her out from that return.

In 1926 her eldest daughter and son-in-law both died of tuberculosis within months of each other, leaving her to bring up her first new-born grandchild. Then in 1938 her eldest son also died of tuberculosis.

These ladies and the millions of other people of the time and all the millennia before, knew what **real poverty** was and struggled through.

Acknowledgements

I feel honoured to be able to thank several good friends for their reviews of aspects of the initial research, the presentations I have built of my findings, their notes and references and now this book.

In particular I thank Bill Young, a very good friend for many years now, for his careful and forensic checking of my blunders and his guidance regarding the understand-ability of the data, as I have tried to present it. Also MS for his checking of my presentations and then the pre-publication edition of this book, chapter by chapter, using his printer's and type-setter's eye to try to avoid blunders on the page, as well as the understanding of the narrative and spotting my many "apostrophic" errors.

I have also carefully checked the graphics and my explanations of these with my Mother in particular, as she has very strong views on politics and social organisation which I must confess are not at all in accord with my own in many respects. This has helped enormously to keep me scrupulously levelled in all facets of my interpretation of my findings.

Also I am very grateful further to Bill Young, my Mother, Rachel Turner and Alaine Mardle for their reading of the first printed draft and their notes and corrections of my errors and the oversights they have found therein and their suggestions for improvements throughout.

I have tried my very best to be even-handed and driven entirely by the "facts", the **best known facts** I could find from the evidence. All in the light of my natural and overpowering scepticism of all loud mantras of faith and ideologies (religious or secular).

If I have failed to be scrupulously honest, even-handed and factually correct then that is my error and no one else's.

Table of Contents

Life Expectancy 181

Summary 201

Afterword 215

References................227

Bibliography, Selected Reading and Internet Data ... 241

Index................263

List of Figures

"What is the use of a book', thought
Alice, 'without pictures...'"

Lewis Carroll
(Charles Lutwidge Dodgson):
Alice's Adventures in Wonderland,
1865

Foreword

"[The English language] *becomes ugly and*
inaccurate because our thoughts are foolish, but
the slovenliness of our language makes it easier for
us to have foolish thoughts... if thought corrupts
language, language can also corrupt thought."

George Orwell:
Politics and the English Language,
1946

Origins of this work

This book, and the project that gave rise to it, found their gestation in an accumulation of headlines and narratives in public discourse that burst fully upon my consciousness in 2017.

The particular words and phrases, and their underlying intent, that drew my attention at the time, were centred upon the chastisement of the owners of diesel internal combustion engine powered motor vehicles (though it is quite clear that much of the narrative around the claimed issues is actually inspired by general dislike, if not loathing, by certain groups of people, of private and personal transport).

At the same time a growing clamour of claims of housing "*shortage*" reached a crescendo as well, though this had been bubbling on and off for a decade before, thanks to the 2007/2008 economic crash.

Then to add to the multi-faceted and sweeping claims about how terrible life is in 21st century Britain (UK), was the oft repeated use of the word "*poverty*" about some lives of economic struggle and hardship, that yet did not seem remotely as "*poor*" or challenging as those of millions upon millions of people throughout Britain's history, nor still billions of people in the world beyond the UK in the 21st century.

Thus, from a consideration of both initial scepticism (a natural state of mind for myself and the essence of the scientific method) and to seek out the best known facts about these and related matters from the evidence, I started researching these topics in terms of established, proven, measured and statistically rigorous sources, whilst also improving my understanding of the semantics and meaning of words used over and over again in public discourse.

Research

The internet, which all too often seems to encourage the amplification of self-referential, introspective and emotive clamour in place of careful, balanced and considered factual research-based discussion and debate, actually proved to be an invaluable tool. With thorough and persistent searching I was able to access hundreds of digital forms of papers, books and data from the most respected academic and research sources from around the world, including many digitised versions of old and new writings of the foremost contributors to the analysis of socio-economic history of the peoples of the United Kingdom.

Thus, this project is not original research by me, but the collation of the research of others, documented in detail in references and bibliography.

The period from 1700 was chosen as the start point, being the effective end of the Stuart age (the reign of Queen Anne permitting) and the 1707 union of England & Wales with Scotland and the formation of the United Kingdom of Great Britain.

The intent finally developed to end the analysis in the year 2019 (fiscal and calendar) before the onset of the Coronavirus Pandemic, as the latter and Government reactions to it, and consequent devastation of the economies of the world, are shocks with consequences yet to reveal themselves in the coming decades.

In particular reaching back to 1700 (the 18th century) appeared a reasonable compromise in so far as reliable data, quantifying most aspects of social and economic history, become very rare before that century.

Declaring preferences and interests

It is an axiom of both research and social and economic discourse that honesty, transparency and factual accuracy are central to the reliability of any claims, arguments or propositions made supporting political or campaigning positions.

It is therefore imperative to use some version of the scientific methodology in the sphere of social, economic and historical research, as best as is possible, even in the light of the data generally being less rigorous than is normally the case in natural science investigations.

As such the key principles I have based all my analysis upon are:

- Science is always sceptical
- Science is never settled
- Consensus is not scientific
- Faith is not scientific

Accordingly, whilst qualitative history is invaluable and enlightening, it is essential that we seek to discover the quantitative measures that support or undermine those qualitative views, historical or contemporary.

As such we start from observation, we then form an hypothesis, which we then test, and once enough observations and hypotheses have been tested producing consistent results, we may start to form a "theory" (or view) with some reliability and evidential support.

Fortunately a large number of social and economic academics from around the world have undertaken decades (if not centuries) of thorough quantitative research in parallel with the many historians; combining the older history with modern (20th century onward) survey based analysis, all underpinned with the data from government records and, of course, the censuses (from 1801) for these 320 years.

Regarding my own "interests", my background is that of a working-class family (blue-collar, TV engineer and factory worker) who are amongst the millions to have benefited from the greatest age of progress and social mobility after the end of The Second World War. I was able to study History, Economics, Sociology, Mathematics and Physics at school then attend university to study Politics. As such I have always been a socially and economically aware person with a keen eye to justice and opportunity, but emphatically underpinned by economic, mathematical and physical reality. The essence of the Enlightenment and liberty.

I therefore declare myself, in my own estimation to be a "radical" in the traditional sense, from a time before the rise of the socialist, communist, and later fascistic mentality with their disparate variants. A radical more in the tradition of John and Elizabeth Lilburne, Mary Wollstonecraft, William Cobbett, John Stuart-Mill and Harriet Taylor; not a modern ideologue of the secular usurpation of those great religious traditions of self-righteous imposition of their faith upon others.

I was fortunate to be able to improve my own position in life by making maximum use of the opportunities of the expanding and transforming technological and economic revolution from the 1980s, in the world of IT, and I must declare that I was never in the position of many households, of being challenged to make ends meet.

From the world of IT I was able to learn the essential power and value of rigorous data processing techniques, which I have tried to use throughout this analysis.

Defining words used throughout

In so far as this book is focussed on the social and economic history of the peoples of the United Kingdom, it inevitably centres mostly on the financial well-being of the people of this nation-state and therefore intentionally focuses on the best known facts about their status from the evidence.

Of course it is another axiom of thought and discourse that all languages evolve. It is therefore important to establish what meanings of certain words will be used within, with some explanation of why they are used this way.

This is essential as all discussion around this is drawn, as if by imaginary gravitational forces, to the word "*poverty*" and its fellows in the modern English language.

Since all such terminology is never black and white, but is composed of infinite shades of grey, the word "*poverty*" will be used throughout in its more traditional sense, rather than that meaning adopted by certain academics and campaigners in modern times of "*relative poverty*"; this latter is centred around the multitude of methods that almost always reduce to measures more akin to inequality rather than "*real poverty*", as though the two were the same thing: which they most certainly are not.

Thus "*relative poverty*" is a valid attempt to establish the importance of social (and economic) exclusion from the benefits of society through the ages, as opposed to social (and economic) inclusion or participation.

However, it is notable that the modern meanings attached to two of the more emotionally charged words relevant to this analysis and discourse ("*poverty*" and "*pollution*"), have not evolved in any natural way, but have clearly been intentionally re-defined by several socio-politically motivated parties, clearly in order to harness the emotions the words invoke to their chosen causes.

This is of course quite dishonest, and it leaves very large numbers of people in the public both confused and sceptical and thus is all too often counterproductive in the manner of Peter crying Wolf at every rustle of leaves in the trees and undergrowth.

Note: the following definitions in italics are quoted verbatim from their sources, though with my bold emphasis.

Levels of hardship, poverty and destitution

Most people have some conception of poverty that invariably dates back to their years of education, though all too often vague and not well-defined.

Thus as follows, the conceptions I have tried to use here form a type of qualitative hierarchy, attempting to simplistically group shades of grey for practical purposes, clearly their meaning still being essentially relative.

Just about managing - Being a modern term describing a state of household finances in which the key decision makers are managing to pay the important household bills and expenses (food, housing, fuel & lighting and clothing & footwear), but invariably with limited spare to socially participate in all the modern benefits of economic riches.

Hardship - Being a state of household finances in which the key decision makers are struggling week to week or month to month to pay the important household bills and expenses.

Breadline - Being a state of household finances resulting in the poorest condition in which it is seen as acceptable to live. Being closely related to **subsistence**, defined by Oxford 2019 as *"the action or fact of maintaining oneself at a minimum level"*, as in "on the breadline".

Poverty - Being a state of household finances of *"not having enough material possessions or income for a person's needs"* (Merriam-Webster).

- *"The condition of having little or no wealth or material possessions; indigence, destitution, want (in various degrees)."* (Oxford Shorter English Dictionary 3rd edition 1983 from 1972 revision).

- *"the state of being extremely poor"* (Oxford 2019).

- *"lacking sufficient money to live at a standard considered comfortable or normal in a society"* (Oxford 2019).

This latter being akin to the modern term *"relative poverty"*, being:

- when a person cannot meet a minimum level of living standards, compared to others in the same time and place.

Where **Poor** is defined as:

- *"Having few, or no, material possessions; wanting means to procure the comforts, or the necessaries, of life; needy, destitute; specifically (esp. In legal use), so destitute as to be dependent on gifts or allowances for subsistence. In common use expressing various degrees of poverty. The opposite of rich or wealthy."* (Oxford Shorter English Dictionary 3rd edition 1983 from 1972 revision).

- *"A person is considered poor if his or her income level falls below some minimum level necessary to meet basic needs."* (World Bank)

Destitution/destitute - Being *"a state of poverty so extreme that one lacks the means to provide for oneself"* (Oxford 2019).

- *"Bereft of resources, "in want and misery"; now, without the means of bare subsistence, in absolute want."* (Oxford Shorter English Dictionary 3rd edition 1983 from 1972 revision).

Now often called *"absolute poverty"*. Often referred to as **distress**:

- economic distress is a condition in which an individual cannot acquire the essential resources for life, because they are unable to meet or cannot pay their financial obligations.

- *"severe problems caused by not having enough money, food, etc."* (Oxford 2019).

- *"Absolute poverty is the complete lack of the means necessary to meet basic personal needs, such as food, clothing, and shelter"* (Unesco).

We also have the advantage of some historical attempts to codify and define key words in the English language, particularly referring to the first attempt by Dr. Samuel Johnson in 1755, (here quoted verbatim).

Dr. Johnson 1755, defined **poor** as -

"(pauvre, French. Povre, Spanish) Not rich; indigent; necessitous; oppressed with want, (Pope)."

Where **Indigent** is defined as -

"(indigens, Latin) 1. Poor; needy; necessitous (Addison). 2. In want; wanting (Philips)."

And **Indigence/Indigency** *"(indigence, French. indigentia, Latin) Want; penury; poverty (Burnett)"*

We also have **pauper**, which appears regularly throughout older documentation and literature, defined by Dr. Johnson in 1755 as -

"(Latin) A poor person."

This latter evolved in the course of the eighteenth and nineteenth centuries to mean, more specifically, someone who called upon support of the "Poor Law" guardians in their *"distress"* and *need.* Thus in a later, much expanded edition of Dr. Johnson's dictionary, updated by Henry Todd (published in 1818), pauper is given as -

"(Latin) A poor person; one who receives alms."

This referring back to, and creating continuity with, the time before the establishment of the Elizabethan "Poor Law" 1558-1601, which were laws codified to address the disparate acts from the reign of Henry VIII upon the dissolution of the monasteries during the Tudor Reformation, the church previously being the most common giver of alms.

A particular word used extensively in the past, but now evolved is **Vagabond**, in modern terms recently colloquially and commonly known as a tramp and now a rough sleeper in public discourse.

Dr. Johnson 1755, defined **Vagabond** as – *"Adjective [vagabundus, low Latin. vagabond, French], 1. Wandering without any settled habitation; wanting a home. 2. Wandering; vagrant. Plus n.s. [from the adj.] 1. A vagrant; a wanderer, commonly, in a sense of reproach. 2. One that wanders illegally, without a settled habitation."*

"Shortage" and "Pollution" (air-quality)

Given the primary triggers for this research, analysis and book included claims of a *"shortage"* of housing (with a multitude of consequent issues that are claimed for this *"shortage"*) and claims of terrible *"pollution"* (air quality) causing deaths and ill-health (many pointing to the modern penchant for private transport in the form of motor cars); it is also essential to offer some precise meaning to these two words.

Shortage – *"Being a state of deficiency in quantity; the amount by which a sum of money, a supply of goods, or the like, is deficient."* (Oxford Shorter English Dictionary 3rd edition 1983 from 1972 revision).

In relation to housing, the claim implicit in the oft-used term *"housing-shortage"* is invariably meant to describe the relatively reduced home building rate since the 1980s in general, but more particularly during the first two decades of the 21st century.

Shortage in this case refers to a shortfall of available housing (dwellings) in relation to demand for homes from the public.

The primary evil claimed to be consequent upon this *"shortage"* are the large increases in house prices since 1997, therefore lack of "affordable", usually social housing, and subsequent over-crowding due to un-affordability.

Pollution – *"Being the action or condition of polluting, to make physically impure, foul or filthy; to dirty, stain, taint, befoul."* (Oxford Shorter English Dictionary 3rd edition 1983 from 1972 revision).

This research is limited entirely to the processes of pollution of the atmosphere, rather than the land, rivers or sea, since the narrative as mostly perpetuated in public discourse to 2019 is of some form of terrible health-debilitating and mortality-inducing air quality, focussed here upon road transport, as this is targeted as the worst *"polluter"* in the public narrative.

The imputation in the narrative seems to be that in some way such air-quality is worse than at some point in the past, though this is generally implied in the form of the narrative rather than being explicitly stated. The imputation is never substantiated.

The evolution of language

Referring back to the very first words of this foreword, being the quote from George Orwell (Eric Blair), we see innumerable examples of the slovenliness of language due to the foolishness of thought.

"Poverty"

From this discussion it is clear that the definitions of *"poverty"* and related terms are both social constructs that evolve over time as social and economic conditions change, but also point strongly towards an over-arching concept of a state of life and well-being in which hardship, need and want of the necessities of life are a reality for many and morally should be a concern for all.

In the early centuries the well-off and commonly even the less well-off also often applied very strong condemnatory moral judgement upon those in *"poverty"*.

In general many social, economic, political and philosophical commentators not only regarded the *"poor"*, in the manner of the bible, as an inevitable part of all societies, but also subject to some form of judgement upon their moral character. Thus, as the centuries passed, so emerged the concepts of the deserving and undeserving *"poor"*.

From these categorisations and definitions we also derive the often used terms of privilege, deprivation and disadvantage, these being closely related to the more academic terms of social inclusion/participation and hence social exclusion or "*relative poverty*".

Housing "shortage"

Regarding housing "*shortage*", almost the whole of the public discourse has ignored the core origins of the house price inflation, namely the boom of demand due to an enormous growth of easily accessed and relatively cheap (and ultimately cheapening) credit in the market from the mid-1990s onwards.

"Pollution" and air-quality

Regarding air-quality and its "*pollution*", this work concentrates upon those pollutants that are scientifically proven to cause lung irritation to air breathing mammals, particularly Nitrogen Dioxide (NO_2) and particulates and the trend over time of emissions and concentrations of these in the atmosphere of particularly densely populated cities. The yet more serious emissions of Sulphur Dioxide is touched upon, but thanks to the deprecation of the use of coal, and the improvements in the refining and burning of oil, this has thankfully fallen to comparatively minuscule levels in the 21st century in the UK.

> Note that the modern conflation of "*pollution*" with the presence of Carbon Dioxide (CO_2) in the atmosphere or its emission into the atmosphere, ignores the chemical molecular reality of CO_2.
>
> Thus it should be noted clearly that Carbon Dioxide is intentionally not discussed in relation to atmospheric "*pollution*" as, despite the US Supreme Court's 2007 ruling, the consequent US Environmental Protection Agency re-definition of CO_2 as a "*pollutant*" and widespread misuse of the word "*pollution*" in relation to CO_2 this, as with many such rulings and illogical, counter-scientific and counter-factual ideas in the 21st century, contradicts physical, chemical and biological reality!
>
> CO_2 is not a pollutant, it is one of the key constituents and sustainers of all life on Earth since the planet's formation, alongside Oxygen for almost all animal life, and of course water in its three states.

Introduction

*"Better 'first drafts of history' can be gleaned
from data...and from vital statistics."*

Steven Pinker:

Enlightenment Now,

2018

Synopsis

Events unfold before our eyes and we can either attempt to ignore them or, if we have an interest, attempt to understand them.

Herewith I am collating together the work and analysis of the academics, and the government departmental statistics and surveys over the years and centuries to attempt to present the best known facts about the quantifiable social and economic history leading to and consequent upon those events, and the actual evidence of the status of the much discussed housing "*shortage*", "*poverty*" and "*pollution*" (air quality).

Whilst there is a vast spectrum of vitally important topics that are within the realm of social and economic life and well-being, this work restricts itself to quantifiable data and information that bear directly upon these three much vaunted topics.

Understandably the further back in time we delve the less certain the data that is available to us (if any) to quantify historical events and the trends through time. This is inevitable as almost all economies and peoples throughout the world, including the UK, were less well off than today and as such had fewer available resources to devote to administrative and data gathering procedures.

It has thus fallen to academics to gather more and more evidence (often by proxy) of otherwise known events and trends that are documented in more qualitative ways than quantitative, in much of history, important and informative as these qualitative histories are.

What is covered within

The data used in this book is not based upon my own original research, but a collation of the outstanding research of the best qualified academics, individuals and departments of governments, throughout the world, who have and do study and analyse the economy of the UK and its constituent nations and peoples, over a very long period of time.

The book (and its structure) thus covers the following core topics.

The first five chapters (population, economy, income, inequality and living costs) establish the underlying numbers and changes over time that form the foundation of the discussion of the three topics of housing "*shortage*", "*poverty*" and "*pollution*" (air quality).

Each of these three topics is then explored in detail in the subsequent three chapters. A concluding chapter then presents the starkest representation of three centuries of progress, the life expectancy at birth and beyond, in years, of the people of the UK.

The findings of the best known facts and the improvement of the material quality of life for almost everyone living in the UK in 2019 is then summarised.

Finally this is followed by an afterword offering an analysis of the best known mortality effects of the Covid-19 pandemic of 2020 to 2021.

Population

The central history that underpins all others is the history of the population of the United Kingdom (focussing mostly upon their largest bordered components of Great Britain and England).

Population change over time is again well researched (particularly thanks to the seminal works of the late Professor Sir Anthony Wrigley and the late Dr. Roger Schofield), but is strongly underpinned for the period of this study by the nationwide introduction of the decadal census from 1801 and then registration of births, deaths and marriages from 1837.

Rates of population change over time and their drivers, including the aforesaid births and deaths, plus net migration to or from the country are discussed. The age demographic of the population and the long term life expectancy are both also highlighted.

Economy and State

The economic history will focus on the best measures of the annual results of the wealth creation efforts of individuals and organisations in the form of Gross Domestic Product or GDP (a set of measures and methods that have unfortunately been changed several times by successive governments, so do contain the usual uncertainties).

Also that component of the economy that is controlled by government bodies over time, through a multitude of forms of taxation etc. (Revenue) and the corresponding government expenditure (Spending) patterns over time. In addition the magnitude of debt carried by the nation as a whole, both at national level, but later touched upon within households, will be covered, as inevitably debt has implication for some sense of solvency and the need to actually service that debt with the creditors. This latter reducing the ability to spend on immediate consumption or otherwise accumulate savings and capital.

Of particular interest in relation to government controlled spending are historical military spending and the gradual evolution of greater social protection spending in the last century or so. It is this latter that has more direct implications for the social and economic well-being of the population, subject to the government of the nation and its policies, and are investigated in more detail in the third chapter **Earnings and Income**.

Also touched upon are the underlying shifts in the components of the nation's economy in the form of the move away from agriculture as the largest component of the economy, to the growth of industry and manufacturing, and in more recent decades the move again towards greater contribution from the service sector.

In each case there have been measurable declines and growths of contribution to the economy and of course employment, all with dramatic consequences for the population, their incomes and well-being accordingly.

Earnings and Income

The key driver for most people's economic and in turn social well-being, beyond their health, are their earnings and consequent income, since comparatively few have any independent form of "capital/asset" that could yield a "non-earned" income such as rent or profit.

The whole question of earnings and consequent income is of course very complicated, simply in so far as the enormous variance of working patterns in a large population, and the huge variance of those patterns over time is particularly extreme as we research deeper into the past.

Immediate questions arise of how we identify full-time working (a definition of which itself alone is highly changeable) versus part-time working, shift working, piece-working upon results and so-on, all with and without any bonuses and benefits.

Even these patterns change dramatically, for example the "normal" full time working week is generally agreed to have become much shorter for most earners over the decades and centuries.

In modern times (approximately three decades or perhaps marginally more) there is slightly better availability of regularly captured data, but data from the past has been the subject of very complex and detailed research and itself subject to great debates in the world of economics in academia.

This analysis has picked out three main threads of that thorny issue in order to keep the over-all trend as simple and consistent as possible. Firstly the work of Professor Gregory Clark (and the MeasuringWorth organisation) and his proposition for the average earnings of all "workers" including both "white collar"/"middle class" administrative workers and all "blue-collar"/"working-class" including agricultural labourers. Secondly the work mostly of the late Professor Charles Feinstein which focuses very heavily on all "blue-collar"/"working-class" including agricultural labours, but excluding the "white-collar"/"middle class" administrative workers. Finally as a separate sub-set of the Charles Feinstein series, at least until the eve of The Great War, a specific series of earnings analyses from Gregory Clark and Charles Feinstein amongst others (including A. Wilson Fox's analysis captured and slightly supplemented in the British Labour Statistics Historical Abstract, 1971) of agricultural labourers is considered. This allows us to track the relative changes of these series as well as to point back in the second chapter **Economy and State** to the otherwise documented changes in the balance of the economy and employment over the centuries covered.

In these cases the values tracked by the researchers are all, in effect, "full-time" employed and thus do not truly represent some magical average of weekly earnings regardless of hours worked per week or any other remunerations. They do thus miss the inequalities present in society within the very large share of the earning population between men and women for example, amongst several others, including the effects of mass unemployment at any point in time. But they do offer a consistent trend through time that does provide a well understood picture of improvement and progress over these centuries.

Income Inequality

We also have available the interesting and very useful, but sadly flawed, social tables of Gregory King (1688), Joseph Massie (1755/1759), Patrick Colquhoun (1798/1801/1803), William Ray Smee (1846) and Robert Dudley Baxter (1867); by using these tables, all being carefully analysed and updated using many other records that inform, by Professors Peter Lindert, Jeffrey Williamson and later Professor Robert Allen, we can start to see inequality trends over the early centuries.

These earlier tables are then combined with later analysis of Inland Revenue data by Professors Arthur Bowley, Peter Lindert/Jeffrey

Williamson and Peter Scott/James Walker (for 1911); plus the analysis of Peter Scott/James Walker along with R. B. Ainsworth (for 1937/1938), and again Scott/Walker (for 1949), and of course the Central Statistical Office (CSO) and Office for National Statistics (ONS) and Inland Revenue/Her Majesty's Revenue and Customs (HMRC) from 1992 to-date.

All this has been extensively analysed further with yet more supplemental information by the late Professor Anthony Atkinson, plus his collaborators.

All offer good correlated analysis of the previous Gregory Clark/Charles Feinstein et al. series, and allow us to glean some extended distribution of earnings analysis, in addition to the basic mean of weekly and annual earnings over time.

The question of the inequality of financial condition, both income (earnings) and wealth are very important pointers to potential economic, social and life outcomes for people.

It is probably almost universally agreed that too much inequality is very damaging to both social cohesion as well as to most peoples' ability to live a fulfilled life in any given society.

Slightly more controversial, thanks to the regular conflation of inequality with "*poverty*", is the idea that too much equality (at least attempts to enforce it) is liable to be as damaging to social cohesion and most peoples' ability to live fulfilled lives. This latter negative view of "too much equality", is, in the long term, thanks to the general likelihood that natural human incentive and enterprise is eroded, and can lead to the productivity of the economy as a whole being reduced.

Inevitably the debate then centres around the relative value judgements of "too little" and "too much"!

By using the social tables to represent the best known distributions in the more distant past, plus the analysed information from Inland Revenue/HMRC data, as documented above, gives the researchers a powerful tool to look at trends in, at least, earning and income inequality over slightly more than three centuries.

The representations of inequality include several widely used tools, including the Gini index, which attempts to give a single measure of inequality, where a Gini of 0 (or 0%) represents "complete" equality in which all of the recipients receive exactly the same income (or own the same wealth) and its-obverse, a Gini of 1 (or 100%), in which a single member of the group receives all the income (or owns all the wealth). Thus the higher the Gini, in general, the higher the level of inequality.

This is often supplemented with various ratios when the incomes of the top 10% of the recipients are compared with the bottom 10%, thus the 90/10 ratio, or similarly the 90/50 and 50/10 (where the 50% is also known as the median) which offers more nuance by identifying some level of varying inequality over the whole range.

All of these percentages or shares can be further disaggregated to increase our understanding of degrees of inequality from the very top to the very bottom of income, wealth and expenditure patterns.

Two supplements to these are then provided.

Firstly the Lorenz curve that represents what share of the population receive what share of the total income, in which unity is equivalent to a Gini of 0. Secondly a very useful representation, if achievable from the data, is to show what percentage of the income recipients (or households if such is available) are in receipt of calculated amounts of money (per week or per year) at each or at least critical points in time.

These methods can be used for income (earnings), disposable income and expenditure and also wealth.

For wealth, for the majority of people and households, another very useful indicator is the percentage of households who are owner-occupiers over time, and in most advanced economies, that percentage of renters of a private versus "*social*" or some form of collective or subsidised renting.

A mix of the methods are used within to help the reader understand the trends of inequality over time and reveal the most recent general state of inequality in the UK.

Cost of Living

Critical to the financial and social well-being of people is what is known as the "cost of living", in the form that people have to pay for the goods and services they need and choose to consume. The limiting factor, of course, is derived from the level of earnings and income at each equivalent point in time compared to the prevailing costs of the goods and services they need/desire to purchase.

These costs vary over time (almost always increasing, at least in the long term), but it then becomes necessary for earnings to increase in order to prevent people from becoming poorer in real terms. It is this process that gives rise to "inflation".

The academics have calculated many "Cost of Living Indices" (CLI) for the past along with government departments that gave rise ultimately to the "Retail Prices Index" (RPI) and its more modern variant the "Consumer Price Index" (CPI), plus the latter's multiple sub-variants including the "Consumer Price Index including Housing (owner occupied)" (CPIH).

By both tracking the prices of as many goods and services as practical over time, and changing the balance and weights of the items tracked to reflect real household and personal spending patterns as the economy develops and grows, a reasonable single index, or collection, can be built to allow an approximation of the "real" or effective change in standards of living experienced by people over these years.

This allows us to track "*the value of the pound in your pocket*", to paraphrase the late Harold Wilson.

Perhaps the most simple that is available, in a fairly reliable form, covering the whole 320 years of this analysis, is the price of bread.

Though for early years even its calculation is often heavily reliant on the wholesale grain market prices in some cases.

Of course "*man cannot live by bread alone*" and fortunately prices of other important items are moderately well tracked and have been well analysed for older history by dedicated academics. Also a general analysis of household spending patterns over time, linked to these goods and services, further substantiate the trends of the cost of living for people.

For modern times there are also major items that can be tracked and understood, including the cost of buying houses and flats, plus the cost of buying cars, these being the two largest expenditures, at least as single items, that the majority of people face in their lifetime.

In fact it is notable that the inflationary measures and pressures of house prices particularly, often yield very different values over time from the measure of consumable commodity goods and services, such as food and clothing.

Further complicating the cost of housing is that current interest rates for mortgages (and any deals that a prospective purchaser may be able to agree with a lender) often do not directly reflect the full purchase price of the house or flat, thus the ultimate cost of buying (servicing the mortgage debt), and even on occasions the rent a tenant might pay, do not move directly in line with the inflationary movement of other prices or earnings. Thus the importance of the ONS calculated CPIH in addition to the CPI.

Housing - "Shortage", Occupation, Ownership, Mortgage and Rental, Prices and House Building

Food and warmth (in the very temperate and in fact rather cool and damp climate of the UK of the last 320 years) are a human being's first essential source for the sustenance of life.

In a modern geographically non-nomadic society, the dwelling-place now rates equally with food and warmth as an essential source for the sustenance of life. With technological, economic and social progress these have also been joined by lighting, to artificially extend the length of the productive and enjoyable day.

Thus the whole question of housing comes to the fore both as a home and hearth as a personal and family benefit, but also as a form of market and a commodity over time.

Inevitably therefore, the quantity of housing is closely related to the size of the population and the essential number of households (and thus an idea of the number of people per household), plus of course the size and quality of housing for maintaining health.

Fortunately as with all other essential indicators of core social and economic health and progress, various academics and government departments, especially the late Dr. Alan Holmans, have researched, collated and analysed in detail the status of housing in the United Kingdom, covering the majority of the period within this work.

We are thus able to see not simply our consistently falling number of people living in each household, on average, as well as the rates of annual completed construction of housing; but also good estimates for the twentieth century onwards of the share of owner occupation against those who are renting. Before The Great War, owner-occupation was, of course, restricted to a very small minority of households.

These then inform the central measure and analysis of supply and demand for housing, and thus reveal any theoretical "*shortage*" at any point in time.

However the matters of supply and demand are equally, crucially, informed by the cost of housing, in the forms of rental costs or purchase price, and thus the availability of credit and loans and the cost of servicing same, namely mortgage repayment rates. These latter payments are driven by prevailing supply and availability of credit in the economy and the prevailing rates of interest charged to the borrower by the lender.

We will see that this latter relationship appears to be the principal key to the recent (from 1997) matter of the "*shortage*" of housing and the huge and sustained house price inflation relative to the 4 decades before 1997, rather than a dearth of actual supply of dwellings caused by inadequate building rates.

It was precisely this relationship that led directly to the steady fall of the cost of borrowing, which underpinned the growing demand for a naturally in-elastic supply of housing (housing cannot be created in days or weeks) and consequent burgeoning household debt. All this leading directly to the financial crash that began in 2007, which resulted in the collapse of building rates and collapse or near collapse of a large number of financial institutions worldwide.

The result was the return to national debt, but for the first time due to a non militarily-induced unprecedented financial failure. Such debt still remains uncorrected in many western economies to this day, a quarter of a century since the spiral started in 1997, including in the UK. In fact the national debt burden has been greatly increased by the government's choice of actions to "protect" and then support people in the wake of the spread of the pandemic that started in 2020.

Further, a sound and consistent analysis of the cost of housing and the servicing of the debt (mortgage) can be undertaken, thanks to the nature of the post Second World War housing market and the prevalence of long term comparatively well funded and stable Building Society institutions, offering a good historical record, supplemented by comparative analysis of proxy building cost data, collated by the Bank of England. Mortgage and long term interest rates allow us to calculate a consistent measure of theoretical sustainability of housing purchase by households since mid-Victorian times.

The UK's housing market is thus represented generally on a set of criteria that illustrate similarity and dissimilarity in recent times in access to and cost of housing.

Poverty - Expenditure and Social Protection

Poverty (see the discussion of the meaning of words earlier in the **Foreword**) is a very contentious and emotionally charged issue (and in fact a very emotionally charged word in itself).

It has ranged from being seen as some sort of punishment meted out to the "indigent" and "feckless" by God, to the result, in modern times, of crass, and often deliberate neglect by government, and all points between.

It is axiomatic that very few people actually wish to be poor, though some do choose to live in poverty for various moral and social reasons.

It is therefore essential to find meaningful and consistent ways to attempt to identify, measure and numerically represent the presence of poverty (whether *"real"* or re-defined as *"relative"*, or preferably both), in a consistent way over time in order to allow both the targeting of protection and assistance to those in need and, to historically see if real progress has and is being made.

By linking the real cost of living for the population of the UK to their real effective earnings, and their real measured spending patterns on the goods and services available at any point in history, represented as best as possible over the range of households at each point in time, a very strong picture of the retreat of real poverty emerges from the historical record.

From these best known facts, we are then able to look further at the various possible contributors and causes of the presence of real poverty, and historically, the various changes wrought in the economy (from all identified sources) that have helped to finally lift the vast majority of the population of the UK out of real, and in fact grinding, life-limiting and life-shortening poverty, over the three centuries plus, to 2019.

Strongly identifiable contributors to the persistence of extreme poverty, for the first 200 to 250 years, are:

- the generally limited productivity of a simpler economic structure and means of production;
- extreme inequality of distribution of those limited resources (GDP);
- and the persistent lack of commitment to bold social protection, apart from a comparatively limited historical Poor Law system.

Subsequently identifiable from the start of the twentieth century (in fact hinted to in the latter decades of the 19th century), the initial persistence of real poverty and then gradual change and long term improvement in the retreat of real poverty are:

- repeated bouts of severe and widespread, and often regionally very severe, unemployment;
- very large shocks and transformations of the more dynamic economic structure, in a very intertwined international system of trade and inter-dependence;
- the substantial improvement to real sustained productivity to-date;
- the reduction of extreme inequality allowing the greater sharing of the

fruits of improved productivity;

- initially slow growth of, but ever greater widespread commitment to, concerted national social protection systems, being the move from the limited and ancient system of the Elizabethan Poor Law to a centralised system of national social protection.

Whilst real poverty, and its even worse incarnation, destitution and homelessness, have not gone away, they have retreated to a much smaller portion of the population than at any time in our measurable and known history.

This is repeatedly, very strongly attested to in the data, as well as our qualitatively documented history.

> Of course the modern persistence of real poverty (albeit reduced compared to the past) can only be tackled by increased enterprise and productivity. Combining increased productivity with modern social protection policies can potentially assist those languishing in real poverty.
>
> This is only possible if its presence is honestly and consistently identified correctly, without the prejudiced, ideological political and campaigning bias that is overwhelmingly prevalent in the clamour of public discourse (along with the gross misuse, and repeated abuse, of the word "*poverty*") as has been the norm in the last 50 or more years.

Air-Quality - "Pollution", Road Transport

Of course all land fauna life-forms, including ourselves, require not just clean drinking water, food, shelter and some form of warmth, but even more immediately, breathable, clean air.

As we have become richer, with much greater income since The Second World War, the populace and politicians have become more aware of the importance of ensuring that our environment in general and our air in particular is as clean as is reasonably possible.

Major and quite devastating triggers for the awareness of this need were writ large in the form of the smog (fog and smoke combined) of the 1950s and 1960s.

As households' real incomes improved after The Second World War, this brought about the burning of ever more coal (and coal/town gas) to heat homes and with which to cook, as well as being contributed to by the greater demand for electricity, mostly from coal fired power stations. In addition the resurgence of industry in the aftermath of The Second World War added its contribution.

Many deaths were attributed directly to the very poor atmosphere, particularly in large cities, and the London smog, in particular, became world famous. The results were the Clean Air Acts of 1956 and 1968.

From 1970 the various government departments made responsible for the environment in which the populace live, began monitoring for as many known air-quality pollutants (as well as river and land contamination issues) as possible.

The result is now a publicly available, continuous, 50 year (plus) record of the quality of the air that we breathe throughout the country and includes the various pollutants to which road vehicles are known to contribute, as well as the various pollutants from direct and indirect use of energy by people in their own households.

This data is used along with the similarly publicly available record of the number of road vehicles and households to show clearly the real status of air quality and the nation's use of road transport over fifty years.

Life Expectancy

The sum of all of the changes and improvements over 320 years might be simply measured against improved health, but is most starkly revealed by the calculated life expectancy of people born or living in the UK, including analysis by constituent nations and their regions and cities.

This again informs public discourse and governmental policies and if properly understood might allow more refined policies to help tackle the worst areas and pockets of lower life-expectancy found in the UK.

The UK has had central registration of births, deaths and marriages since before the middle of the 19th century. From this, and combined with estimates of population, it has been possible to calculate estimated rates of deaths per 1,000 population. Even more usefully, by tracking age at death combined with an estimate of the age distribution of the population, it is possible to calculate a standardised rate of mortality for the relative age of the population.

Such analysis, mostly from the Office of National Statistics (ONS), but also historically collated and published in the "Human Mortality Database", the World Bank and "Our World in Data", allows a very long-term analysis of the improvements in life expectancy, the ageing of the population and also differences by nation and region, sex and ethnicity over time.

Clearly visible in the record are significant impacts such as the world wars, the "Spanish Influenza" outbreak of 1918/19, and also now the Coronavirus (SARS-CoV-2/Covid-19) pandemic. From this the relative magnitude of such impacts, as well as long term trends and in particular the improvements to life-expectancy at all age ranges, not just compared to declining rates of infant mortality, can be adduced.

The overwhelming message that emerges is that the retreat of real poverty, the greater access to better and better housing (and warmth), ever falling real costs of food and cleaner air are having a direct and sustained effect on the quantitative expectancy of life longevity for almost all ages of people, regardless of geography and even regardless of inequality in the UK and its constituent nations.

Even the latest pandemic is not even numerically comparable to the devastating loss of life and health wrought by the "Spanish Influenza" of 1918/19.

Summary

Drawing the elements together there can only be one conclusion for the vast majority of people in the UK; that life has improved in almost every way imaginable (and measurable) over not simply the last 320 years to 2019, but mostly continuously along the way, though with some extremely serious and sometimes regionally very serious halts and even reverses.

The reasons are actually very simple, it is human ingenuity, aspiration, enterprise and trade that have led to vastly improved productivity in every walk of work and life.

The exploitation of every type of energy that has been discovered from our own physical labour, the harnessing of very powerful animals with which we share the environment such as oxen and horses, the careful breeding and selection of plants and animals to improve yields, paralleled by the discovery of the ever greater ways to extract energy from wood, then coal, oil and gas has lifted humanity from the simple hand to mouth brutally short life, to longer and longer, healthier and more fulfilled lives, with ever greater opportunity for the vast majority of people in the UK and thankfully the world.

This is abundantly writ large in the UK's history from the very early 16th and 17th century advances in trade and small scale industrialisation that then led to the "explosions" of productivity growth during the 18th, but especially from the 19th century onwards.

Afterword

In the year 2019 we were the inheritors of 320 years (and much more) of vast improvement in all aspects of life, even the pandemic that started in 2020 is nothing compared to all known equivalent pandemics from previous ages be it the "Spanish Influenza", Plague or so called "Black Death", all of which caused more death and devastation when they struck.

Health and mortality data for 2020 to 2021 are presented in detail in the Afterword and compared to the previous century and also some international comparisons are offered with selected comparable developed nations.

References, bibliography and further reading.

I reiterate that this is not a work of original research, but a collation of the outstanding research of the best qualified academics, individuals and government departments throughout the world, who have and do study and analyse the economy of the UK and its constituent nations and peoples, over a very long period of time.

I have attempted to document and of course fully acknowledge all of the sources used to build this work.

Thus an extensive reference, bibliography and further reading collection is provided that the reader, who is so motivated, might choose to pursue in order to find more and more detail to inform themselves of the best known facts.

The references document the multitude of data sources that are used in each chart, collection of charts and corresponding text.

Note also that all chart and table titles are replicated in full in the previous list of figures, as originally so labelled. But in an attempt to make tri-chart or double chart pages more readable the title, label and legend text for such charts has been enlarged and thus on occasions some titles have been abbreviated to make both such text and the charts themselves fit on each of their pages.

All of the topics that are discussed are covered in the form of narrative discussion with graphical illustrations in the form of charts, where useful. I have consciously eschewed, as much as possible, pages and pages of tables, as I know this is not easily digested by most readers. Of course all charts are by definition derived from such underlying tables and my collection of such, related to all the topics herein discussed, is now huge.

There are a very few exceptions to this, in which I have used a few such tables, and even these are intentionally coloured using red, orange, green and bright pink fonts or background coloured blocking to draw the readers' eye to the patterns within the table, rather than the reader be fogged by the detail of the numbers in the data itself. The colours selected are cast as consistently as possible across tables to illustrate trends.

Those researchers, academics and authors are the discoverers and documenters of the amazing history of over three centuries of progress that just happened to start making itself felt first on the world stage in the islands that we call the United Kingdom of Great Britain and Northern Ireland.

What is not covered within

There are of course many, many other vitally important topics that directly inform and represent the quality of life lived by the many people of the UK that are not actually covered by this work.

There is simply not space or time to cover everything, and in fact important as these matters are, they generally did not receive quite the volume or consistency of clamour in the recent public discourse, compared to the core issues of housing "*shortage*", "*poverty*", "*pollution*" (air quality) and "*austerity*" and life expectancy. In addition in that public discourse these preceding four essential underpinning principal topics have been so poorly misrepresented in relation to the current and historically best known facts, that the focus simply had to be the correction of their ill-informed and grossly inaccurate misrepresentation, thus these many other topics have been left out of this volume accordingly.

Such topics are all complex and each would need substantial research and analysis in themselves and of course include, in just this small list:

- Access to education, and of course quality and breadth of education;
- Access to health care, and again quality of care and outcomes;
- Thanks to our living longer, access to age care and nursing in modern times as our bodies and minds deteriorate;
- The whole matter of migration in and out of the UK (far from a new phenomenon, their being no humans in the UK for 10,000 years in the last glacial maximum from 25,000 to 15,000 years ago);
- The rightly very contentious and painful history of both neglect of subject peoples, or even worse the slavery of peoples in the past and the short and long term effects of such abominations.

The many other very important topics, in addition to this short list, I will leave the reader to consider for themselves.

Since starting this project in 2017 momentous events have taken place throughout the world.

In particular a significant health pandemic became known of in the closing days of 2019, with mortality effects being discussed in the Afterword. This was followed in the early spring of 2020 by its growing spread and the consequential growth of varying degrees of caution and near panic amongst populations and particularly in government circles. This latter then drove "unprecedented" imposition of restrictions and the effective "decimation" of economic activity.

During the periods of restriction and since, new populist protests erupted and eventually a new war in Europe began.

The consequences of all of these events and behaviours, both socially and economically, are only now (in 2023) starting to develop, with the long term consequences for peoples' well-being and lives as yet impossible to determine.

The secret now is to continue with the age of enlightenment and reason and science; eschew all forms of self-righteous ideology, bigotry and ignorance and thus recognise reality; seek out real poverty, improve access to the resources needed to maintain and improve the quality of life; ensure all breathe cleaner air through the development of ever better and affordable technologies, and by allowing everyone to live better and longer lives, ensure that all people in the world have a share of the fruits of human ingenuity, aspiration, enterprise and trade, all underpinned with liberty under the rule of law.

I therefore commend this work to the reader as a collation of the best known facts available to all, and for the reader to find any errors of such facts, and also to draw their own conclusions from those best known facts here presented, and in turn other quantifiable information about these topics.

Population

Growth of the population

The seminal research of parish records in the 1970s by Professor Tony Wrigley and Dr. Roger Schofield, that led to the publication in 1981 of their book *"The Population History of England 1541-1871: A Reconstruction"*, has established a sound and reliable view of the growth of the population of England from the reign of Henry VIII and the establishment of the Church of England, via the start of the era of central registration (from 1837) and the detailed censuses (from 1841) to date; effectively also the UK by virtue of England's size as part of the Union.

With the introduction of the central registration of births, deaths and marriages from 1837 and the expansion of the decadal census from 1841, so that names and counts of people, households and locations are available, the historian is able to develop a thorough picture of the growth of the population to date, including the principal drivers of that growth for almost the last 500 years; including improvements to general health, wealth and well-being, as well as longevity of life.

Whilst in this work we are focussed on the period from 1700, it is very useful to reflect on the context of the population of at least England to 1700 (sadly, somewhat less is reliably known about the populations of Wales, Scotland and Ireland in the earlier centuries before that year).

The best known historical analyses strongly suggest that from the time of William I (the Conqueror) to 1700, the population of England grew from an estimated 1.5-1.7 million in 1086 (thanks to the "Domesday" survey) to an initial peak of 4.8 million in 1348, as the "Black Death" arrived in the country; then collapsed by 1351 to slightly over 2.5 million.

Almost half of the population of England being estimated to have died in that plague in just three years.

The population of England then did not return to match that peak of 1348 until the 1620s, subsequently slowly growing to 5.2 million at the end of the 17th century in that turbulent and plague affected time.

The extensive work of Wrigley and Schofield has been well supplemented for the UK for our period of focus, mostly from the "*Glorious Revolution*" in England in 1688, thanks to, for example, K. H. Connell for Ireland ("*Land and Population of Ireland", 1950*) and James Kyd for Scotland ("*Scottish Population Statistics: including Webster's analysis of population of 1755"*, 1952) plus the census for all of the UK from 1801.

Both the ONS and MeasuringWorth have also calculated and collated political boundary-based population measures for the UK (as they have changed in 1707, 1801 and then in 1921), but also attempted to calculate an historically "consistent" set of annual values based upon the post 1921 political boundaries, namely the United Kingdom of Great Britain and Northern Ireland, as though that entity had been extant from 1700.

It is these latter that provide the best picture of growth of the United Kingdom in terms that are most readily understood, for the last 100 years.

This shows us that the "consistent" population of the UK (England, Wales, Scotland and Northern Ireland) has been estimated to have grown from 6.6 million in 1700 to 66.8 million in 2019, whilst England's population increased from 5.2 million to an estimated 56 million in 2019.

A tenfold increase in 320 years for the UK and almost eleven fold increase for England.

The first chart opposite visually illustrates the magnitude of the growth of these populations over 320 years, with the estimate of the population of the "consistent" UK represented in the dark grey line.

That of the UK as constituted from 1801 to 1921 including southern Ireland is represented in the solid mid-grey line, but hypothetically extended back to 1700, as though it had previously been an integrated whole via the mid-grey dotted line, rather than "The Kingdom of Ireland".

England's population as a constituent of the whole is represented in the mid-orange line.

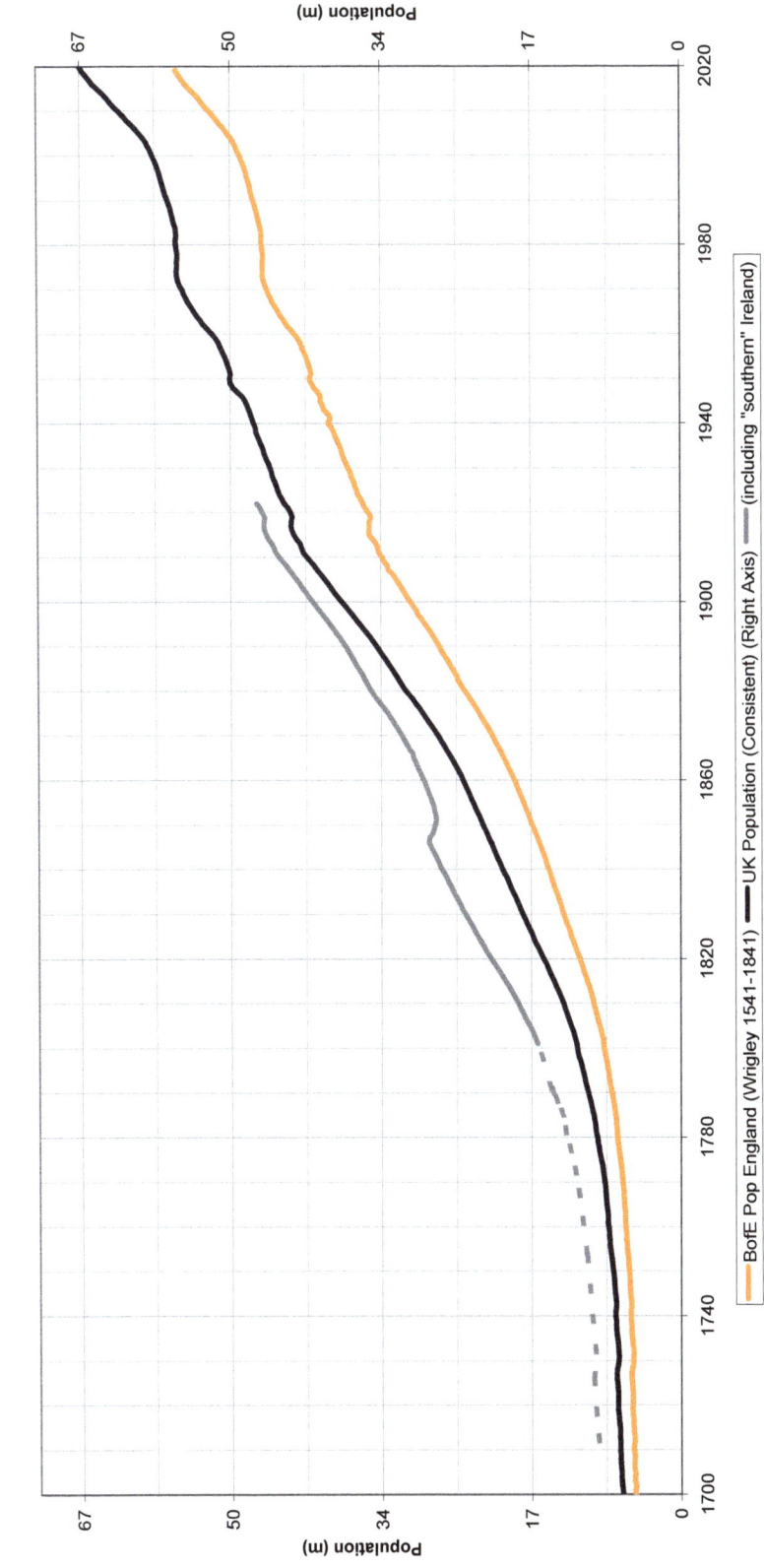

UK and England Long Term History of Population (Millions)

BofE Pop England (Wrigley 1541-1841) ━━ UK Population (Consistent) (Right Axis) ━━ (including "southern" Ireland)

Whilst not shown here, interestingly the populations of both Wales and Scotland exhibit their strongest continuous growth in the period 1700 to about the time of The Great War, both showing much reduced rates of growth thereafter (Scotland more so even than Wales); but England's growth rate after 1920 continues to almost match that of the earlier period.

It should be noted that the population of the island of Ireland tells a radically different story than that of Great Britain, as suggested by the fall of the mid-grey line in the graph on the previous page in the section between the years 1820 and 1860.

The graph opposite for Ireland suggests that from the period 1687 to 1845 (from Connell 1950), via the Census figures from 1821, Ireland's population grew from approximately 2.5 million in 1700 to a peak of approximately 8.3 million in 1845, before the disaster of the potato famine that year (and subsequent failure of government to meaningfully help alleviate the suffering).

The population at first crashed over the subsequent decade to 6 million in 1855, then continued to steadily decline to a low point of approximately 4.2 million in 1926, the final combined census year (this being calculated by combining the populations of the Irish Free State and that of the province of Northern Ireland). Thereafter growing again to approximately 6.8 million in 2019. (In the graph opposite, the island of Ireland is represented in the dark green lines, southern Ireland in the light green lines and the province of Northern Ireland in the violet line).

Thus from even the simplest perspective of the growth of the population of the UK there are clearly multiple complex and varying stories for the constituent nations and even regions and localities throughout the history of these islands.

It is also worth reflecting on the thought that the story of the population of Ireland is a salutary reminder of the effects of the failure of government policy due to the over-bearing preoccupation with fixated ideology (in this case the obsession with theories of "laissez faire" and "Political Economy"), taking the form of effectively disowning responsibility to use its power and authority in a desperate emergency to meaningfully aid the citizens of the nation for which it is constituted.

Of course, there are also as many, if not more, cases of governments interfering in the life of, and dictating to, its citizens equally in the name of over-bearing and fixated ideology (both religious and secular).

A note on population density

Whilst there are many states with population density greater than that of the UK (277/sq. km.), itself greater than that of Germany (233/sq. km.), it is notable that England (434/sq. km.) would effectively rank 6th in population density of the world's countries, after Bangladesh (1,094/sq. km.), Taiwan (652/sq. km.), South Korea (511/sq. km.), Rwanda (467/sq. km.) and the Netherlands (457/sq. km.), if one excludes the city-states.

Connell's estimate of the population of Ireland plus "southern" Ireland and "northern" Ireland (BofE, 1700-1891) plus Census returns (m)

Population of Ireland (Connell 1950) — Calculated Population of Ireland — Calculated Population "southern" Ireland — Population of Northern Ireland (Census Tables/ONS)

Birth rates and death rates

Thanks to the parish records (with their many challenges and inconsistencies) and then central registration of births and deaths, we now have a clear picture in which we can be confident of the effect of the numbers of births and deaths and the consequent rates per thousand population thereof for the past 320 years and their effect on the growth of the population (here we are only using what is termed "crude" death rates, being calculated regardless of the prevailing age of the population, the latter being referred to as "Age Standardised" rates).

A general pattern has emerged from the record that seems to have been repeated throughout the world; as many other nations' territories have developed in the manner as the UK did in earlier centuries.

It is now generally understood that in pre-developing times the birth and death rates tend to be closer to each other resulting in long term slow changes of population. In developing times birth rates amongst populations tend to be significantly higher than death rates, once development and consequent improvements in health and well-being start to be felt.

It then takes several decades before birth rates fall to match the reducing death rates, resulting ultimately in more stable and ever ageing populations after the phase of more rapid population growth slows. These trends can however be very heavily mitigated by delaying marriage as well, so are not entirely determinate in themselves; at least in more religious societies that observe the rituals of marriage before parenthood.

Also both births and deaths still remain vulnerable to many natural and man-made disasters, and Wrigley and Schofield identified many large scale mortality crises in the records they surveyed. We are also aware of several more, particularly in the 20th century with the two "World Wars" and the particularly deadly "Spanish Influenza" pandemic, and of course the latest Coronavirus (SARS-CoV-2/Covid-19) pandemic.

In fact the mortality crises of 1727/30 and 1741/2 identified by Wrigley and Schofield (caused by epidemics), can be seen in the chart on the opposite page in the orange line for "crude" death rate per thousand population on the left of the chart in the period between 1700 and 1740. Thereafter comparatively few crises occurred and the effects of those in the 20th and 21st century were thankfully more limited in historical terms.

It is also notable that the birth rate (the green line in the chart opposite) rose quite steadily from 1700 until about 1820 before beginning its continuous fall from the 1880s onwards.

Both rates strongly suggest the greatest effects of improvements from development seem to have been felt from about 1870 to 1880, shown in the continuous fall of both birth and death rates, though death rates had begun an earlier gentler decline after the 1740s as well.

The gap between birth rate and death rate is referred to as the "crude" rate of natural increase (or decrease).

England & Wales Long Term History of Birth and Death Rates per Thousand Population

England Births per 1,000 —— E&W Births per UK 1,000 —— England Deaths per 1,000 —— E&W Deaths per UK 1,000

Of major significance in the reduction of the nation's death rate is the huge fall in the rate of deaths of live new born infants before their first birthday.

This was a centuries old tragedy for humanity until the effects of development in the forms of hygiene, food and improving health and medicine started to manifest themselves.

These falls are revealed thanks to the detailed records of the central registration of births and deaths available from 1837, and shown in the chart on the next page from 1841 for England and Wales.

The chart opposite shows the death rates by quinquennial age ranges, but with special exception for the deaths of infants under 1 year of age in the bold red line. This record for infants illustrates huge reductions to post-natal infant mortality rates; falling from an average of 168 per thousand of their population age cohort in 1841 to 1904, to just 4 per thousand by 2019. Also very clearly visible is the fall from almost 48 per thousand in 1947 to slightly over 32 per thousand in 1948, the year of the establishment of the National Health Service; making available access to health care "free at the point of delivery" for millions who were previously entirely unable to afford even the most basic health care.

Also clearly visible in the graph in the other colours (blues for the older age cohorts to oranges and yellows for younger age cohorts) are the steady reductions in rates per thousand through time for each in turn. The most recent very visible reduction for the oldest reported cohort of those aged 85 and over at death, is a steady fall in death rates from about 1940.

Further indicators of patterns in the data are the obvious annual variations, these clearly reducing noticeably for all age ranges again mostly from soon after 1951 in this case.

A notable effect in the data from the period 2010 to 2019 is the levelling of the rate of deaths for most age cohorts. It is this effect that has given rise to a slowing of the rate of increase of life expectancy. This will be discussed further in the final chapter, that covers the question of life expectancy in more detail for the period from 1970 to 2019.

The effects of the "Spanish Influenza" pandemic are visible, particularly in 1918 and 1919 in the rise in the red line for infants, but also visible is the substantial death toll of The Great War in the rise in the yellow and orange lines from 1914 to 1918. Also visible is a notable spike in 1940, being the year of the "Blitz".

A further visible effect, almost as a recent "*last gasp*" of major epidemics is the 1951 influenza outbreak. It can be seen to have particularly affected the older age cohort in that year. As a particularly bad outbreak of influenza that year it appears to have raised the annual national "crude" death rate from 11.5 to 12.6 per thousand, with excess deaths of perhaps 45,000, yielding an 8.8% increase (when compared to the averages for 1946-1950/1952-1956 combined).

Of course the reader will be abundantly aware of the return of a major pandemic in 2020. This raised "crude" death rates that year from 9.1 to

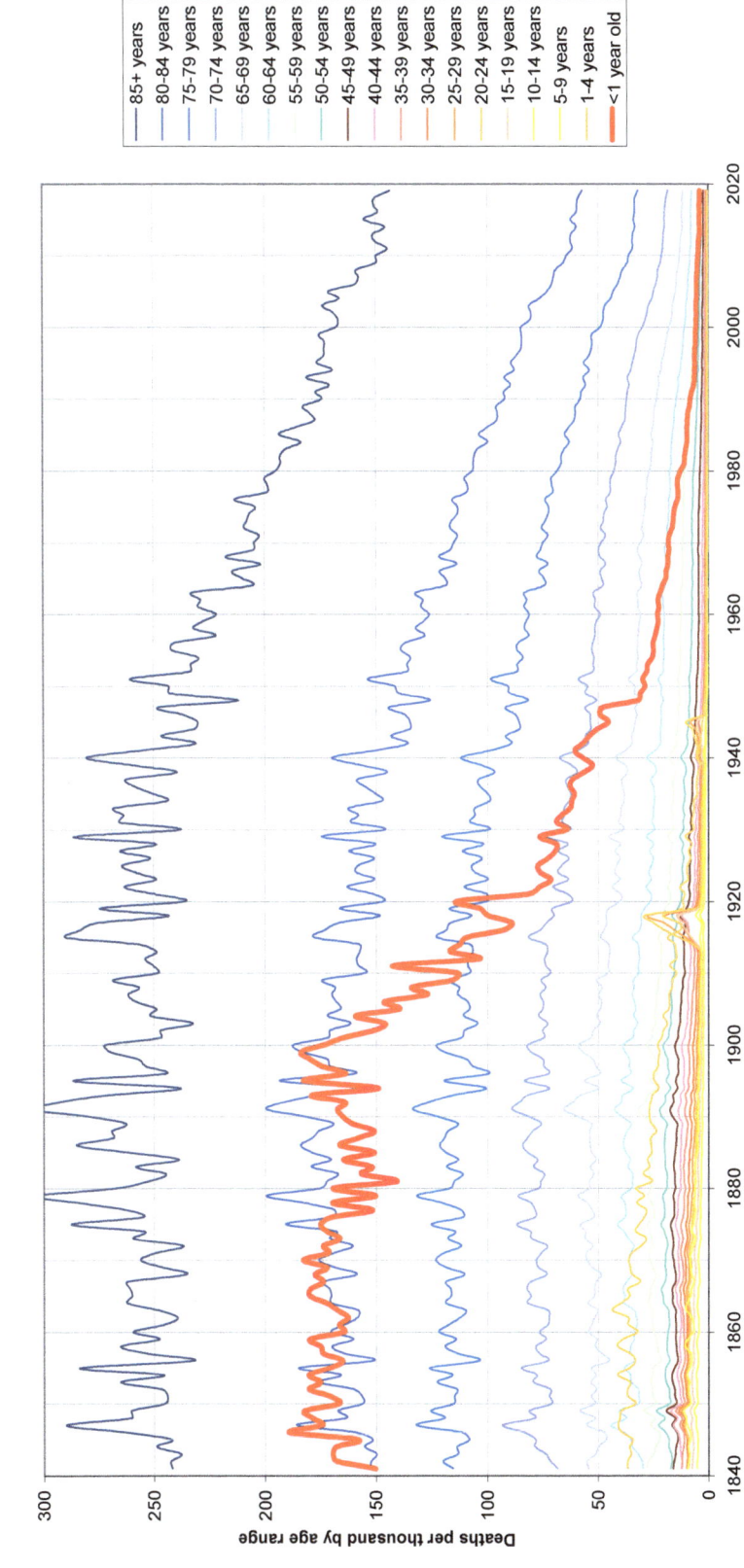

Death Rates per Thousand Population by Age Range for England & Wales (ONS/Human Mortality Database)

Legend:
- 85+ years
- 80-84 years
- 75-79 years
- 70-74 years
- 65-69 years
- 60-64 years
- 55-59 years
- 50-54 years
- 45-49 years
- 40-44 years
- 35-39 years
- 30-34 years
- 25-29 years
- 20-24 years
- 15-19 years
- 10-14 years
- 5-9 years
- 1-4 years
- <1 year old

Y-axis: Deaths per thousand by age range

10.2 per thousand, with excess deaths of some 75,000 in 2020, yielding a 12.1% increase (when compared to the averages for 2015-2019).

Clearly the influenza outbreak of 1951 was also a very serious event with a significant loss of life, however both such epidemics pale when compared to the "Spanish Influenza" outbreak of 1918-1919; which appears to have raised the annual "crude" death rate from 13 to 15.8 per thousand, with excess deaths of perhaps 81,000, yielding a 24.9% increase (when compared to the averages for 1910-1913/1920-1928 combined, ensuring the exclusion of the years of The Great War).

Ageing of the population

All of these changes point strongly to a probable outcome for the population as a whole, namely that over the decades there are many more people surviving for many more years, invariably thankfully in reasonable health for many of those years, thus yielding what is known as an "ageing population".

Also emerging from the research of Wrigley and Schofield is a strong understanding of the long term age demographic characteristics of the population of England. Thanks to those same more reliable central registration of births and deaths combined with the more detailed census analysis from 1841, a very powerful and much more detailed analysis of the age demographics of the population of the UK is possible thereafter.

(**Note**: For this analysis the detailed data for England before 1841 and thereafter for England and Wales is used as generally representative of the UK, though not precisely identical).

As living conditions have improved in every way: housing, hygiene, food, medical facilities, working conditions and technology, so the majority of people born over the decades, as progress has been felt, have lived longer, healthier and more fulfilled lives.

It is this ageing of the population that has been the chief driver of the growth of the population as a whole in the more recent decades.

The difference between birth and death rates that heavily drives growth at first (seen on the previous pages), then clearly narrows from after The Great War. The age demographic shown in the graph on the next page shows the older age ranges expand steadily thereafter (represented by the mid-blue of those aged 60 and over and lavender of those aged 25 to 59 years).

Clearly visible from the start of the 20th century to date is that the actual number of those aged under 25 years largely stabilises to between 16 and 18 million. However, also visible is a dip below 16 million around The Second World War from 1935 to 1957, followed by an increase to over 17.5 million for a period from 1964 to 1986 as the "baby boomers" added to the population and came of age, and a small but visible rise above 17 million since 2010 to-date.

Population (m) England (Wrigley et al), England & Wales (ONS/Human Mortality Database) by age Range + UK (MW "consistent")

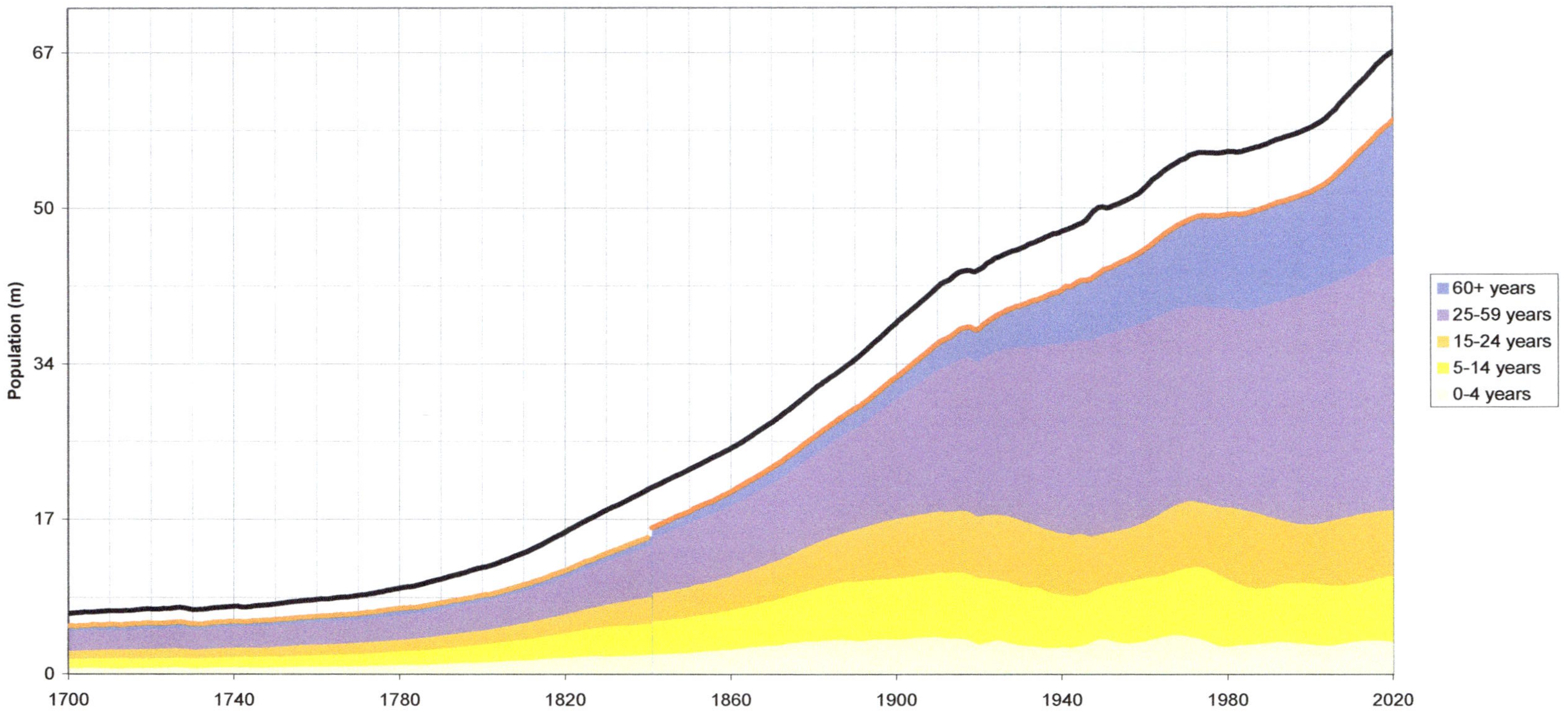

Legend:
- 60+ years
- 25-59 years
- 15-24 years
- 5-14 years
- 0-4 years

Y-axis: Population (m) — 0, 17, 34, 50, 67

X-axis: 1700, 1740, 1780, 1820, 1860, 1900, 1940, 1980, 2020

The latter is mostly driven by the increase of inward migration that has gathered pace since the mid-1990s, helping to check a little of the ageing effect of the population through a return to the growth of the number of those under 25 years of age.

This pattern is repeated throughout the world in currently developing countries leading to the phenomenon known as "peak child".

It is strongly believed that the numbers of people aged under 25 has actually now peaked in the world as it did in the UK at the turn of the 19th and 20th centuries.

An alternative way of presenting the age distribution by age ranges is as a share of the population in each year, rather than the count as in the chart on the previous page. Thus the chart on the next page reveals other information in addition to the previous presentation.

This chart shows that from 1700 to 1820 there is a significant increase in the share of people under the age of 25, this share then stabilising until a little before the end of the 19th century. Thereafter the share of those under the age of 25 years exhibit a notable fall, with the interesting boom after The Second World War, with even the recent increase of inward migration and the resultant mini-baby boom unable to completely check this trend in share of the population.

However, also strongly revealed is the continuous growth of the share of those aged 60 and over, again from the very end of the 19th century; this time notably less interrupted by the so-called "baby-boom" in the wake of the end of The Second World War.

In general, interestingly, the share of the population of those aged 25 to 59 is moderately stable at about 40% to 45% from 1700 to 2019 (ranging from a low of 35%, but rising to 49% in the period of The Second World War and slipping back to a recent level as high as 46% to 47%).

(**Note**: these figures are all for England before 1841 and for England and Wales thereafter, and those for the UK would be slightly different).

This process of the ageing of the population, of course does have many financial and basic care implications as fewer people amongst the population produce the goods and services that constitute the essence of the economy, whilst also needing care for longer as they live longer.

In addition the characteristics of changing and eventual ill-health and causes of death notably change under such circumstances of the ageing of the population.

In particular "new" major disease effects emerge to the fore, as the causes of deaths in the past recede and other, previously less common degradations to health and ultimately causes of death become more common.

The most obvious of these is the rapid growth in the effects of dementia as a more major impact on declining health and ultimately death in later, older years.

Share Population England (Wrigley et al), England & Wales (ONS/Human Mortality Database) **by age Range + UK (MW "consistent")**

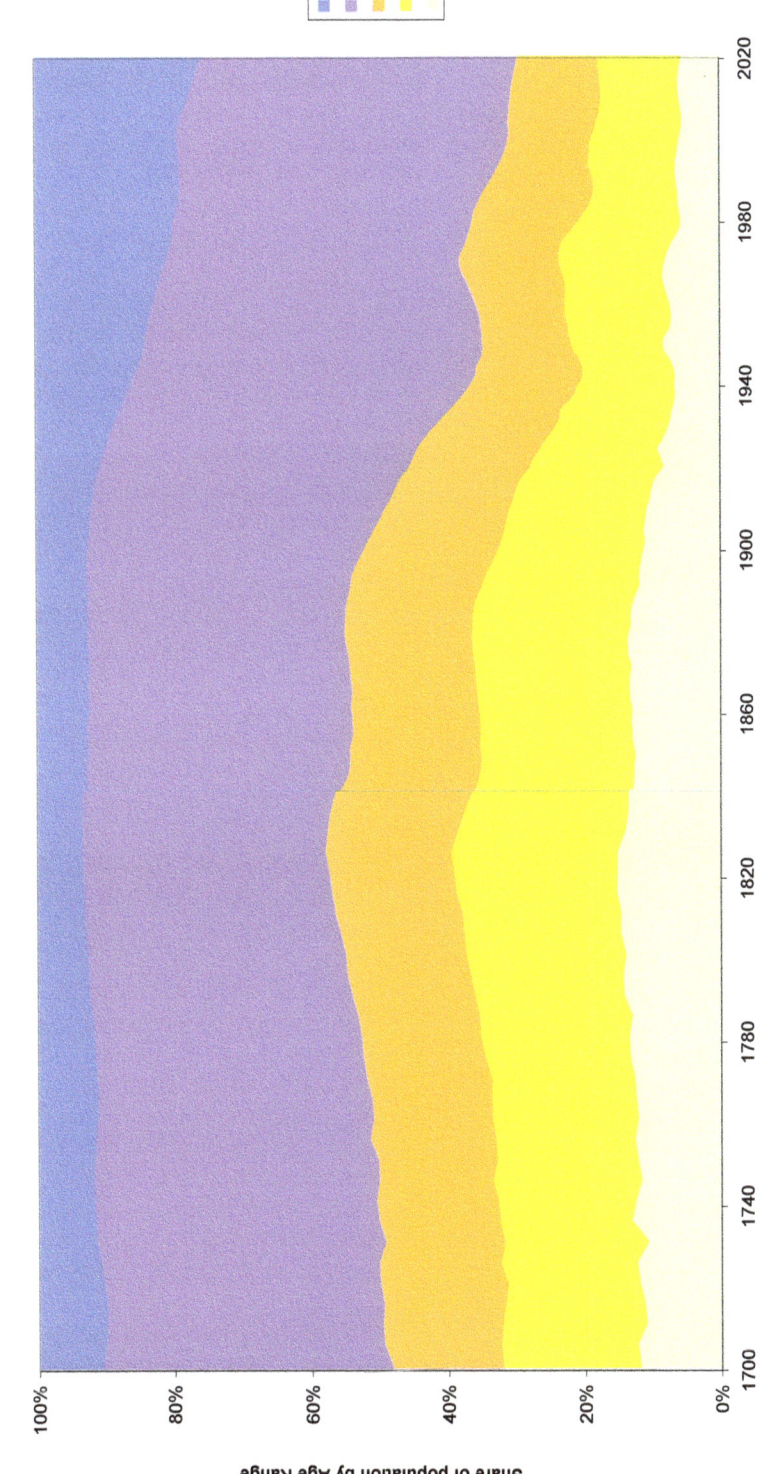

Share of population by Age Range

- 60+ years
- 25-59 years
- 15-24 years
- 5-14 years
- 0-4 years

1700 1740 1780 1820 1860 1900 1940 1980 2020

100% 80% 60% 40% 20% 0%

Calculated life expectancy at birth

Life expectancy calculation is a very useful tool for the demographer and historian, and further indicator of well-being in a population.

It is a statistic that calculates "the average number of years a newborn is expected to live *if mortality patterns at the time of its birth remain constant in the future*" (from Suzuki et al. at https://blogs.worldbank.org - *What does "life expectancy at birth" really mean?*, 2013).

It is not therefore a prediction of the hypothetical life expectancy in the future, but rather a calculation of life longevity for those who die at a point in time.

With the very detailed analysis available for England from 1541, then England plus Wales from 1700, and the whole of the UK for the last 100 years, a very strong image emerges of the huge improvement to life expectancy at birth since 1700. In fact, thanks to the registration data available from 1837, detailed calculations of remaining life expectancy by age for all years can be performed which yields a strong picture of the trend over time in keeping with the improvement for those at birth.

This trend informs us clearly that the improvements are not restricted to infants and children, but in fact apply at all ages throughout life, though those improvements are most dramatic for the very young.

The chart on the next page illustrates this dramatic improvement over the centuries for the life "expectancy" at birth very well.

Clearly visible is the previously mentioned mortality crises of the 1720s and 1730s, as identified by Wrigley and Schofield, in which calculated life expectancy at birth plunged to a low of just 28 years. However, thereafter a steady increase can be seen, at first gradual until the later years of the 19th century, reaching 50 years of age at the start of the 20th century.

From the Edwardian era the increase becomes far more dramatic, though sadly interrupted by the death toll of The Great War and "Spanish influenza" in the period 1914 to 1919, as can be seen in the precipitate fall to just 41 years in 1919.

The rapid increase of life expectancy at birth returns in 1920 to the same level as would have been expected from the pre-Great War rate of improvement, even had those mortality crises not intervened.

A second severe interruption is clearly visible from 1940 to 1945, brought about by The Second World War, thereafter rising rapidly to a new slower rate of improvement following the foundation of the NHS in 1948 and the widespread introduction of penicillin in the 1940s.

Also clearly visible after 1948 is the reduced annual variability caused mostly by significant winter threats to life, mostly of older age cohorts. This was also clearly visible in the age cohort death rates discussed earlier.

As mentioned previously a slowing of the rate of improvement can be seen from about 2011 or 2012 until 2018, before returning to a similar

UK Long Term History of Life Expectancy at Birth (from Wrigley & Schofield/ONS/Human Mortality Database/Our World in Data)

OWID Life Expectancy at Birth

growth in 2019. Thereafter interrupted again from 2020 due to the pandemic previously mentioned (though not shown here).

Migration rates

Of course the other substantial factor that affects the growth (or decline) of a population is migration in and out of a country. This has always been and remains a cause for "concern" amongst the authorities and currently indigenous population of any country. The authorities and people of the UK are no exception to this reaction to migration.

The graph on the next page illustrates the history of the migration rates very well (factored for the size of the population at any time) in the blue line. Note the pink line shows the effect of the rate of "natural increase (or decrease)", namely birth rate minus death rate. Again Wrigley and Schofield calculated that for England until 1841, then that for England and Wales follows until 1900 and thereafter that for the UK is shown.

For the period from 1700 to 1983 the overall net average migration rate was 1.1 per thousand leaving the country every year for lands abroad. This strongly reflects the growth of trade and empire as huge numbers of people sought better and new lives and opportunities outside the UK.

In fact this trend was equally present at almost exactly the same rate from the start of the period covered by the detailed analysis of Wrigley and Schofield, namely the reign of Henry VIII. This whole period from 1541 to the middle of the 20th century clearly well quantifies the impact of the presence of the burgeoning world of trade and commerce and its later incarnation in the form of the growth of empire.

It was this latter that transformed into the Commonwealth that gave rise to well known inward migrations from the Caribbean, India, Pakistan, Bangladesh, Kenya, Uganda and ever wider parts of the world, including of course many nations of the European Union from the UK's accession to that block of nations, ultimately increasing quite significantly following the implementation of the open border policy from 2003 until the UK left the EU in 2020. Since leaving the EU, inward migration has continued at even an even greater rate, though mostly from non-EU citizens.

These inward migrations have all been driven mostly by the desire on the part of the migrants seeking better and new lives and opportunities in the UK. A small share of the inward migration is also driven by those seeking asylum from persecution.

Throughout the period of the first four decades following the end of The Second World War, numbers of those inwardly migrating to the UK were more than matched by those leaving the UK, usually to Canada, Australia, New Zealand, the USA and then also various countries throughout Europe.

Thus a clear net outward migration remained prevalent until 1983 finally turning to a very small net inward migration rate of less than 1 per thousand population until 1997.

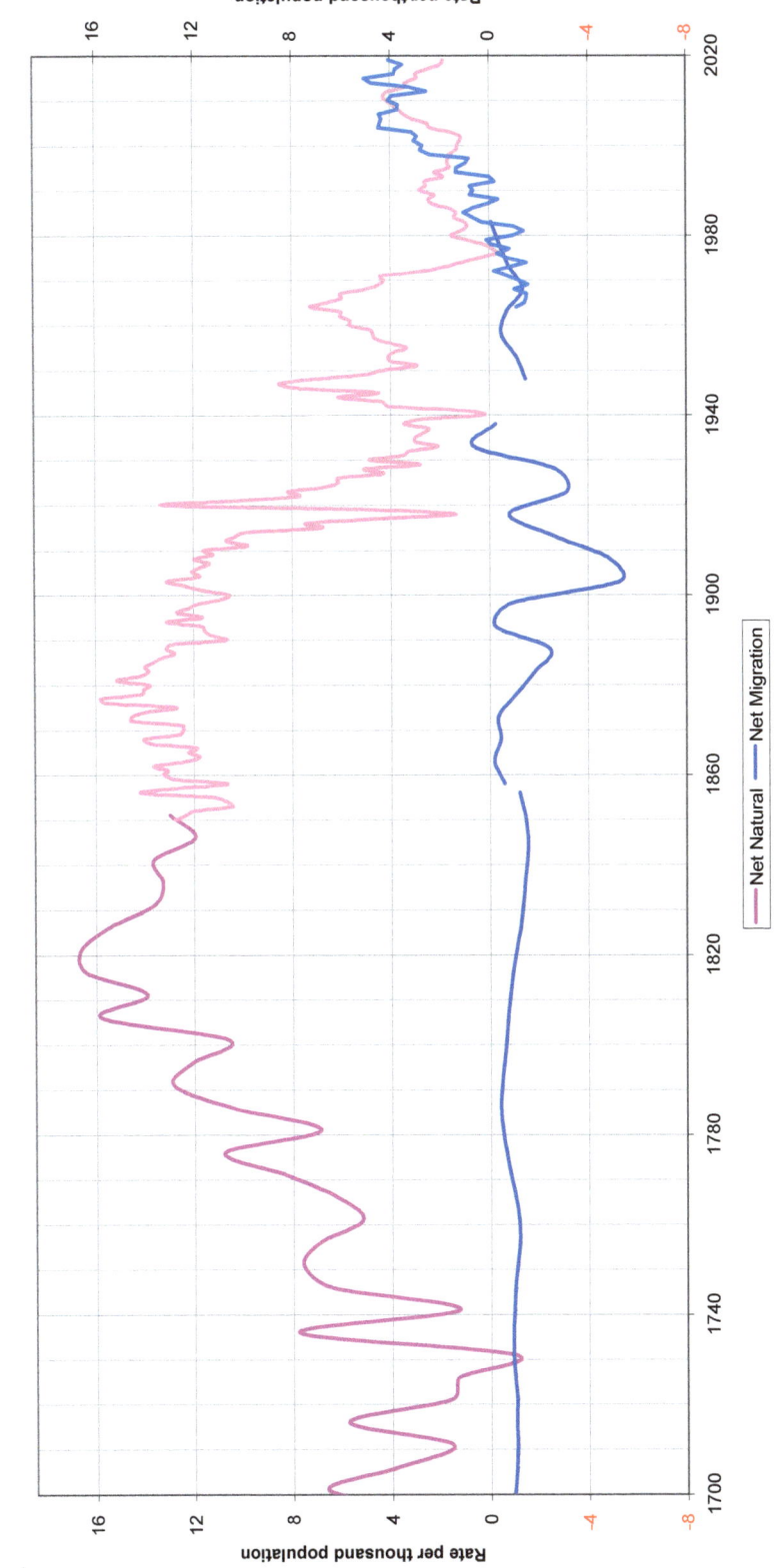

Annual "Crude" Natural Increase (Birth-Death) & Net Migration rates per thou. population - Wrigley et al & ONS/Human Mortality Database

Rate per thousand population

— Net Natural — Net Migration

Of very particular note is the rapid increase of the inward migration rate to an average of 3.7 per thousand of the resident population per year, from 1998 to 2019 (peaking in 2015 at over 5 per thousand of the resident population). From the "Long Term International Migration" analysis by the Home Office and ONS for the same years, the share of inward migrants who are seeking asylum is approximately 11 percent.

This is the basis of the slight relief from the effects of the ageing of the population, revitalising the population of the UK, even resulting in an increase of the birth rate during most of the first two decades of the 21st century. This also helped the staffing of the NHS and care homes and many other of the critically important roles needed in a well functioning society in the 21st century.

However the opposite side of that coin has been a notable increase in the disquiet felt by a naturally culturally conservative resident populous (the majority of humans are generally naturally conservative, at least culturally).

This has been very prevalent throughout the period since The Second World War and been felt very strongly in the notable areas in which the new inward migrants have tended to settle, and continue now to inevitably settle as the more recent migrants gravitate to communities that they themselves recognise culturally.

These tendencies sadly bring out the very worst facet of the conservatism and tendency to prejudice in human beings as they often feel threatened by such changes in their communities.

It should be noted how the English, Scottish, Welsh and Irish have behaved in exactly the same way throughout the last centuries when emigrating to other lands seeking better lives and opportunities outside the UK.

Economy and State

*"The Industrial Revolution, however,
was...more even than an acceleration of
economic growth. It was a revolution in
men's access to the means of life, in control
over their ecological environment, in their
capacity to escape from the tyranny and
niggardliness of nature."*

*"The uniqueness of the historical
Industrial Revolution is that it opened the
road for men to complete mastery of their
physical environment, without the
inescapable need to exploit each other"*

Harold Perkin:
The Origins of Modern English Society,
1969

Growth of the economy

From the formation of settled agricultural societies and the growth of over-arching stable hierarchies of authority within defined boundaries, human societies and then "nations" have tended to formalise a concept of "The Economy". Originally centred around the household and family, perhaps extending to the tribe, this is encapsulated in the concept of the management of expenditure or resources.

The generally accepted modern measure of the value of the nations' economy, that is used in the 21st century is what is known as the Gross Domestic Product (GDP) of the defined economy, being the monetary value of all the products and services produced over a defined (and consistent) time period, generally being a year.

For most of the 18th century it was still the case that the economy of

41

the nation was not intensely managed and accordingly, as with population analysis, academic researchers have had to work very hard to collate meaningful statistics that correspond with those we more readily understand and accept from the end of the 18th century onwards.

Critically important to that idea of the size of the economy, and the possible benefits accrued to the members of the population thereof, is the aggregate value of the economy each year, from all of the production of goods and services, trade and then consumption of those products, being expressed in monetary terms (GDP).

As population has grown within the UK, inevitably the total size and value of "The Economy" has grown.

However, these values not only need to be factored by the size of the population, but also the "real" value of the monetary tokens of exchange that are used within a society over time.

In the UK, for our purposes, that monetary token of exchange has remained the Pound, at least for England and Wales and then later used in the other nations as unification took place (albeit converting from pounds, shillings and pennies to pounds and pence in 1971).

All will understand that over time money tends to become "de-valued" thanks to various forms of inflation. Thus in household terms one year a loaf of bread might cost 1 pound, but the next year that same loaf of bread might cost 1 pound and 10 pence. This is inflation.

Inflation applies equally to an economy as a whole, but the mix of items that are produced, traded and consumed at a national level are of course somewhat broader than those of a household. This results in a different calculation of the rate of inflation for the economy than that for consumer prices. From this we derive the "GDP deflator".

Using our now well understood increase of population to produce the average annual value of GDP per person we must also apply the effect of inflation over time, using the GDP deflator, to arrive at an average "real" value of the economy per person from 1700 to 2019.

Thus in the chart on the next page we see the growth of the population of the UK, as defined by consistent borders that came into force from 1921, in dark grey, growing from 6.6 million in 1700 to almost 67 million in 2019, with the values in millions on the left axis.

Correspondingly we can see the "real" value of the economy per person (in modern pounds), catering for the effect of inflation using the GDP deflators, as calculated by academics such Charles Feinstein and Gregory Clark, combined in modern times with that from the people at MeasuringWorth, the ONS, HM Treasury and the Office of Budget Responsibility (OBR). This is represented in the aqua blue/green line in the chart, extending over the same time period, and represents the average "real" value of the economy per person per year, with those values in thousands of pounds per year on the right axis. In 2019 this "real" value of GDP reached almost £33,300, compared to just £1,800 per person in 1700, an increase of approximately 18 fold.

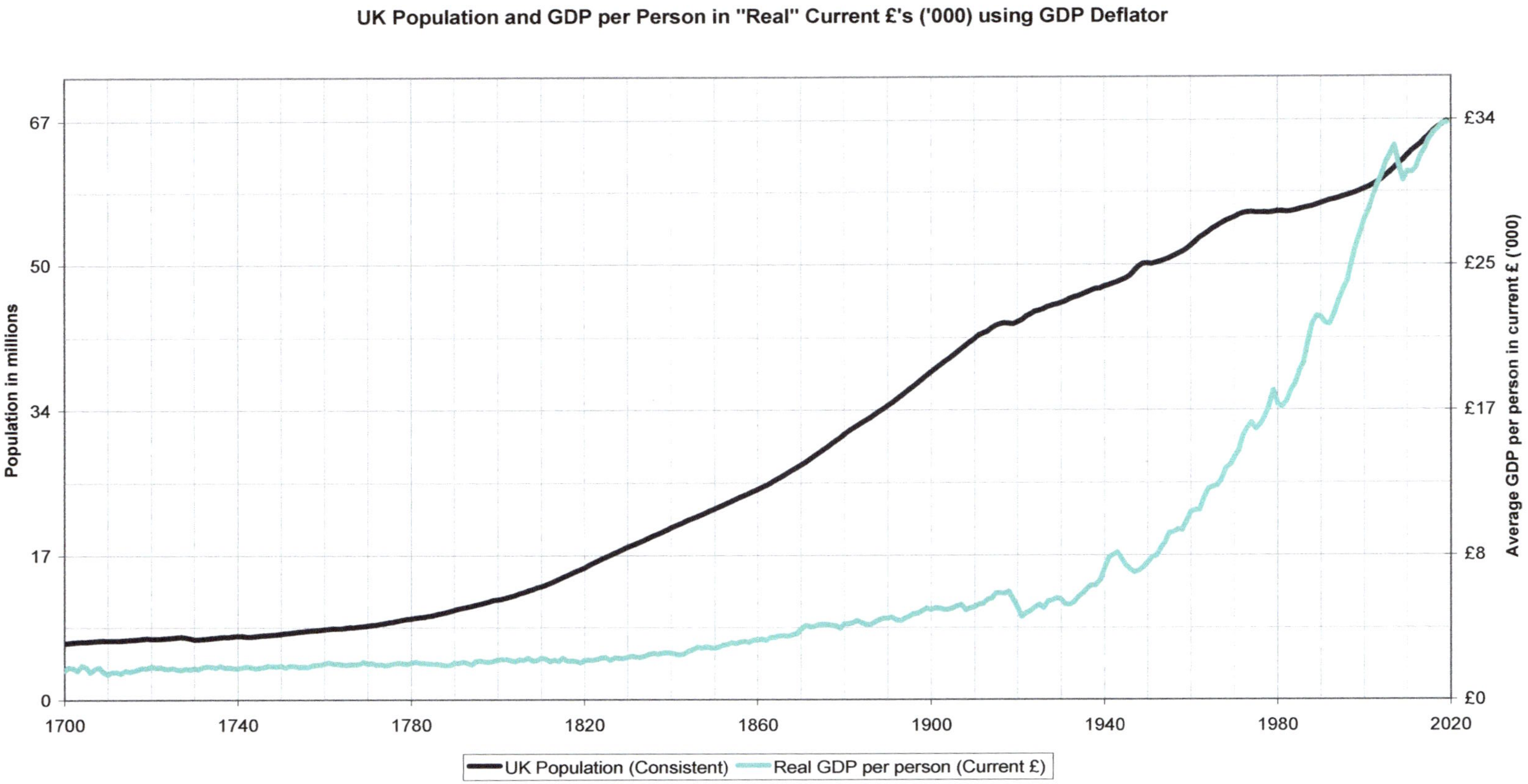

UK Population and GDP per Person in "Real" Current £'s ('000) using GDP Deflator

Average GDP per person in current £ ('000)

£34
£25
£17
£8
£0

2020
1980
1940
1900
1860
1820
1780
1740
1700

Population in millions

67
50
34
17
0

UK Population (Consistent) ——— Real GDP per person (Current £)

Clearly visible in the "real" value of GDP per person are the effects of various downturns, including the years after The Great War, The Second World War, the effects of the oil crisis of 1973 through to the "The Winter of Discontent" in 1979 and the effects of the 1989-1992 house price inflation and crash and the UK's ejection from the ERM mechanism.

However, most obvious is the effect of the 2008 economic crash, before which "real" GDP per person had peaked at almost £32,000 in 2007 but fell to a low of less than £30,000 per person in 2009 (falling to the same "real" value as in 2003). This was accompanied by an even more significant impact to national debt and average earnings, discussed in the coming pages and the next chapter respectively.

Economic transitions

All economies are composed of many different elements and for our purposes, to illustrate the composition as simply as possible, they are grouped into three broad categories of agriculture, industry and services.

It should be noted that there has been a great deal of debate in academic circles about the relative contributions from even these three broadest categories, so the representations here only form a general indication of change over time.

The first and oldest, and once certainly the largest component, is agriculture (though incorporating forestry and fishing to encompass the whole process of growing and gathering food and other facets of land management and consequent related production, for example timber).

This category is represented in the first chart at the top of the next page and coloured in green. Clearly agriculture, in the form of the production of food for a continuously growing population since 1700, remains a vital component of the health and well-being of the nation, but in terms of its economic contribution to the economy, it has obviously declined since the levels of the first half of the 18th century, then being slightly over 40%, but now measured at less than 1% of the economy at the end of the second decade of the 21st century.

Even more contentious is the growth of industry and manufacturing. All are aware of the concept of the Industrial Revolution, regarded generally to date from the second half of the 18th century, but there has been much debate centred on the rates of growth from that time. Three major academic contributors are represented in the middle chart and are encapsulated by Deane and Cole from 1962 in the top purple line, then that compiled in the Bank of England "Millennium Database" in the middle brown line (sourced mostly from Broadberry *et al.* from 2015), then that from Harley and Crafts from 1992 in the bottom burgundy line. All three however show that the greatest effect of that revolution in production did not begin to be felt strongly until after the end of the Napoleonic wars.

We stand on much firmer ground for the later years during the peak of manufacturing industry and its decline after The Second World War.

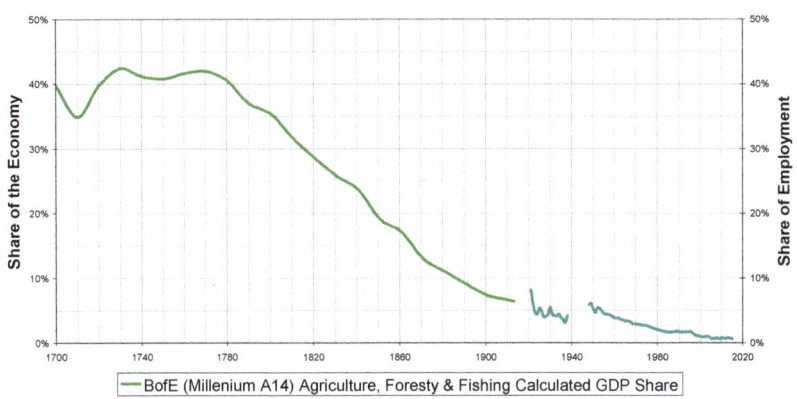

The decline of Agriculture as a contribution to the Economy and Employment

BofE (Millenium A14) Agriculture, Foresty & Fishing Calculated GDP Share

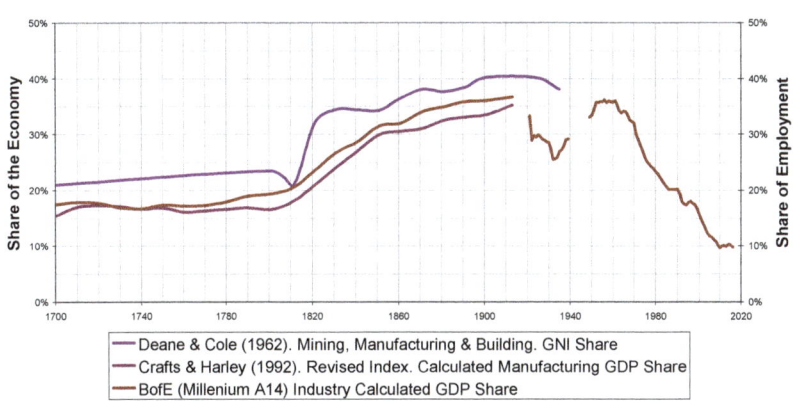

Growth and decline of Industry as a contribution to the Economy and Employment

Deane & Cole (1962). Mining, Manufacturing & Building. GNI Share
Crafts & Harley (1992). Revised Index. Calculated Manufacturing GDP Share
BofE (Millenium A14) Industry Calculated GDP Share

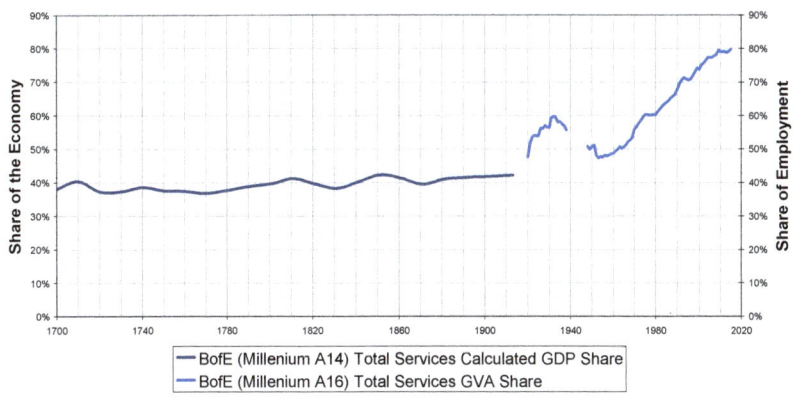

The growth of Services as a contribution to the Economy and Employment

BofE (Millenium A14) Total Services Calculated GDP Share
BofE (Millenium A16) Total Services GVA Share

Manufacturing contribution has now fallen from a post Second World War peak of 35% in the 1950s to just a 10% contribution to the economy at the end of the second decade of the 21st century.

Of huge significance, as a result, is that all types of services, from retail, education, health and social care etc., have grown from a surprisingly large 40% contribution during the 18th and even 19th centuries, booming to an estimated 80% or more at the end of the second decade of the 21st century. These being represented in the chart at the bottom of the previous page with the blue lines.

Although not shown here for the sake of simplicity, estimates of share of employment within the economy for each of the three broad groupings each tend to show correspondingly similar shares of total employment.

A state of war

At a national level the economy is of course also intimately linked to that authority that we call the State and its' Government.

In the millennia before 1700, the probably apocryphal claim associated with Louis XIV, the Sun King of France: "*l'état, c'est moi*" , was effectively a reality (Attributed by Jacques-Antoine Dulaure in his 1834 *Histoire physique, civile et morale de Paris*).

At least in early feudal times, the King effectively owned the whole land and granted his lands to his supporters. A prime example of this in practice being expressed in the Domesday Book of 1086, commissioned by William I (the Conqueror).

Therefore for most of the history of England, Wales, Scotland and Ireland that authority was an absolute monarchy, but by 1700 the authority had finally become constitutional, thanks to the violent and devastating civil war in the early 17th century and the subsequent "Glorious Revolution" of 1688.

As such the primary focus of the state was, and largely remained until the start of the 20th century, the prosecution of wars for a multitude of aggrandising reasons and in support of complex political machinations of the monarch and the governments of the time.

The wars prosecuted and the general lifestyle of the monarch were expensive and as such the state imposed taxes on as many of their subjects as they could, to provide the necessary funds.

As such it is not unfair to view the State as being in "a state of war" for much of history.

This is represented in the chart on the next page by the blue line, being estimated military expenditure as a share of the GDP, and the obvious effect on total government expenditure as a share of GDP in the dark green line.

The total revenue taken by the government as a share of GDP is also shown in the light green line. The gap between the dark green and the light green being the first and most obvious shortfall that ultimately gives

The Growth of the State - State Revenue and Spending plus Military Spending as % GDP

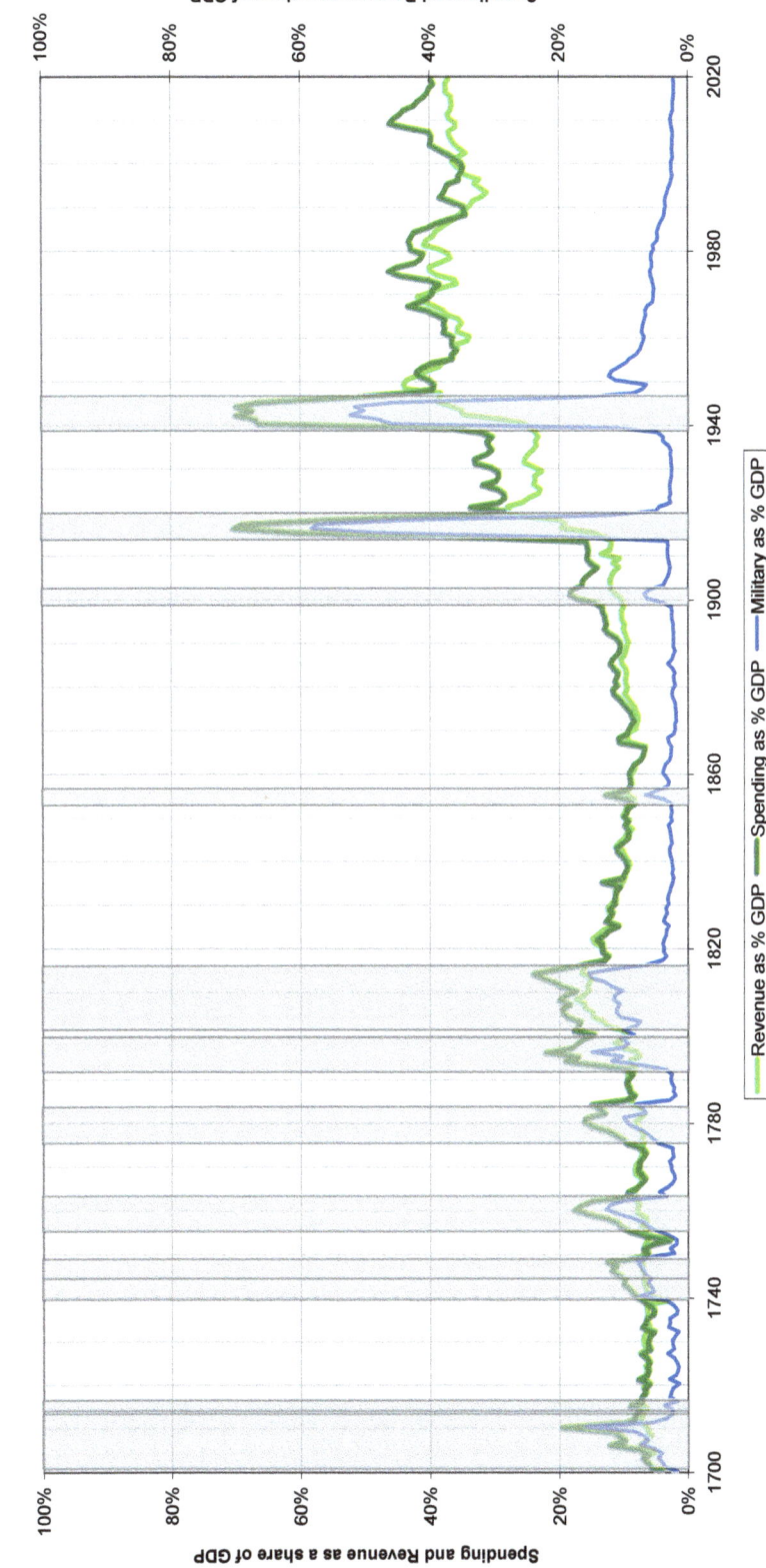

Spending and Revenue as a share of GDP

Revenue as % GDP — Spending as % GDP — Military as % GDP

rise to both the annual deficit and the National Debt (or Public Sector Borrowing Requirement, amongst other measures).

To illustrate the effect of wars on government expenditure, these are highlighted in the selected grey blocks, which chronologically represent:

- The War of the Spanish Succession (1701 to 1714)
- The first Jacobite Rising of 1715
- The War of Jenkin's Ear (1739 to 1748)
- The War of the Austrian Succession (1740 to 1748)
- The second Jacobite Rising of 1745
- The Seven Years War (1756 to 1763)
- The American War of Independence (1776 to 1783)
- The French Revolutionary Wars (1792 to 1802)
- The Napoleonic Wars (1803 to 1815)
- The Crimean War (1853 to 1856)
- The Boer War (1899 to 1902)
- The Great War (1914 to 1918)
- The Second World War (1939 to 1945)

Fortunately there have been comparatively few wars of quite such magnitude in which the UK has been involved since The Second World War, though the immediate post war decades were marred by the Malayan Emergency, The Korean War, The Suez Crisis and of course The Cold War. The fiscal effect of these can also be seen in the small uplift of the blue military expenditure line in 1950 followed by a steady decline.

Even the more recent involvement in the Falklands conflict, Balkan wars, Gulf War and the Afghanistan and Iraq conflicts have been comparatively limited, at least in their fiscal impact.

The fiscal effects of this huge military expenditure are illustrated in the chart on the next page in the growth of National Debt as a share of GDP in the pink line.

This clearly tracks these wars as it rises from 20% of GDP in 1700, through the 18th century, peaking at 220% of GDP in 1820 (that is more than twice the annual size of the economy). It then gradually falls to 30% of GDP on the eve of The Great War, as the debt is cleared, then surges thereafter, until peaking at 250% of GDP in 1946, after The Second World War. Military expenditure as a share of government expenditure is also shown in the yellow line to re-emphasise the close relationship.

Interestingly, there are two notable increases to national debt that are non-war related periods of growth of debt.

The first was a relatively small rise in the 1930s from 170% of GDP in 1929 to 190% of GDP in 1932, as a result of the worldwide economic depression triggered by the "Wall Street Crash".

The second is the result of the worldwide economic crash of 2008 when National Debt as a percent of GDP soared from 34% in 2007 reaching 84% of GDP in 2019.

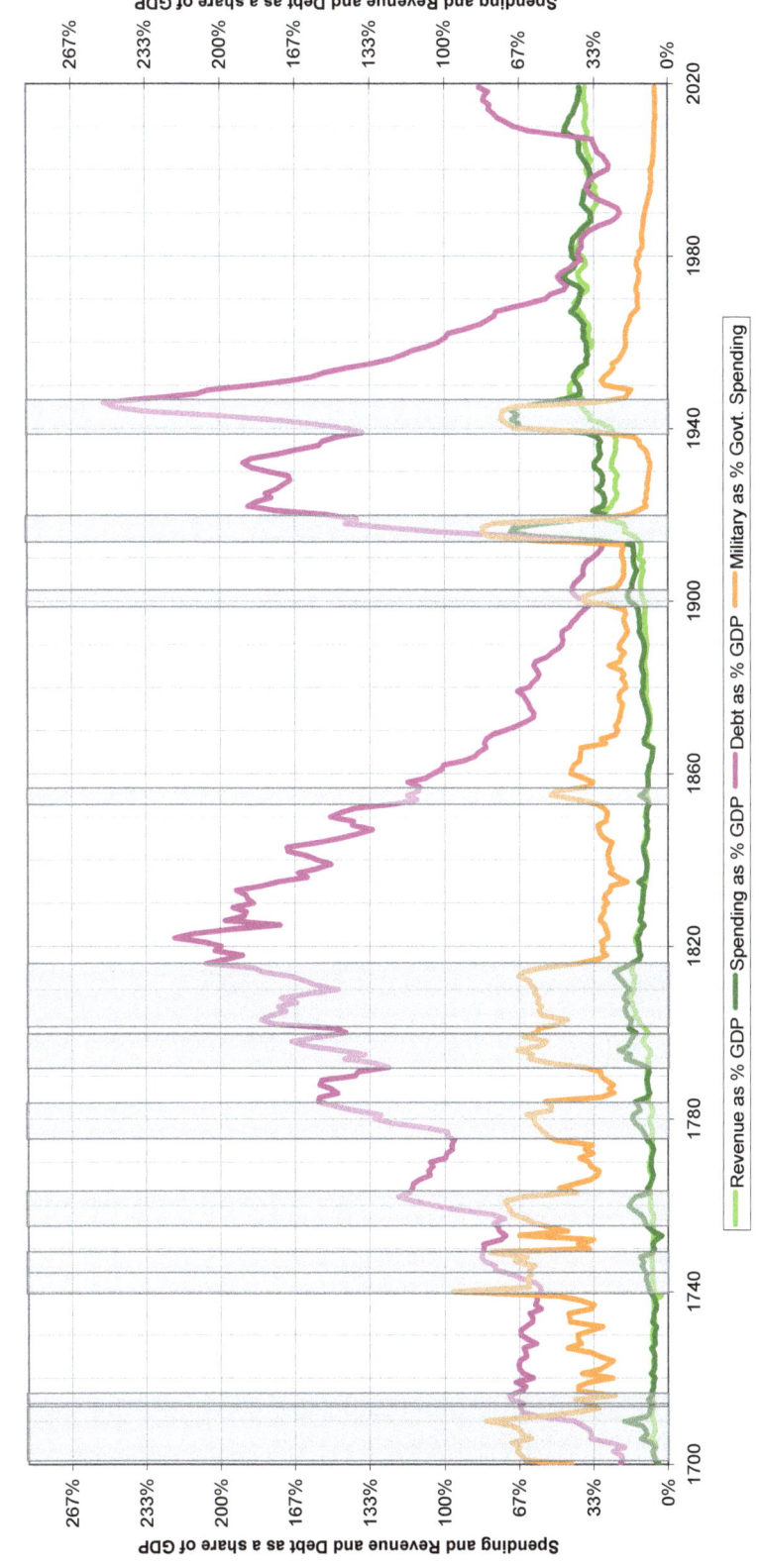

A State of War - UK Debt, State Revenue and Spending as a % GDP plus Military as % Govt. Spending

Spending and Revenue and Debt as a share of GDP

Revenue as % GDP — Spending as % GDP — Military as % Govt. Spending
Debt as % GDP

National Debt can be thought of, in household terms, as the nation taking out loans over long periods, on which interest must be paid to the lender (the international markets). This should not be confused with the current budget deficit carried by the government in any year, which might be thought of as more akin to an overdraft.

Public sector employment

In addition to the share of the economy occupied by government revenue and spending, the government also employ people to conduct and administer their business.

This extends from core government functions and senior officers to all forms of administrative civil servants, armed forces, and also in the 20th century, employees of nationalised industries and corporations, health care employees and state school teachers.

The estimates of such employment over time, again shared in the Bank of England Millennium Database, are illustrated in the chart on the next page as a share of total "gainful" employment in the whole economy.

The total including armed forces is represented by the green lines (light and olive), whilst excluding armed forces by the blue lines. This closely corresponds with the estimates and measures of expenditure on wars previously discussed until the post war period.

Further confirmation of the impact of the new policies, from the 1945 election of the Labour government led by Clement Attlee, can be seen in the share of employment by those corporations that were nationalised, within the non-armed forces blue line. The purple line illustrates the share of state employment excluding the share employed by the state-owned corporations and armed forces, and clearly shows the growth as a result of nationalisation followed by the denationalisation particularly from the time of the Thatcher premiership.

Represented within the purple line as well is the growth of state employment including state education and the National Health Service, but this also includes the underlying share employed to service state administration.

The historical trend of the component of state employment that explicitly excludes all employment by armed forces, state corporations, public sector teachers and clinical staff in the NHS (including an allowance for front line NHS support staff) is not easy to ascertain and an up to date estimate for 2019 of about 10% of all employed for state administration is presented in the sand coloured diamond at the far right of the chart.

Growth of the state

Returning to the question of National Debt and its funding, needless to say, the debt incurred is generally repaid at some time, but it must also be serviced in the form of interest payments.

Estimates/measures of Public sector employment as a share of all employment

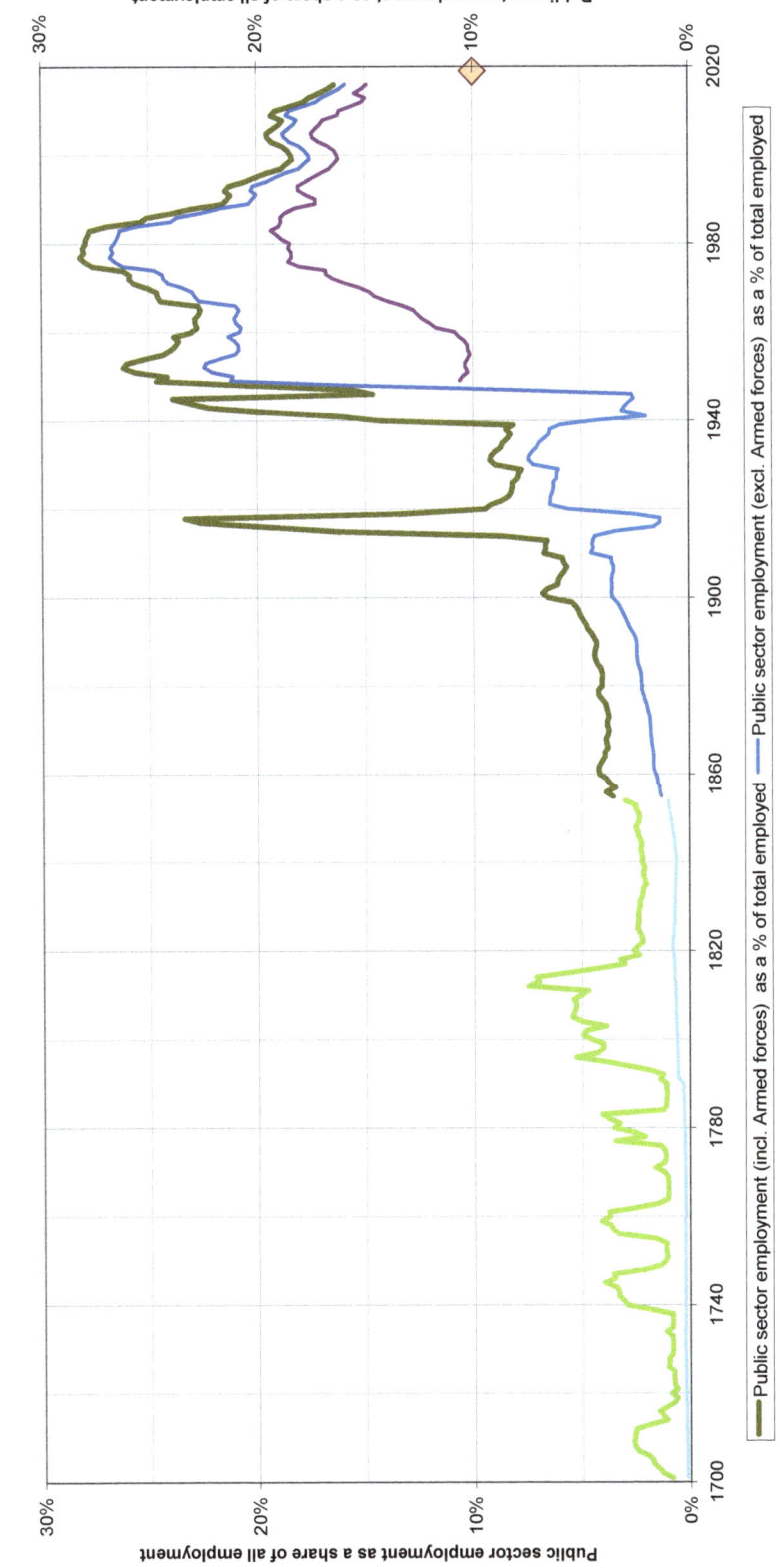

Public sector employment as a share of all employment

— Public sector employment (incl. Armed forces) as a % of total employed —— Public sector employment (excl. Armed forces) as a % of total employed

In the very colourful chart on the next page the primary components of the spending by the government as a share of GDP are illustrated.

Very notable in the chart is the dearth of data about the internal overhead of government expenditure before 1800.

This was also a time before any form of income tax was imposed, this being first introduced in 1799 by William Pitt "The Younger" as a means of finding extra funding for the very costly wars with France. This was repealed in 1816, but was re-introduced permanently in 1842 by the government of Robert Peel.

The mid-blue block at the top of the stack is a re-presentation of that illustrated in the previous two charts in the blue and yellow lines, being military (or Defence) expenditure. The aqua blue/green block below defence, represents the interest that governments have had to pay to their creditors to fund the debt previously discussed.

It can be seen that this has clearly fallen as the debt burden has fallen, but notable in the second decade of the 21st century, the interest burden is very small in relation to the large increase of the debt burden as, internationally, interest rates have been strongly suppressed since the twin peaks of 1980 and 1990. It should be noted that the twin peaks themselves had immediate significant corrective impacts on the housing markets (by stopping house price inflation), but with the subsequent suppression of interest rates, other consequences for the housing market have been experienced since 1997 (see the sixth chapter **Housing**).

Clearly visible is the growth of related social expenditure by government from the later decades of the 19th century, represented by the blocks of salmon pink (Education), orange (Health Care/NHS), pale blue (Old Age Pension), light blue (Social Welfare), bright pink (Transport) and light pink ("Protection", including police and courts).

The total shares for these six primary social and infrastructural provisions in 2019 represent approximately 27% of the GDP and 67% of total government expenditure, accordingly.

It is also interesting to note the vicissitudes of government spending and revenue in the decades since The Second World War, from the establishment of The Welfare State including the NHS, as alternative philosophies of fiscal largesse and rectitude have held sway.

This is quite clear in the effect on the share of government spending and revenue rising and falling over time.

Peaks of spending have tended to occur when the Labour Party have been in government, whilst reductions, in the light of attempts to reduce at least the government deficit by curbing spending, when the Conservative Party have been in government.

International events have both strongly mitigated and exaggerated this trend. For example between 1948 and 2019 total government spending as a share of GDP had been reduced to a low of less than 35% in 1988 during the Thatcher premiership and again in 1999 during the Blair premiership, but peaked at 46% of GDP in 2009, in the aftermath of the 2008 crash.

Government Spending and Revenue as a % of GDP

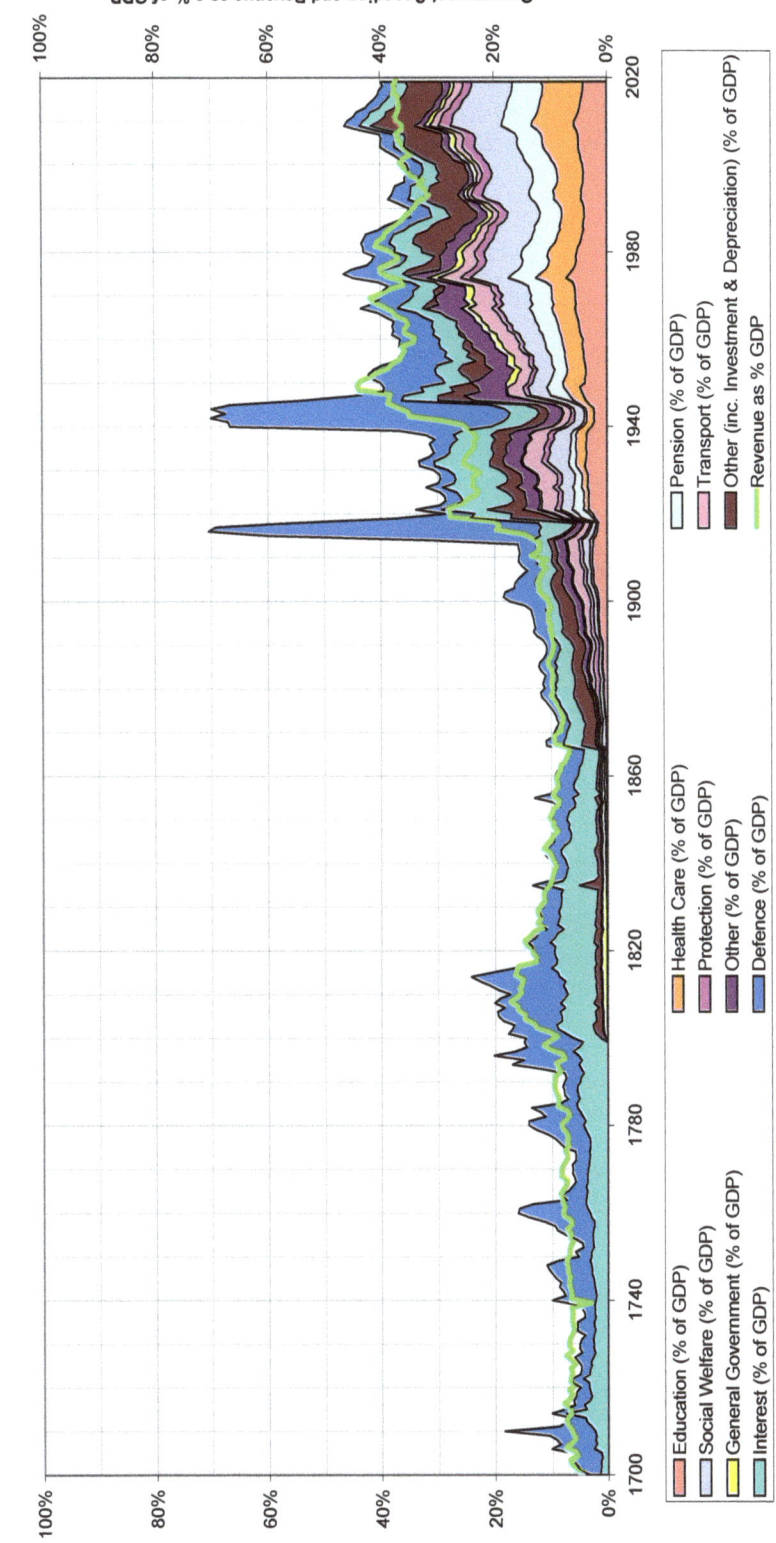

Government Spending and Revenue as a % of GDP

Government Spending and Revenue as a % of GDP

Legend:
- Education (% of GDP)
- Social Welfare (% of GDP)
- General Government (% of GDP)
- Interest (% of GDP)
- Health Care (% of GDP)
- Protection (% of GDP)
- Other (% of GDP)
- Defence (% of GDP)
- Pension (% of GDP)
- Transport (% of GDP)
- Other (inc. Investment & Depreciation) (% of GDP)
- Revenue as % GDP

However in the light of the return to large debt after 2008 and severe budget deficit of 7.2% of GDP in 2009, the coalition and subsequent Conservative governments reduced this to a short lived credit in 2018 and a low of 0.6% of GDP in 2019, by generally reducing government spending back below 40% of GDP in 2018 and 2019.

Poor Law and social protection

The Poor Law was conceived during the reign of Henry VIII in the aftermath of the English Reformation, the dissolution of the monasteries and the establishment of the Church of England.

Until this revolution, alms to assist the poor were almost entirely the preserve of the church.

Ultimately the 1601 Poor Relief Act was introduced, which consolidated the various pieces of legislation from the 1530s to the end of the 16th century, providing a new approach to aiding those in poverty and destitution. This law and its predecessors were entirely conceived as parish responsibilities and funded through local provision by a parish based Poor Law "rate", imposed on local land owners and businesses.

As most people tend to be very adaptable and mobile, following opportunities for work and pursuit of business by migrating geographically as they needed, a side effect of the establishment of the Poor Law centred on parish authorities, was the refusal of relief for anyone who fell on hard times whilst resident in their "non-native" parish.

These laws were supplemented often, but particularly by the 1662 Relief of the Poor Act that gave "non-natives" who were resident in another parish access to poor relief in hard times.

Historically, provision of social spending as a share of GDP, via the Poor Law, is represented in the chart on the next page in the orange and pink lines.

An estimate of the share of the economy spent on poor relief is derived from the best known data quoted in Mitchell (*British Historical Statistics*, 1988) and Boyer (*The Winding Road to the Welfare State*, 2019), this consistently showing that the share peaked in the decade before the 1834 Poor Law Amendment Act at approximately 2% of GDP.

Thanks to the 19th century campaigns against relief outside the workhouse, ever harsher conditions of access to, and conditions within, workhouses and the growing moral stigma accompanying the idea of turning to the Poor Law for help, there was thereafter a tendency for fewer people to claim relief. Thus the share spent fell thereafter to significantly less than 1% of GDP, as it had been throughout most of the 18th century, until the outbreak of the French Revolutionary Wars.

The central state provision of social protection from the first decade of the 20th century onwards (including some support for education from the later 19th century and later health care) is shown in stark contrast in the red line, clearly showing the growth of the share of all social protection.

Historical Poor Law Relief and State Social Spending (Education, Health, Pension and Social Welfare) as a % of GDP

Social Protection Spending as a share of GDP

— Expenditure on Poor Relief as % GDP — Govt. Education, Health, Pension + Social Welfare as % GDP

Clearly seen in the red line though are the reduction in total provision as a share of the economy during the two World Wars, as well as a reduction following the 1976/77 IMF crisis, subsequent "Winter of Discontent" and the election of the Conservative government under Margaret Thatcher. There is a clear return to growth of spending as a share of the economy from 1990 to 2009, but followed by another substantial fall from 2010 under the coalition administration and subsequent Conservative governments to 2019.

State provision of social protection

From the evolution of political and social thinking throughout the 18th and 19th century, which was substantially still driven by earlier religious and moral thinking about God's ordination of the social order and the resulting undeserving poor, to the growth of the middle classes and self-help social, charitable and political thinking, emerged a more radical Liberal Party and crucially a greater political awareness amongst working class people, with stronger unionisation, and a broader franchise that ultimately led to the growth of the Labour Party, founded in 1900.

These trends led to the first major breakthrough in the social "protection" element of spending following the election of the Liberal government of 1906.

Particularly as a result of the zeal of David Lloyd-George and Winston Churchill, many provisions were introduced including: school meals for children; the introduction of early national pension provision from 1908; extending minimum wages to agricultural workers from 1909 and compulsory national insurance for the provision of some health care and unemployment benefit from 1911 (at least for a large number of workers, if not all).

Whilst comparatively restricted in coverage and benefit, these reforms were the true start of what we now think of as the "welfare state".

A side effect of the introduction of the measures was the limiting of the powers of the House of Lords as a result of the 1911 Parliament Act which thereafter prevented the un-elected House of Lords being able to block legislation from the elected House of Commons.

Following the end of The Great War the scope and extent of social provision was further expanded, and even extended to building of social housing under the banner of the "Homes fit for Heroes" policy, encapsulated in the 1919 Housing Act (see the sixth chapter **Housing**).

Looking in more detail at the share of people in receipt of Poor Law and later state social protection, a different picture emerges from that of the share of the economy (GDP) spent on poor relief and social spending.

Note that in the previous representation of social spending, the full provision of education and health is also added to pension and social "welfare" as a share of the economy.

Of course, in the modern era, education with the provision of national

Estimate of Percent of Population in receipt of Historical Poor Law Relief and State Social Protection (Pension & Welfare)

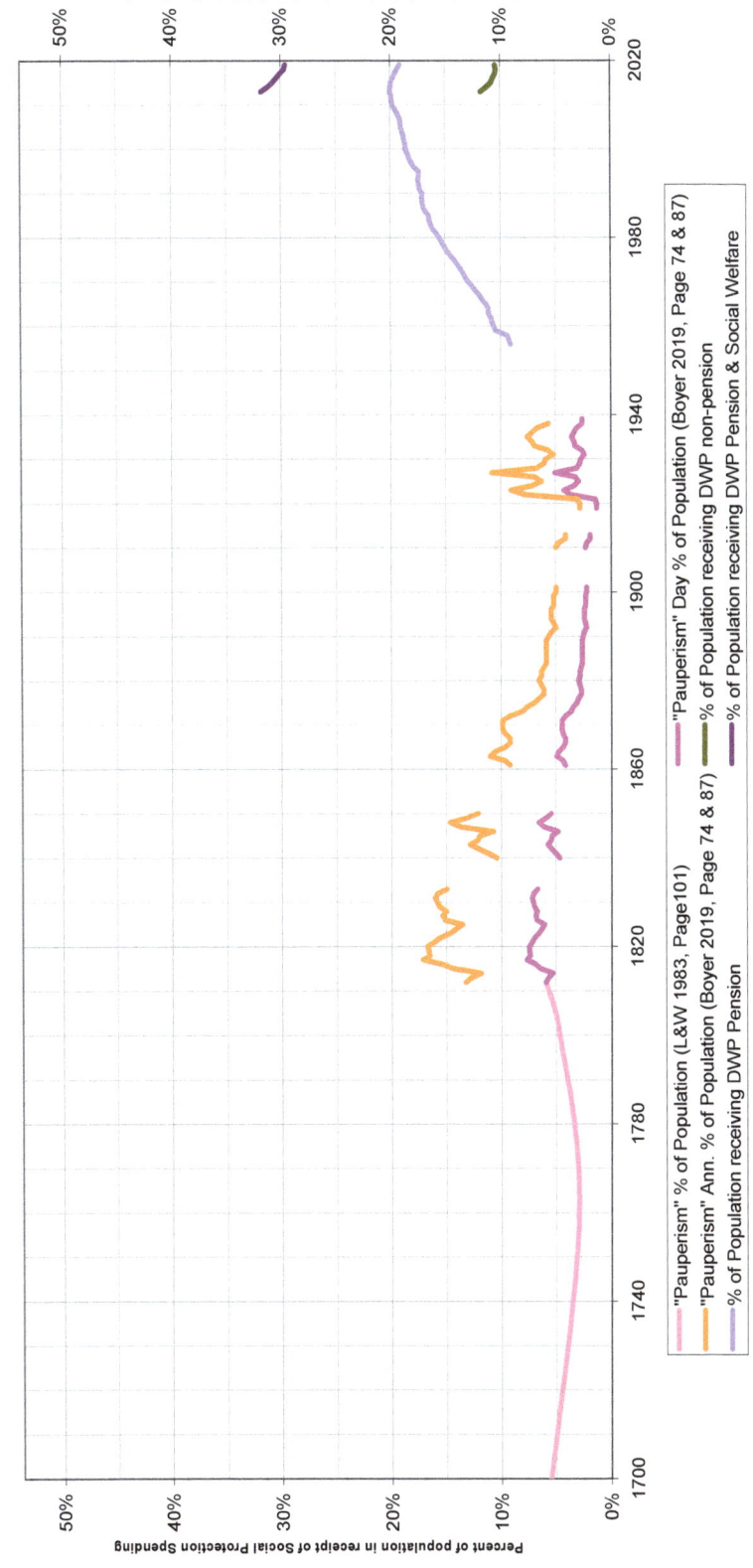

Legend:
- "Pauperism" % of Population (L&W 1983, Page 101)
- "Pauperism" Ann. % of Population (Boyer 2019, Page 74 & 87)
- % of Population receiving DWP Pension
- "Pauperism" Day % of Population (Boyer 2019, Page 74 & 87)
- % of Population receiving DWP non-pension
- % of Population receiving DWP Pension & Social Welfare

schools, and health care with the creation of the National Health Service, are available to everyone, but since no such provision was made by any state authorities, either centrally or locally before the late 19th century, and in the first decade of the 20th century with limited health care funded via national insurance, these two components are excluded for this analysis for the period after The Second World War, in order to offer a "like-for-like" comparison of Poor Law compared to equivalent modern social protection provision.

Thus in the chart on the previous page the focus switches to just the provision of pensions and other social "welfare" spending including unemployment, disability, incapacity, child support and housing benefits.

In addition to the data quoted in Mitchell and Boyer above, we have earlier historical estimates of "pauperism" from Lindert & Williamson (*Reinterpreting Britain's Social Tables 1688-1913*, 1983).

Using these data we are able to estimate the share of population that were in receipt of poor relief and pre-Second World War assistance, on a daily basis represented in the pink lines, peaking at 8% in the 1820s.

However, as with the modern estimation of those people sleeping rough on the streets, there is a very clear distinction between the spot counting of numbers on any given day, compared to the number, and consequently percentage of the population, who may have been forced to turn to the Poor Law (or find themselves sleeping rough) at some time during the year.

For the Poor Law and pre-Second World War assistance this latter derived from the data analysed and presented in Boyer 2019 (from Lees, 1998), is represented in the orange line, clearly peaking at approximately 17% in the 1820s, over twice that of the day rate.

The provision of pension support in old age, and the other social "welfare" benefits mentioned above, which are now the administrative and reporting responsibility of the Department for Work and Pensions, are represented as shares of the population in receipt of each collection of benefits by the lavender coloured line for pensions, currently just under 20% of the population, the green line for the other aforementioned social "welfare" at approximately 10% of the population, resulting in a total of 30% of the population in receipt of these particular social provisions in the purple line. Functionally almost twice that of the peak of poor relief.

This is of course because the provision of social protection is significantly more accessible in the first two decades of the 21st century than in the three centuries from 1700 to the end of the 20th century.

An analysis of national net worth

We conclude our analysis of the growth of the economy by looking at the estimated net worth, or some might think wealth, of the UK as a whole, which, as "net" worth/wealth, represents an idea of the "value" of the economy and the nation, after all debt commitments are accounted for.

Bank of England Millennium (A57) Net Wealth (to 1996) and ONS UK National Real Net Worth (from 1997) per capita in £'000s

Although only usefully available in various forms since the end of The Great War, the chart on the previous page attempts to show the "real" growth of this net worth as a series by representing the historical analysis from 1920 to 1997 from the Bank of England Millennium Database in the pink line, and the ONS analysis of the national balance sheet and the net worth in the red line to 2019.

By applying the same GDP deflator to the net worth estimates, as used previously for the annual nominal production, trading and consumption values, and by dividing by the size of the population, the analysis tends to suggest that the UK's citizens on average ended the second decade of the 21st century theoretically worth over 10 times more than 100 years ago in 1920.

However clearly visible again in this analysis is the huge impact of the 2008 crash, the limited recovery and again a notable failure to achieve further improvement in 2019.

In addition the inequality of the distribution of net wealth is greater even than that of annual incomes, though still dramatically less than in decades before The Second World War.

In general the history of the economy and the state throughout a period of firstly constitutionally and franchise limited authority, and then gradually with a wider and wider franchise, forming a more "representative democracy", tended to yield significant benefits to a greater and greater number of citizens.

This has not shown any signs of compromising the ability of the economy to grow in productivity and consequent outcomes for those citizens.

It is often argued that in fact the acquisition of government revenue by taxation and its redistribution and expenditure is able to perform many stimulations to economic growth and also to mitigate many of the worst effects of economic crises that occur all too frequently.

In the modern era this is now often seen as axiomatic by many.

It has in fact seen a return, in the first decades of the 21st century, to a way of thinking and behaving that is nearly identical to the post Second World War consensus.

It remains to be seen how long it takes for the previous consequences of growing bureaucracy and the even more dangerous tendency of the corruption of thinking in the light of greater and greater state power in the 1970s, to start to undo the gains of the last few decades.

It is possible that these many and various unintended consequences are already coming to the fore in the third decade of the 21st century!

Earnings and Income

"Annual income twenty pound, annual
expenditure nineteen nineteen and six,
result happiness. Annual income twenty
pounds, annual expenditure twenty
pounds nought and six, result misery."

Charles Dickens:
David Copperfield,
1850

Historical wages for labourers

Perhaps in the late 20th and early 21st century we are aware that a greater share of the population are in receipt of "unearned" income than ever before: from returns from share ownership (dividends), returns from land and property ownership (rental income), receipt of pensions, both private and state, and of course state paid benefits for the disabled, incapacitated and unemployed, along with the other similar state aids.

However it remains the case that the vast majority of people in receipt of income, receive this income as earnings in exchange for their "labour", be it physical (once categorised as "blue-collar" and who constituted the "working class") or mental (once categorised as "white-collar" and who tended to make up a large portion of the "middle-class").

Therefore our first view of the improvements of real incomes over time is to focus on the best estimates of average (mean) earnings by that majority of people who exchange their labour for earnings, particularly for the 18th and 19th century, in exchange for their physical labour. We will also touch upon the distribution of those incomes as well, but return to this distribution in more detail in the next chapter to inform the reality that lies behind the average (mean). Note that these data are before the deduction of direct taxation (income tax and national insurance), which was not introduced permanently until 1842 by the Peel government.

Despite the development of the UK economy throughout the 16th and 17th centuries towards ever greater commerce and industry; at the outset of the 18th century the UK remained a strongly agricultural nation, albeit less than those previous centuries and less so than most of its fellow European nations in the 18th century.

As such, historians and economists have been at pains to establish a reliable history of the earnings of agricultural labourers who continued to constitute a substantial share of the workforce, but were gradually supplanted by the greater participation of urban factory labourers throughout the 19th century. The latter began to grow in both numerical and social significance from the last two decades of the 18th century, thanks mostly to the growth of the cotton industry, and industrial iron production.

The foremost researcher in the later 20th century responsible for some of the most trusted analysis of labourers incomes was Charles Feinstein, building upon, refining and enhancing the earlier work of the likes of Arthur Lyon Bowley at the start of the 20th century, who himself further built upon the analysis of A. Wilson Fox, Leone Levi, Josiah Stamp, Robert Dudley Baxter and William Ray Smee amongst many others.

Their research has been further strongly supplemented and extended by many other historians in the late 20th century and the opening decades of the 21st century, particularly including Gregory Clark, and interestingly some detailed analysis by Jeffrey Williamson, Peter Lindert , Sarah Horrell, Jane Humphries and Margaret Lyle amongst others.

Several of the mentioned historians have accordingly also equally focussed their researches on this growing group of urban labourers as well, alongside the agricultural labourers, particularly Charles Feinstein.

These allow us to see a strong pattern that reflects the shift of the economy towards manufacturing and the growing populace employed to support the new methods of production and commerce, centred on the new urban mechanised, water, steam and coal-powered factory system.

This inevitably changed the balance of demand and remuneration for the labours of the workers over the first two centuries of the period we are representing.

In the sequence of the charts on the next page are shown the best known estimates of the average weekly money wages (in shillings per week) of agricultural labourers in the green line in the top chart, and the average of all labourers, both agricultural and urban in the pink line.

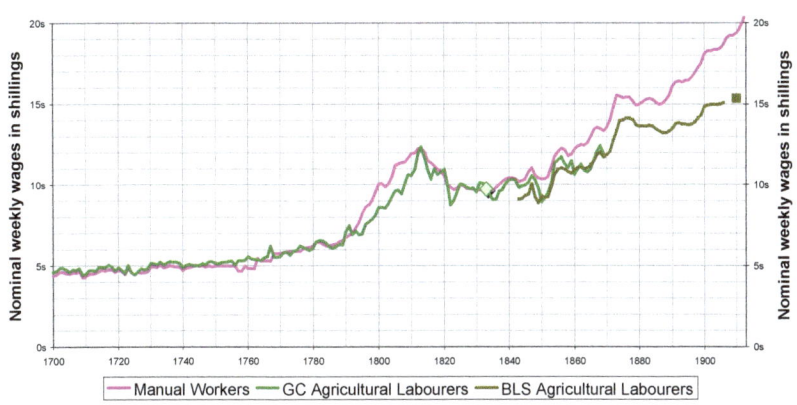

Average nominal weekly wages (shillings per week) for wage earners

Legend: Manual Workers — GC Agricultural Labourers — BLS Agricultural Labourers

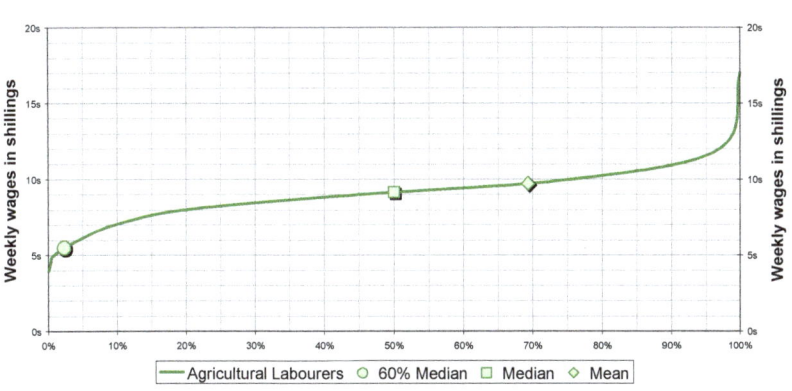

Distribution of agricultural labourers "winter" weekly wages (shillings per week) weighted by parish from 1834 Poor Law Commission Rural Queries (Lyle, 2007)

Legend: Agricultural Labourers ○ 60% Median □ Median ◇ Mean

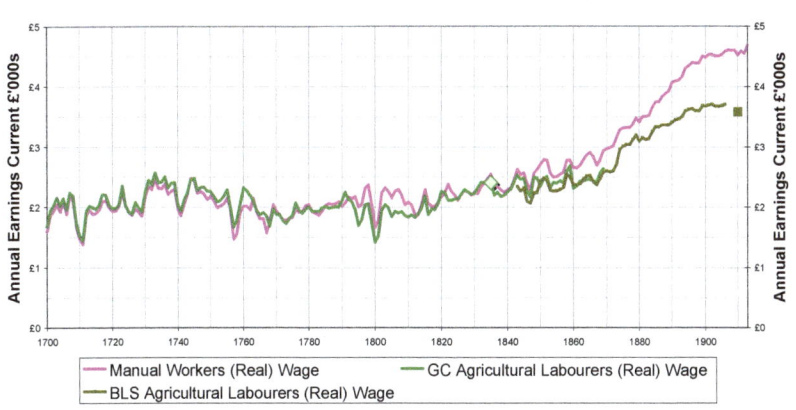

Average "Real" annual earnings (in current £'000s using CPI)

Legend: Manual Workers (Real) Wage — GC Agricultural Labourers (Real) Wage — BLS Agricultural Labourers (Real) Wage

63

It is important to clarify the composition of these two lines.

The green lines, derived from the work of Gregory Clark (GC) (1700 to 1867) and A. Wilson Fox - British Labour Statistics (BLS) (1843 to 1903), are a representation of only agricultural labourers money *"winter"* wages (about 9 months of the year), excluding summer and harvest extras and supplements, and excluding benefits in kind such as food, beer and cider. The pink line, from Charles Feinstein and quoted in the Bank of England Millennium database, however, is a composite for all manual labourers, both urban and agricultural.

Despite these two different compositions, the clear indication that emerges from the early years following the end of the Napoleonic Wars in 1815, is that the average earnings of the composite of all labourers increased at a greater rate than that for only agricultural labourers, through to the eve of The Great War.

The middle chart offers an estimate of the distribution of agricultural winter wages, from the rural returns of almost 900 parishes in answer to one of the questions asked by the Poor Law Commission in 1833/34. Although not weighted by number of labourers it does still show a strong picture of inequality, even within the range of agricultural labourers wages, before Poor Law reform was enacted in 1834.

Margaret Lyle in her fascinating 2007 analysis of these returns (*"Regional agricultural wage variations in early nineteenth-century England"*), from which these data are derived, also extends this variation to its regional impact for all of England, including very informative maps.

We are even able to see the effects of this regional variation upon demand for labour in the 1860 analysis by David Chadwick, Treasurer of Salford (*"On the rate of wages in Manchester and Salford, and the manufacturing districts of Lancashire, 1839-59"*). Chadwick's analysis supports the estimates of higher wages for agricultural labourers in the countryside around Manchester and Salford than the lower agricultural wages in much of the south and south west of England, for example.

The lower chart represents the same data as the first chart, but now normalised to current "real" monetary values, using the cost of living index for those years from Charles Feinstein, and expressed as annual average "real" wages in thousands of pounds. This clearly illustrates the effects of particularly difficult economic times in 1708/11, the mid 1750s and the time of the French Revolutionary and Napoleonic Wars in 1800.

Whilst all labourers saw their real remuneration grow from the 1820s onwards, it is very clear that urban labourers were benefiting significantly more than agricultural labourers, as the composite of all labourers, expressed in the pink line, grew two-and-a-half fold, compared to significantly less than two fold for agricultural labourers only.

In the chart on the next page we now add the historical analysis of Gregory Clark, from the MeasuringWorth website (spliced with the 21st century ONS analysis from the *"Monthly Wages and Salaries Survey"*) in which the blue line presents "real" mean earnings for the whole economy.

Average "Real" annual earnings (in current £'000s using CPI)
(including middle class, all manual workers only and agricultural labourers only)
Indicating that current real average in 2019 is 13-15 times higher than in 1700-1800

The average annual "real" earnings for both middle-class white-collar earners, and all the manual labourers, is shown in the blue line.

Again this is a composite and has the side effect of obscuring the much greater remuneration of many of the middle classes in relation to even the growing group of urban labourers. Note also that focus on agricultural labourers is lost in the general historical analysis from the outbreak of The Great War as the share of employment by agriculture had fallen to below 8% of all employment by then (now fewer than 1% in 2019).

This trend is strongest from the 1870s to the period after the end of The Second World War and corresponds to the greatest growth of the new salary earning middle classes, yielding a 13 to 15 fold increase in average "real" earnings by 2019 compared to the early 18th century. It was this late 19th century growth that also gave rise to increase in owner occupation of housing, particularly from the inter war years, as more and more families and households were able to afford to own a home of their own. This latter phenomenon is discussed further in the sixth chapter **Housing**.

Also clearly visible is the severe impact on average earnings of the 2008 economic crash.

The average earnings for the whole economy (from the ONS "*Monthly Wages and Salaries Survey*" reported since 2000, as supplied in their *earn01* table), shown in "real" terms in the blue line (normalised using the ONS calculated annual CPI), were in 2019 slightly less than £28,000 per annum (being calculated from the average of £537.46 per week from each of 12 months of that year multiplied by 52 weeks for the year), whilst for 2008 were slightly over £28,800 (being calculated from the average of £435.41 per week from each of 12 months of that year multiplied by 52 weeks for the year, and factored by the CPI deflator of 78.57/100).

The chart on the next page illustrates more detail for earnings in the 21st century using the same ONS data from "*Monthly Wages and Salaries Survey*" *earn01* (seasonally adjusted, SA) and *earn03* (not seasonally adjusted, NSA) tables, now represented as "real" average weekly earnings (AWE) (normalised using the ONS calculated monthly CPI).

This shows the whole economy average in blue by month from January 2000 to December 2019 for all earnings (the same source for the annual average represented in blue in the previous chart described above, being the seasonally adjusted value).

Also shown is a re-weighted estimate of the composite of the 2007 Standard Industry Classification (SIC) gainfully employed in Agriculture and Manufacturing in pink, being the nearest similar grouping as presented in pink in the previous charts (though no longer just labourers in the respective industries). In addition the average earnings for SIC 2007 Agriculture (plus Forestry and Fishing) is shown in green. These are not seasonally adjusted (being taken from *earn03*, thus the variability).

Again the two show a substantial continuing gap, but seem to indicate that earnings in Manufacturing, relative to the whole economy average, has increased since the 1980s.

"Real" (CPI) Weekly Earnings Whole Economy, Manufacturing & Agriculture, Agriculture and Accommodation & Food

Average "real" weekly earnings (£)

—— Agriculture & Manufacturing - earn03 NSA —— Agriculture etc (A) - earn03 NSA —— Accommodation, Food Services (I) - earn03 NSA —— Whole Economy - earn01 SA
—— Agriculture & Manufacturing - earn03 NSA —— Agriculture etc (A) - earn03 NSA —— Whole Economy - earn01 SA

As a final reference, the least well paid SIC 2007 grouping of the Accommodation and Food Service sector is shown in light sandy brown and clearly shows how workers in this sector are significantly lower paid, even compared to the agricultural workers.

The industry weights given by the ONS for Agriculture indicate fewer than a 1% share of all gainful employment, whilst the share for manufacturing fell from a 16% in 2000 to an 8% share of all gainful employment at the end of 2019. The industry weight for "Accommodation and Food Services" indicates that the share for these workers has grown from 6% share of all gainful employment in 2000 to 7.5% share of all gainful employment at the end of 2019.

Household disposable income

Instead of wages, salaries and earnings for individual earners (before tax deduction), another perspective on incomes that shows the real effects on material livelihood, is household disposable income, regardless of its origins and after direct taxation.

These data are derived from regular government annual surveys since 1961, though with the addition of a special survey conducted in 1953/54 as rationing effectively ended after The Second World War and analysed in detail by Ian Gazeley and Andrew Newell.

They were known as Family Expenditure Surveys (FES), later being supplemented by a new survey from 1994/95 known as the Family Resource Survey (FRS), and in the case of FES merged with the older National Food Survey (NFS) in 2000 to become the Expenditure and Food Survey (EFS), then enhanced and renamed as the Living Costs and Food Survey (LCFS) in 2008.

FES/EFS/LCFS are notably much more detailed in their analysis of expenditure, but cover smaller samples of households compared to the less detailed but more widespread coverage of households of the FRS.

In addition to these surveys, a further methodological analysis has been applied to these data known as the Households Below Average Income (HBAI). The purpose of the HBAI is to analyse the relative status of the population of the UK by household in order to identify trends in and prevalence of "*relative poverty*" throughout the UK (classified to be those receiving less than 60% of median income), and additionally to accord with internationally agreed methods of identifying such conditions of life.

To achieve the best guide to such relative material well-being, a process known as equivalisation is applied, in which the size and age range of the members of each household are factored using a consistent expected "need" and thus the relative well being of various households may be more "fairly" compared.

This methodology has been applied to FRS data from 1994/95 by the Department for Work and Pensions, and constitutes part of what is known as "National Statistics", being used to guide government policy.

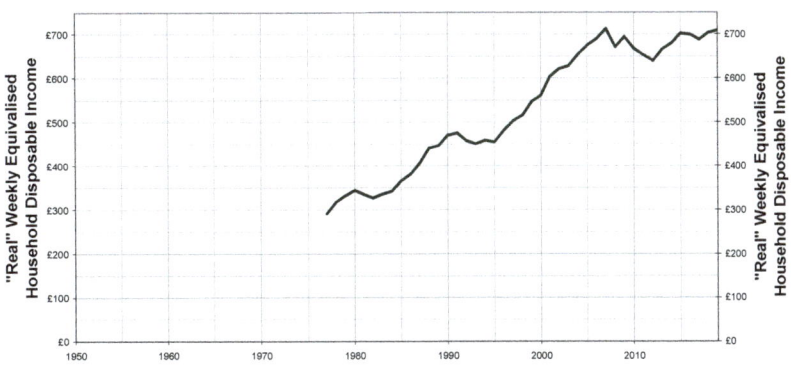

ONS "Real" (CPIH) Mean Equivalised Household Disposable Income of Individuals, UK, 1977 to 2019/2020 - Before Housing Costs

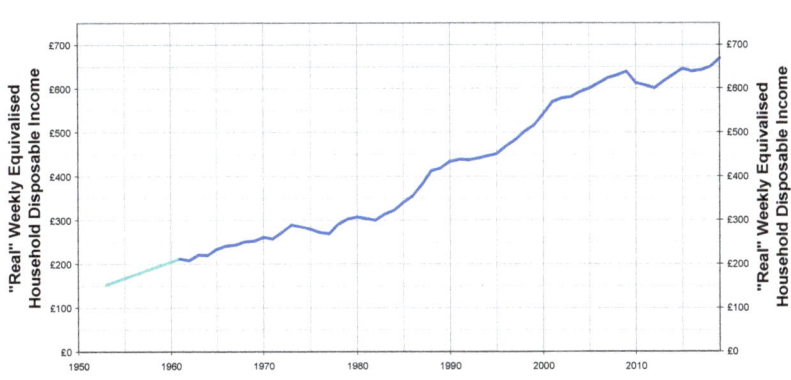

IFS (HBAI) (1953/54, Gazeley & Newell) "Real" (IFS) Mean Equivalised Household Disposable Income - Before Housing Costs

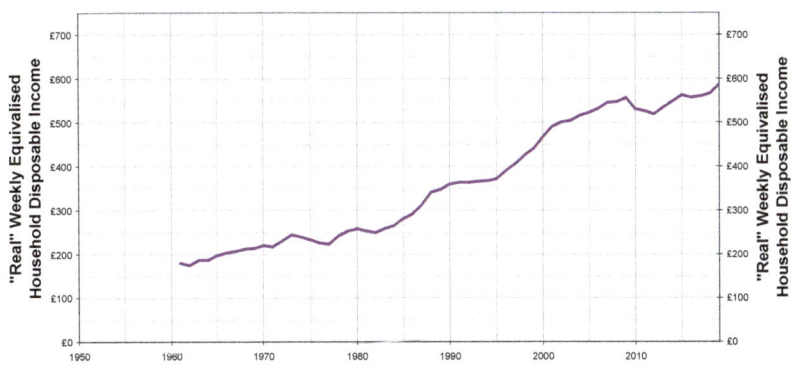

IFS (HBAI) "Real" (IFS) Mean Equivalised Household Disposable Income - After Housing Costs

69

Additionally, the Institute of Fiscal Studies has extended the analysis backwards to the first FES data from 1961.

The three charts on the previous page represent three trends of "real" (using the ONS consumer price index) equivalised mean household disposable income from these surveys.

The top chart shows "real" mean data from that published annually by the ONS for equivalised households for years from 1977, but does not use the HBAI methodology. It suggests that, on average, households are almost 2.5 times better off in real terms in 2019 compared to 1977.

The middle chart shows "real" mean data from the IFS for equivalised households *before housing costs* (BHC) are accounted for, using the HBAI methodology. This also indicates that, on average, households are about 2.5 times better off in 2019 in real terms than in 1977.

The data also suggests households are over 3 times better off in 2019 when compared to 1961. Also spliced to the data in the aqua line is the nearest equivalent available for reference (though not HBAI) from the older 1953/54 analysis and indicates an improvement of almost 4.5 fold in real disposable household income in 2019 compared to the year of the near complete end of rationing after The Second World War.

The lower chart shows "real" mean data from the IFS for equivalised households, this time, *after housing costs* (AHC) are accounted for, again using the HBAI methodology. This indicates that, on average, households are 2.6 times better off in 2019 in real terms than in 1977.

The data suggests households are almost 3.3 times better off in 2019 when compared to 1961. In this case the data for 1953/54 is notably less comparable and has not been represented accordingly for this analysis.

For reference, the relative improvement for individual real earnings in 2019 is slightly less than a two fold increase compared to 1977 and just over a 3.1 fold increase compared to 1961.

Notably all three again clearly show the huge impact of the economic crash of 2008.

It should be noted also that although data are more sparse, the long term trend in the costs of food versus housing have changed since the 18th century, and in particular through the 20th century, in which housing has grown to dominate household expenditure as a portion of disposable income whilst food has become significantly cheaper at the same time. This will be explored further in forthcoming chapters.

Social protection income

Whilst the Poor Law offered the most basic of social protection income to families and individuals in dire need, it was not very generously funded or provisioned for most of its existence. It was not until the first decade of the 20th century that provision for people began to increase in real terms and it took the centralisation of the administration of such social protection to achieve real improvements over the 110 years since 1908.

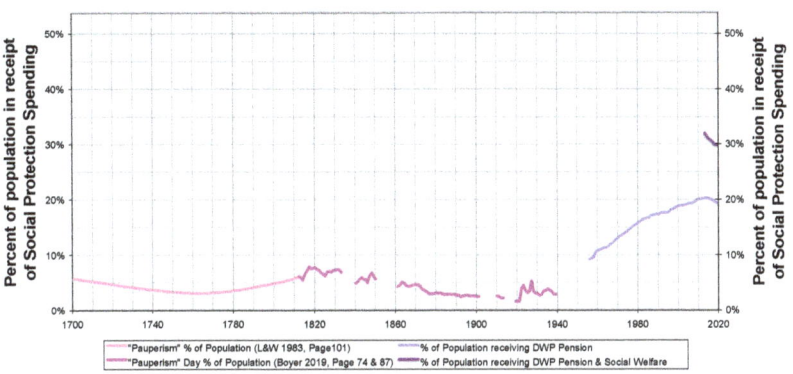

Estimate of Percent of Population in receipt of Historical Poor Law Relief and State Social Protection (Pension & Welfare)

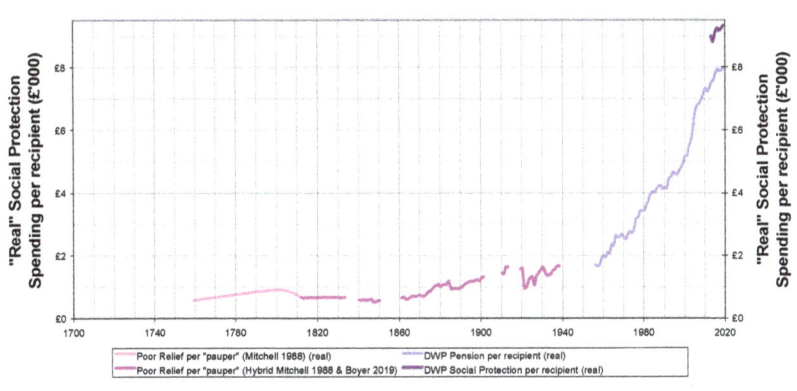

Estimate of "Real" (CPI) Average Annual Historical Poor Relief and State Social Protection Payment per Recipient - (£'000)

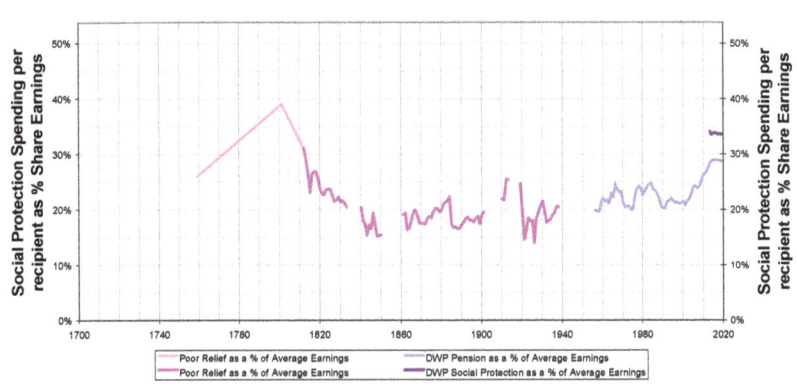

Estimate of Historical Poor Relief and State Social Protection payment per recipient as % of Measuring Worth/ONS Earnings

Although not as extensive as modern data, early estimates of Poor Law relief and numbers of recipients are available from the work of Peter Lindert and Jeffrey Williamson (1983), Brian Mitchell (1988) and more recently George Boyer (2019).

From these data simple estimates can be made of the share of the population in receipt of such social protection income, the average value of the income received by those recipients and how that income compares to the prevailing average earnings of the working population as a whole.

These respective estimates are represented in the three charts on the previous page from top to bottom.

The first chart at the top indicates the share of the population in receipt of Poor Law relief in the pink lines, then central government administered (now by the Department for Work and Pensions, DWP) since the establishment of the welfare state in the lavender line (Old Age Pension) and all recipients of all social protection spending in the violet line (only available from the DWP since 2013).

This suggests that the share in receipt of social protection has grown from a peak in the decade after the end of the Napoleonic Wars of 7.5% of the population, then rising to 30% of the population in 2019 from all centralised social protection income from the DWP (of whom 20% are in receipt of Old Age Pension). This now represents 4 times as many people in receipt of such social protection in 2019 than in 1820.

The second chart in the middle suggests that the amount received per recipient has increased from an early Poor Law peak in the early years of the Napoleonic Wars in 1803 to 1805 of about £860 per year ("real" pounds), steadily increasing from the last decade of the 19th century, then climbing to an average £9,300 per year for all recipients of all centralised social protection spending from the DWP in 2019 (£8,000 per annum on average for those in receipt of Old Age Pension). All amounts are quoted in "real" 2019 pounds, again normalised using the CPI measure of inflation.

In the third chart at the bottom of the previous page these estimates are then placed in the context of their "real" values compared to the estimated "real" value of average earnings. This suggests that at the height of the French Revolutionary/Napoleonic Wars in 1800 to 1805, the Poor Law appears to have paid recipients on average almost 40% of the value of average earnings, whilst in 2019 the overall average income for all recipients of social protection spending yields an average proportion of 33% of the value of average earnings.

This tends to correlate with the general appearance of the system of extending the Poor Law relief administered by local magistrates and Poor Law guardians during the French Revolutionary and Napoleonic Wars, that has become known in modern times as the *Speenhamland system*. This was an attempt to alleviate the obvious increase in pauperism and destitution as a consequence of the severe economic effects of these major wars, and it should be noted that it was this response that led to the clamour to reform the Poor Law that resulted in the 1834 Act.

Average spending on benefits and tax credits at different ages in 2010-11 (DWP/ONS/OBR) in £'000

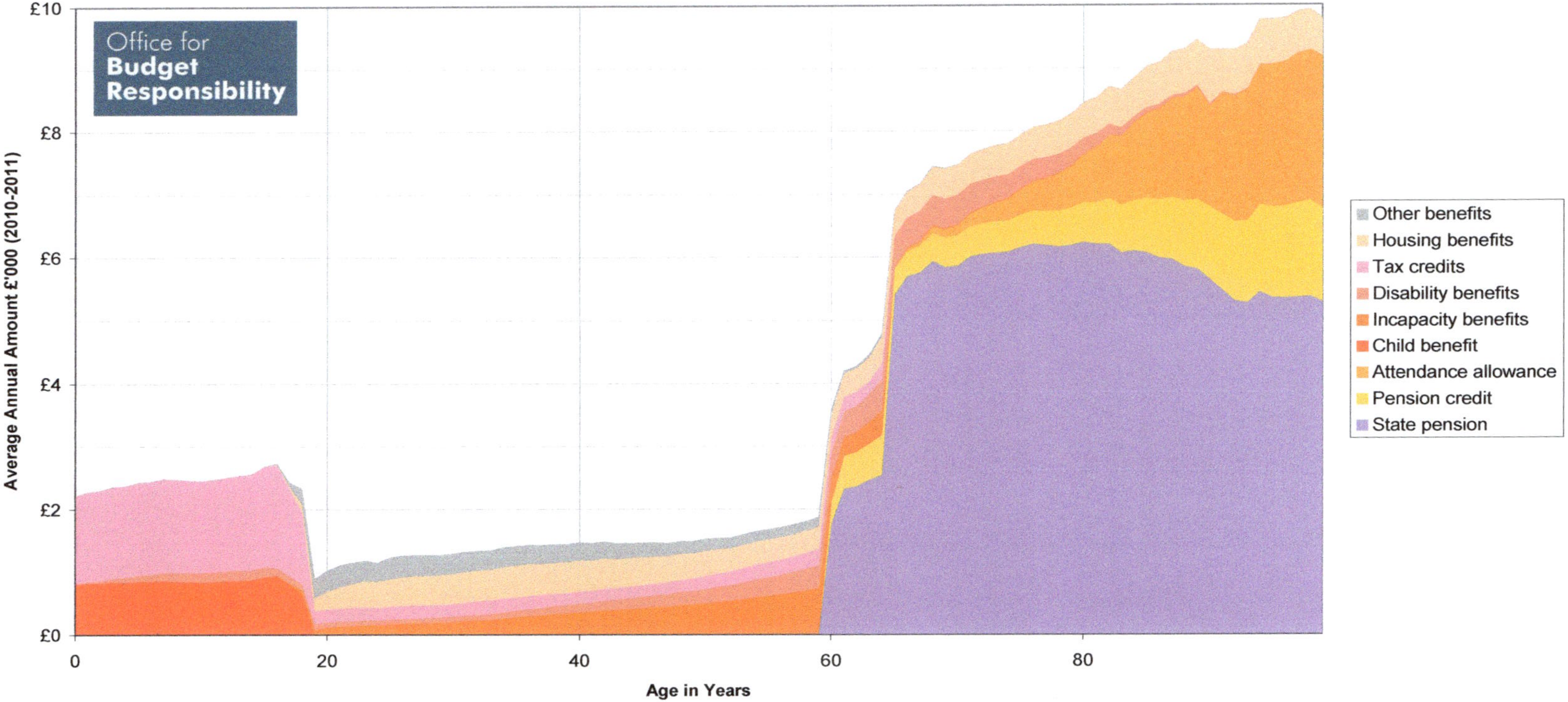

Office for
**Budget
Responsibility**

Legend:
- Other benefits
- Housing benefits
- Tax credits
- Disability benefits
- Incapacity benefits
- Child benefit
- Attendance allowance
- Pension credit
- State pension

Y-axis: Average Annual Amount £'000 (2010-2011)
£10, £8, £6, £4, £2, £0

X-axis: Age in Years
0, 20, 40, 60, 80

There is also a very important caveat to these estimates in that George Boyer's estimates, from Lynn Hollen Lees' 1998 *"The Solidarities of Strangers: The English Poor Laws and the People, 1700–1948"*, suggesting that the number of people in receipt of Poor Law relief in any given year is in fact more than twice those calculated from the day count. Even in the 21st century this seems to be generally reflected in those thought to be "rough sleeping" when spot counts are undertaken compared to estimated numbers moving in and out of sleeping rough in any given year.

Finally in the chart on the previous page, a view of the average spending on social protection benefits and tax credits at different ages for 2010/11 yields a very powerful pointer to both the income needs of people and the modern role taken by the state to address these needs.

This final chart on the previous page is derived from a report by the Office of Budget Responsibility (OBR) *"An OBR Guide to Welfare Spending"* (from 2017 and 2018) and calculated by the OBR with DWP and ONS for the year 2010/11. This strongly shows the growth in receipt of social protection income in older age, but also the support given when people are at school and pre-school age.

Thus the Old Age Pension element again in lavender shows strongly, but as we become less able bodied our need for assistance grows as well. Similarly from age 18 to retirement we see the least average dependence on social protection income.

It is interesting to consider that in the light of developments over 320 years, reflected in the average (mean) earnings, disposable income and social protection incomes to the end of the second decade of the 21st century, that more than 80 years ago, Arthur Lyon Bowley, one of the foremost researchers into the real changes to incomes in the 19th and early 20th century, prefigured the view of Steven Pinker that opens the summary chapter.

In Bowley's seminal 1937 book *"Wages and Income in the United Kingdom Since 1860"*, when discussing his thoughts for the name of his book, wrote on page *x* (10) of the introduction:

"The word Progress prejudges the results; it might be that there was retrogression. Also the idea of progress is largely psychological and certainly relative; people are apt to measure their progress not from a forgotten position in the past, but towards an ideal, which, like the horizon, continually recedes."

The objective reality is undeniably that materially, in relation to the best known facts derived from the evidence about individual earnings, household disposable incomes and social protection incomes, progress has been real and substantial, even allowing for the many interruptions and set-backs throughout the last 320 years.

The horizon remains as far away as ever, but the failure to remember and understand the truth about the journey so far, is to guarantee a failure to find the best ideas to aid the new journey towards the horizon.

Income Inequality

"The nations of the world vary hugely in income inequality and in the happiness of people living in them. A recurrent theme in political debate suggests a causal link: that income inequality reduces happiness. That claim, however, comes to shipwreck on the rock of the facts."

Kelley and Evans:
Societal Inequality and Individual
Subjective Well-being,
2016

Perception of inequality

Psychologically, perceived inequality and actual inequality can and do influence people's view of their lives and in turn their sense of well-being and happiness.

This is well understood by psychologists and repeatedly observed in human behaviour, as frequently as the negativity bias and its polar opposite, the positivity bias. These latter being a generalised tendency for individuals, and all too often in turn collected groups of people, to swing from one to the other, or polarise into groups adhering to one or the other sentiment, often in response to loudly acclaimed popular discourse.

Whilst these tendencies are frequently unfounded in reality, they nonetheless regularly grip the public mood and dominate the public discourse, the media and politicians, in turn reinforcing their effects.

The purpose of this chapter is to collate and present the best known facts derived from the evidence of the reality of income, earnings and expenditure inequality, as well as the previously quoted averages. These data, being calculated by the academics for earlier centuries and, in the late 20th and early 21st century, sourced from detailed surveys of people's real incomes, earnings and expenditure, are now explored accordingly.

Trend of income inequality

To illustrate the trend of income inequality economists and academics are able to represent this using several types of measure.

The first and simplest method to illustrate income inequality is a method known as the Gini index, coefficient or ratio, as developed by Corrado Gini in 1912. It is a method by which an estimate of inequality is mathematically derived from the frequency distribution of a data set, usually of income, or real consumption expenditure, and is represented by a single number ranging between 0 and 1, or 0 and 100, or 0% and 100% (the three are mathematically the same, such that it does not matter which is chosen as the final representation).

A Gini of 0 (or 0%) represents a state of "absolute" equality in which every member of the group receives an identical income, whilst a Gini of 1 (or 100, or 100%) represents a state of "absolute" inequality in which one member of the group receives all the income, whilst no one else in the group receives any income at all.

In the chart on the next page a very long term estimate of the Gini values for England, Great Britain, and ultimately the UK is given in which the blue lines illustrate the historical values calculated by Peter Lindert and Jeffrey Williamson in their detailed work in the 1980s, whilst the light orange and sandy coloured lines are those published by the Inland Revenue from its Survey of Personal Incomes (SPI) and the ONS Gross Disposable Income from the Family Expenditure Surveys (FES/EFS/LCFS, FRS/HBAI/ETB etc.), effectively illustrating the level of inequality of income before the effects of direct taxes. The lines in green illustrate the end result of the effects of direct taxes, illustrating the re-distribution of the gross, pre-tax income from the same ONS source, as well as the analysis by the Institute of Fiscal Studies.

Clearly visible in the trend is a suggestion that income inequality is thought to have increased a little throughout the 18th and most of the 19th century, peaking perhaps in the 1860s (or perhaps, as some suggest, in the 1880s), and falling most dramatically as a result of the economic shock and after effects of firstly The Great War and then The Second World War. These trends are of course also directly related to the era from the election of the Liberal Party to government from 1906, then subsequently the Labour Party in 1945 and the establishment of the welfare systems with their accompanying redistributive taxation increases.

Guide to Inequality in England, GB and UK Using the Gini Co-efficient

Legend:
- Lindert & Williamson 1983 Aggregated (Revised)
- Lindert & Williamson Aggregated 1983 (Revised) UK
- Inland Revenue (SPI)
- ONS Gini Gross
- IFS (BHC)
- ONS Gini Disposable

The second approach to showing the trend of income inequality is to calculate the share of total income received by particular shares of the population, usually from the top percentages of recipients downwards. Thus the top 0.1%, the top 1%, the top 5%, the top 10% and so on.

Any chosen percentage of the populace is valid, but it is best that it be usefully illustrative of the trend over time if that is the intent, as in this case.

In order to keep the chart shown on the next page as simple as possible, estimates of just the top 10% of the population are given, again in the blue lines from Peter Lindert and Jeffrey Williamson, but then from the work of the late Tony Atkinson in the light orange line for share of income before direct taxation, and the bright green line after taxation.

Here the peak of inequality is shown as possibly occurring a little later in about 1880 and the effects of direct taxation are shown as the consistent difference between the light orange and light green lines as calculated by Atkinson.

Note that the two data sets, the Gini and the Top 10% share tend to suggest a generally similar pattern over time, though Atkinson's figures for the inter war years do suggest a different pattern for the top 10% of income recipients than either his top 5% or top 1%. (None of these are shown here, as explained, for the sake of keeping the charts simple).

Also strongly suggested in both sets of data is the period after the end of The Second World War, which seemed to exhibit at first substantial fall in income inequality until the end of rationing in about 1953/54, then a continued steady fall until the period of least inequality in 1976 and 1977. From 1979 this low point starts to grow again, peaking strongly in 2007, before the effects of the 2008 economic crash draws inequality back to a more steady state until 2019. Sadly Tony Atkinson's figures stop for 2012, as he died in 2017. Some supporting indicators of the steady trend are also available from the ONS in their own calculation for the top 1% until 2019, though again not shown here for simplicity's sake.

Income inequality from social tables

Thanks to the work of Gregory King in the 1690s (and various contemporary fellows), then Joseph Massie in particular in the 1750s and later Patrick Colquhoun in the first decade of the 19th century, historians have been lucky to have estimates of distribution of income, estimates of population and estimates of the numbers of households in various "social" groupings (as loosely defined by each contemporary analyst).

It must be noted that each of the analysts were not looking at their estimates dispassionately, but rather generally proposing behaviour and policies to their respective governments; in short, campaigning.

Modern historians and analysts have used these social tables, but always very carefully, thanks to these campaigning biases of the contemporary authors, and have produced reasonable modern variants.

Guide to Inequality in England, GB and UK using the top 10% shares of income

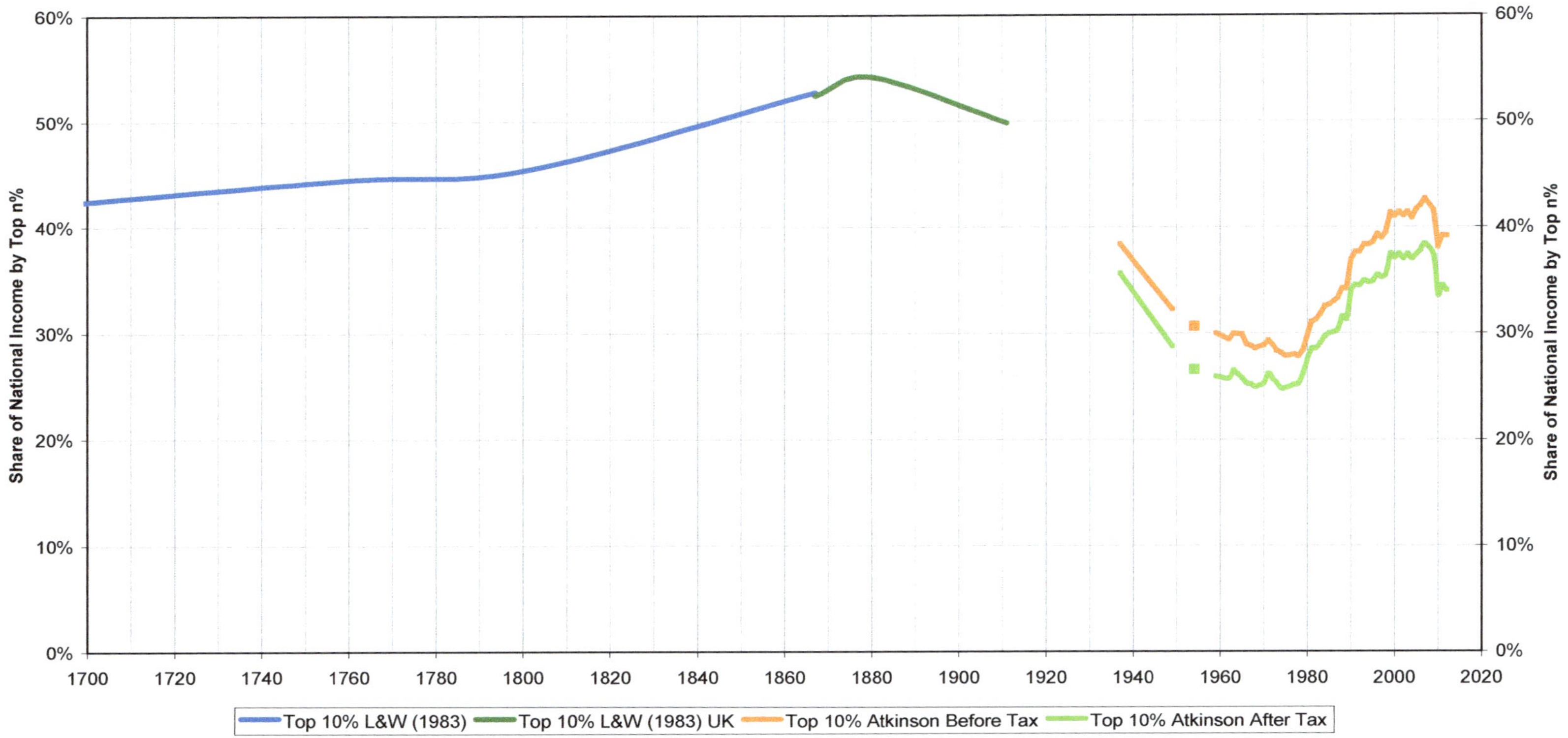

Share of National Income by Top n%

Legend:
— Top 10% L&W (1983)
— Top 10% L&W (1983) UK
— Top 10% Atkinson Before Tax
— Top 10% Atkinson After Tax

From these modern variants, particularly thanks to the work of Peter Mathias in 1957, then the extensive work of Peter Lindert and Jeffrey Williamson in the 1980s, being recently revised further by Robert Allen in the first two decades of the 21st century, we are able to tease a simple and useful pointer to income inequality from the start to the end of the 18th century in three useful charts representing approximately 1700 (actually thought to represent 1688 to 1695), mid-century (1755 to 1760) and end of century (1798 to 1803).

In order to present this graphically we use another representation of inequality developed by Max Lorenz at the start of the 20th century. It is most closely related to the previously used percentage of the population in receipt of percentage of income, in which the "top 10%" were represented through time.

The approach using the Lorenz Curve shows the theoretical range for all members of the population being represented but at a single point in time. In this scheme "absolute" equality is represented, as for example, 25% of the recipients receive 25% of the income, 50% of recipients receive 50% of income etcetera, where the equivalent for the Gini index is 0 (or 0%). In the three charts on the next page this "absolute" equality is represented by the dark grey dashed line in each case.

For each, simple cumulative shares of households and income from each social table, as revised by Lindert and Williamson in 1983, have been calculated and are represented in each chart accordingly. The further the coloured curve from the dashed grey line the greater the level of inequality pertaining in that era.

The chart at the top of the page is a representation for data from Gregory King's estimates in the orange line for the late 1680s to 1690s.

The chart in the middle of the page is a representation for the data from estimates derived from Joseph Massie's work in the 1750s to early 1760s, as collated and represented by Peter Mathias in 1957 and shown in the pink line.

The chart at the bottom of the page is a representation for the data from Patrick Colquhoun's estimates for the turn of the 18th to 19th century, and shown in the salmon pink line.

As in the case of both the Gini index and the top 10% shares trend, the three tend to show at most a small increase in inequality of incomes over the course the 18th century.

This is unsurprising in the context of the now generally accepted thinking of a revolutionary, but actually comparatively slow development of the industrialisation of the economy that eventually so dramatically changed every aspect of society.

What all three analyses (Gini, top 10% and Lorenz Curve) tend to emphasise is that society throughout the 18th century remained very unequal in relation to income inequality, as it had been for many hundreds of years.

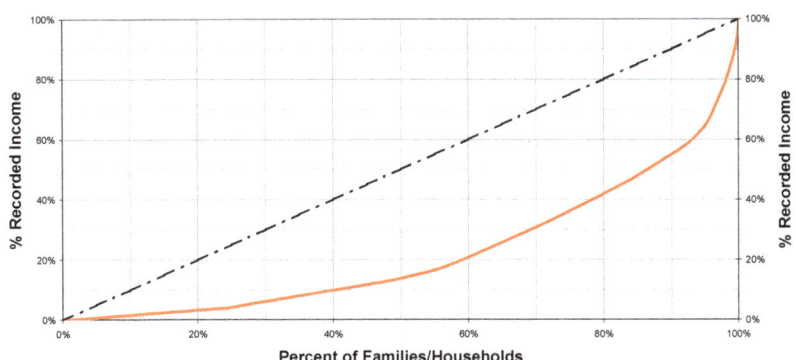

Lorenz Curves derived from Social Table Revisions for Households by Peter Lindert and Jeffery Williamson - 1688 (Gregory King)

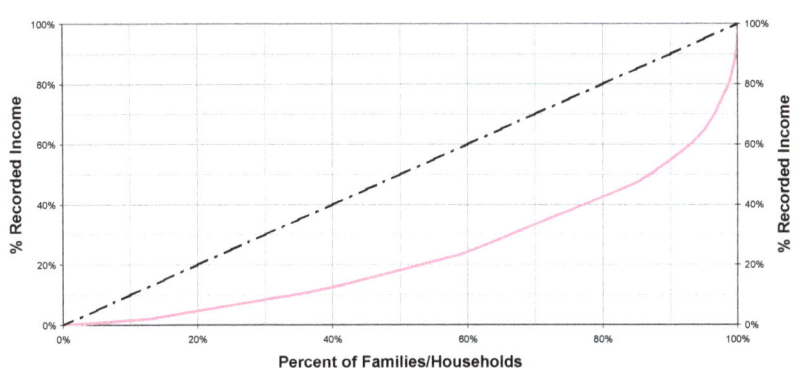

Lorenz Curves derived from Social Table Revisions for Households by Peter Lindert and Jeffery Williamson - 1759 (Joseph Massie)

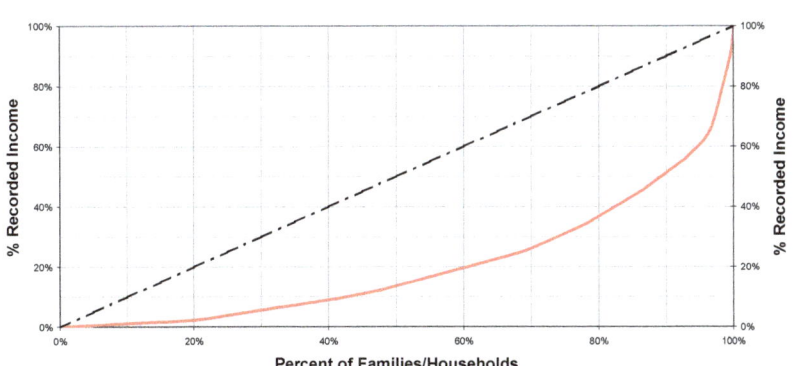

Lorenz Curves derived from Social Table Revisions for Households by Peter Lindert and Jeffery Williamson - 1801 (Patrick Colquhoun)

Income inequality for individuals

Frustratingly, the contemporary analyses of 19th and even 20th century incomes and earnings were invariably undertaken in slightly different ways, and accordingly in each case this makes direct comparison more difficult, particularly with the 18th century. Thus the best long term comparison remains that presented in the Gini and top 10% trend charts.

However, for the 19th century to date we do have a series of analyses that are capable of yielding some comparable equivalents, though the modern data must be extended mathematically to approximate a comparable analysis.

Although William Ray Smee undertook a very useful analysis of incomes in the aftermath of the Peel government's permanent introduction of the income tax in 1842, his analysis, although supporting the idea of the underlying trend, cannot easily be made extensive enough to yield a representative chart. It does however point to a developing tendency to increased income inequality during the era from the start of the industrial revolution.

The three charts on the next page are now presented as distribution charts in which the percentage of income recipients at each "real" annual income level are represented. These incomes are normalised to modern income equivalents using the usual CPI for each year and thus allow us to make a simplistic comparison of income distributions compared to the last published from the HMRC SPI that represents the year 2018/19.

However there is a limitation in the modern data published from Survey of Personal Income (SPI) analysis, in that it is only published for those who actually had a tax liability for their incomes in the year in question. It thus entirely misses the substantial number of people whose annual income is not, for whatever reason, liable for a tax payment in that year. Another caveat to trying to achieve some form of comparability over the decades is that until the decades after the end of The Second World War very few people were in receipt of social protection benefits and thus such recipients should not realistically be incorporated in modern distribution analysis if the objective is to attempt some form of comparison over time, no matter how limited that comparison is in practice.

For these reasons an analysis of the change in tax liability over the decades suggests, in a simplistic estimate, that in 2018/19 the taxable only distribution from the SPI only encapsulates about 75% of those in receipt of income (excluding those exclusively in receipt of social protection benefits). Thus the figures for this last year are extrapolated from the tax threshold downwards by a one third increase in "representation" and are shown in the blue line in each chart.

Exactly as with the previous Lorenz curves for the 18th century, the following distribution curves represent inequality by the depth that the curve falls into the bottom right corner of the plot area.

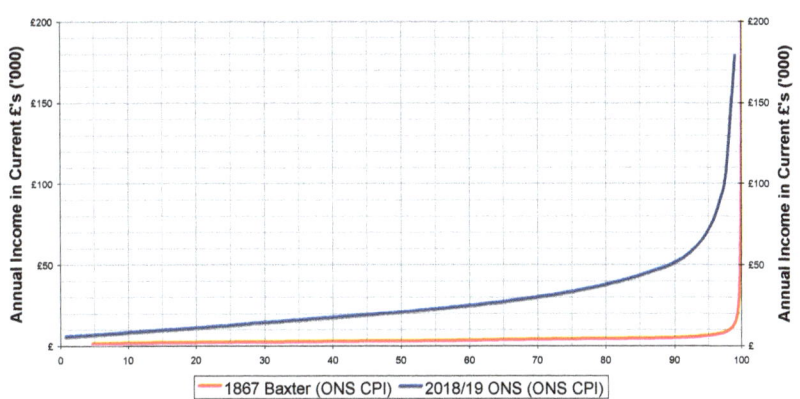

Compare real earnings/income distribution (CPI)

— 1867 Baxter (ONS CPI) — 2018/19 ONS (ONS CPI)

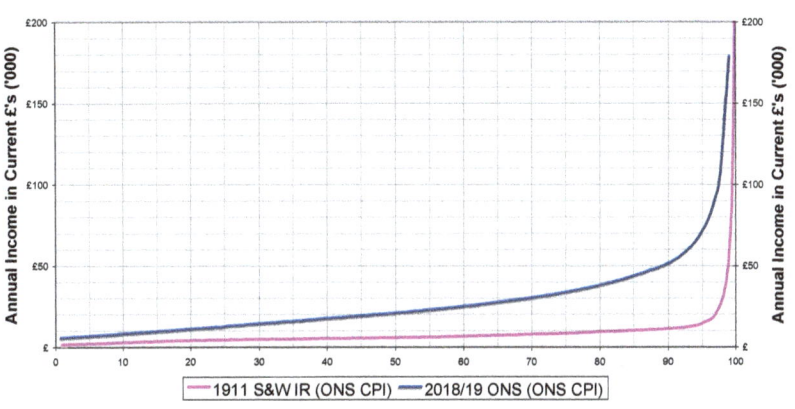

Compare real earnings/income distribution (CPI)

— 1911 S&W IR (ONS CPI) — 2018/19 ONS (ONS CPI)

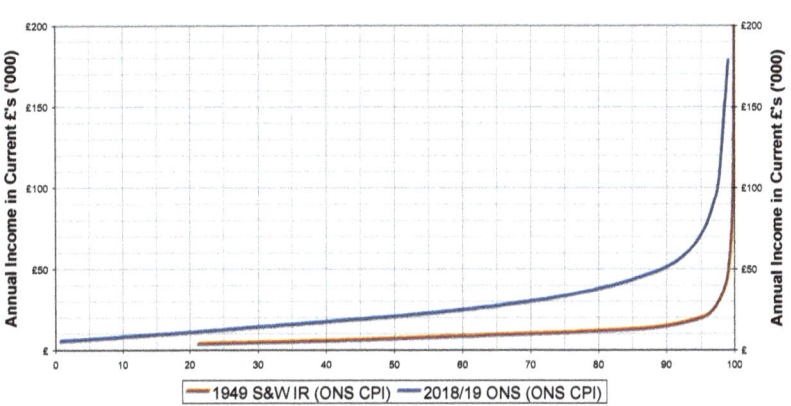

Compare real earnings/income distribution (CPI)

— 1949 S&W IR (ONS CPI) — 2018/19 ONS (ONS CPI)

The oldest substantial and most useful analysis that is able to yield a representative chart of personal income inequality is derived from the work of Robert Dudley Baxter in the 1860s. This was extensively analysed by Peter Lindert and Jeffrey Williamson in the 1980s and Peter Lindert has even made a very powerful spreadsheet of their findings available for download from the University of California – Davis website.

In the first chart at the top of the previous page, this data representing Baxter's analysis of UK incomes in 1867, as processed by Lindert and Williamson, yields the red income distribution line, which can be adequately compared to the blue line for 2018/19, 150 years later.

It clearly strongly suggests the much greater levels of income inequality in the 1860s in the UK than at the end of the second decade of the 21st century.

The second chart, in the middle of the previous page, is another very useful analysis, this time from work undertaken by the Inland Revenue for the pre-Great War Liberal Government of Asquith for the year 1911. It was an analysis of incomes used to support the famous "people's budget" of that year and the Parliament Act that was introduced to limit the power of the House of Lords. The data from this analysis was used by Arthur Bowley, Josiah Stamp and Guy Routh, later by Anthony Atkinson and most recently in 2018 by Peter Scott and James Walker. Again the data has been extensively analysed by Peter Lindert and Jeffrey Williamson and again a very useful spreadsheet of that analysis has been made available by Peter Lindert as before at the same website.

By applying the Lindert disaggregation of the untaxed majority of income recipients in the data for 1911 from the Scott and Walker table of data, the resulting income distribution is represented in the pink line in the chart in the middle of the previous page, as normalised to modern incomes using the CPI for that year.

It also clearly suggests continuing income inequality in 1911 compared to 2018/19, but does actually tend to show a fall in inequality compared to 1867.

Finally in attempting to present such a series of changes in personal income distribution from 1867 to 2018/19, the data presented by Scott and Walker from Inland Revenue analysis for incomes from 1949 is similarly processed, normalised and presented in the chart at the bottom of the previous page in the brown line.

The data for 1949 again clearly suggests that income inequality was still significantly greater than that of 2018/19, but again had reduced compared to that of 1911.

Interestingly the data presented by Scott and Walker from the extensive survey by the Inland Revenue of 1937/38 incomes tends to exhibit a very similar distribution to that of 1949, implying the first general trend in the reduction of income inequality had begun in the later decades of the 19th century, but had been given significant impetus in the aftermath of the shock of The Great War.

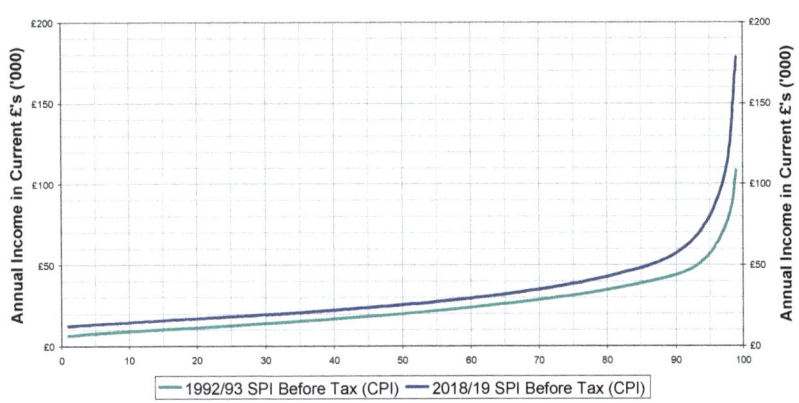

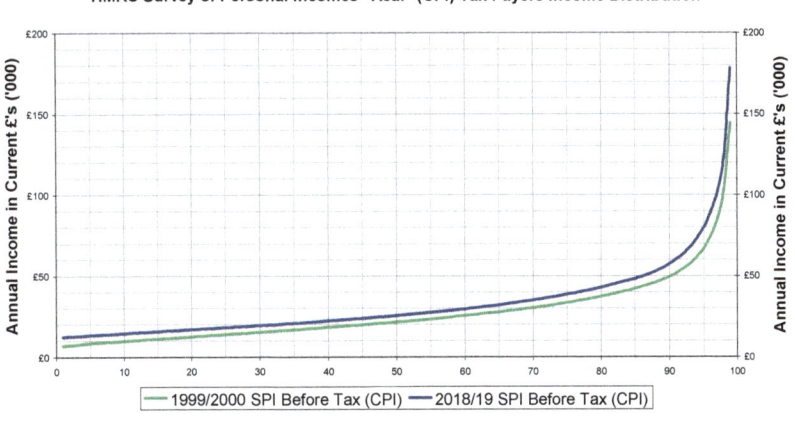

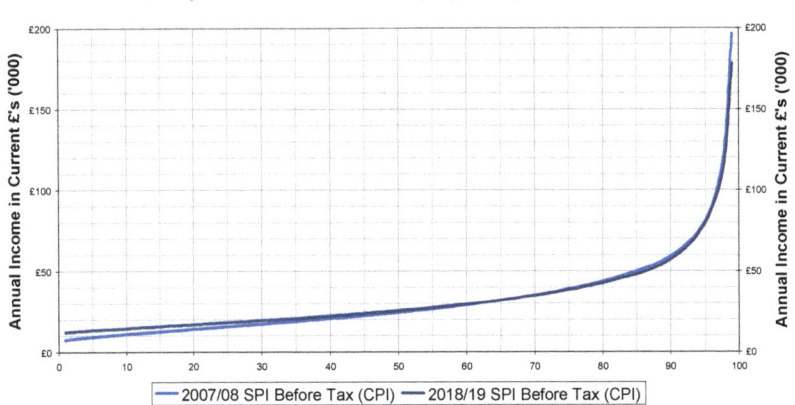

Survey of Personal Incomes

We now focus particularly on the analysis of tax payers' income inequality, before tax, from the HMRC Survey of Personal Incomes. In the charts on the previous page we see a pattern of comparatively stable income inequality, at least since 1992, when comparing just those liable for tax upon their incomes. Note the data for fiscal year 2018/19 was previously used in an extended form, estimated to include non-tax payers.

For the selected years, the first contrasting 1992/93 (in teal green) with 2018/19 (in dark blue) in the chart at the top of the previous page, the most significant trend is the general increase in real incomes across the income distribution (as normalised again using the ONS CPI), rather than a significant change of inequality across the distribution of taxable incomes.

The trend from 1992/93 to 2018/19 is also supported by the intermediate analysis for 1999/2000 in the chart in the middle of the previous page, in which that year is represented by the sea green line, supporting the previous general uplift in real incomes, but hinting at notably greater increase for the top 10% as the sea green line is close to the dark blue line on the right of the middle chart.

The notable exception to that medium term trend is that within the 27 year period there was an increase of tax payers' income inequality to the year before the 2008 economic crash. This is illustrated in the chart at the bottom of the previous page in which that distribution from the 2007/08 SPI is illustrated in the royal blue line, and is contrasted to the distribution from the 2018/19 SPI, again in the dark blue line. Note the notable gap between the royal blue and dark blue lines below the median (50th percentile) point in the middle of the chart.

This pattern is therefore fully in support of both the calculated Gini Index shown at the start and the top 10% chart shown after the Gini Index.

Household income inequality

Unfortunately equivalent representation of personal income data for the crucial period of the 1950s to the 1980s is not readily available and thus, to show the relative changes to income inequality of the 70 years from the period after the end of The Second World War to the end of the second decade of the 21st century, different data must be used in the form of household disposable income and total expenditure.

Of course this data is even more useful in many other ways as it does take account of the changes wrought by the introduction of the welfare state and the consequent changes in taxation regimes over the decades.

It also offers a view of the real spending capability of households in the modern age rather than simply the incomes of individuals, who make up various different households, all with different needs.

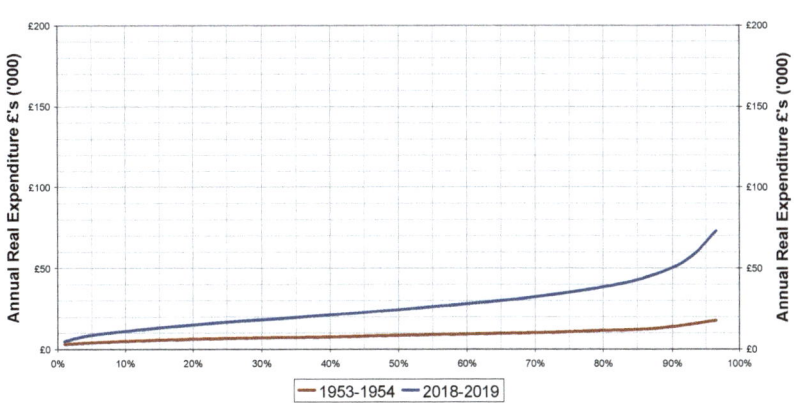

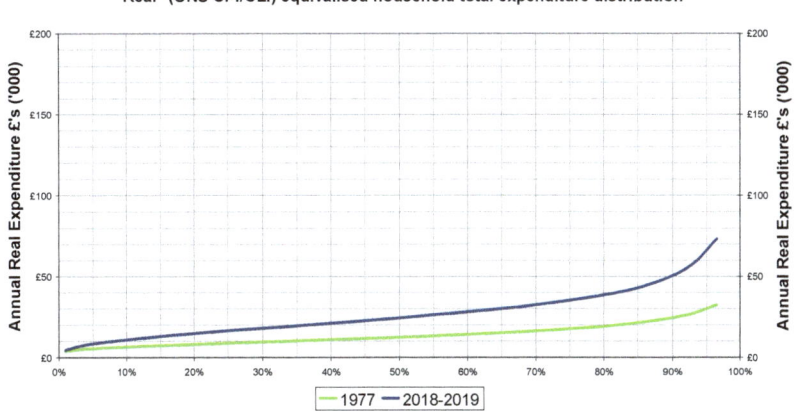

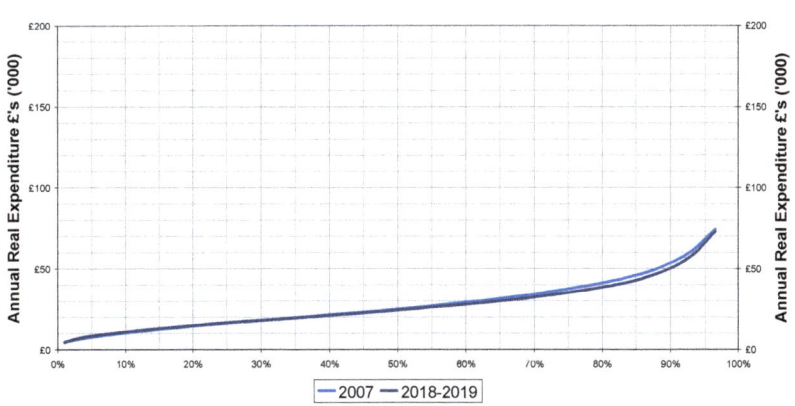

To provide a consistent picture of that real spending capability, a process known as equivalisation is used to show the real effects of a household's total income in relation to the size of the household.

Clearly a single person household in receipt of £25,000 per year would be in a theoretically better position than a four person household for example consisting of 2 adults and 2 children on that same £25,000 per year. Equivalisation is a process of estimating some equivalence of needs within each household in order to place each household on a distribution curve that caters for their estimated needs in relation to their total household income.

It should be noted that inevitably there are almost limitless ways in which such equivalisation may be calculated and in this analysis the same method has been carefully applied to the data using the best information available for each study year since the first detailed survey of 1953/54.

Note that since the Family Expenditure Surveys (FES), including Expenditure and Food Surveys (EFS) and Living Costs and Food Surveys (LCFS), are focused on expenditure, we use equivalised total expenditure accounted for by each household as the nearest equivalent of income in the three charts on the previous page.

Now we are able to show change incorporating the years from the end of rationing in 1953/54 in the chart at the top of the page, illustrated in the dark red/light brown line (the closest year to the previous personal income analysis of 1949), and again 2018/19 in dark blue.

The first very strong picture that emerges is that very significantly, almost all households are noticeably better off in "real" terms in the last year of the second decade of the 21st century than in the year 1953/54. But a theme to which we shall return starts to become clear as well, that households in the lower 3 to 5 percentile range are not showing signs of much benefit from the huge levels of progress since the end of The Second World War.

The chart in the middle of the previous page contrasts the year 1977, illustrated in the lime green line, to that 2018/19 in the dark blue line, and is widely found to be, by all known measures, one of the years with the most equal distributions of incomes in the measured and known history of the United Kingdom.

This is then extended in the chart at the bottom of the page to a comparison again of the year 2007 in the royal blue line to that of 2018/19 in the dark blue line, producing a not dissimilar distribution to that of personal incomes previously discussed for those years.

Inequality After Housing Costs (AHC)

Data from all household expenditure analysis, including sporadic older historical analyses, has highlighted another long term trend in the form of the ever greater dominance in household budgets of their expenditure on housing, compared to previous eras when food dominated expenditure.

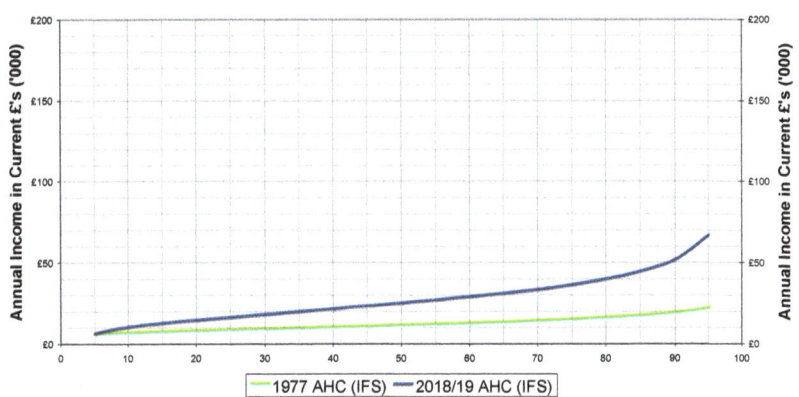

"Real" (IFS CPI) equivalised household disposable income (After Housing Costs)

1977 AHC (IFS) — 2018/19 AHC (IFS)

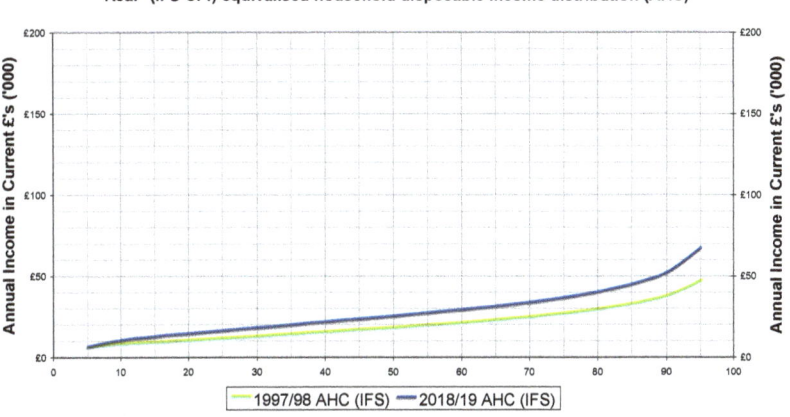

"Real" (IFS CPI) equivalised household disposable income distribution (AHC)

1997/98 AHC (IFS) — 2018/19 AHC (IFS)

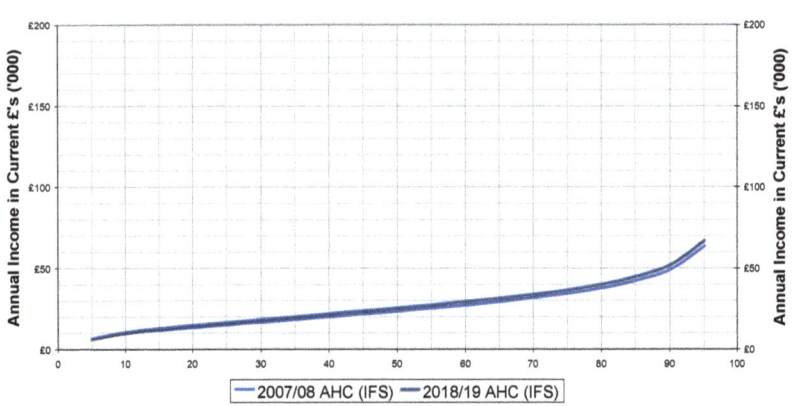

"Real" (IFS CPI) equivalised household disposable income distribution (AHC)

2007/08 AHC (IFS) — 2018/19 AHC (IFS)

By turning to the extensive analysis undertaken by the Institute of Fiscal Studies, using the Households Below Average Expenditure (HBAI) methodology, extended back to the first regular Family Expenditure Survey from 1961, we are able to view a consistent pattern of equivalised household expenditure and income, after expenditure on housing is accounted for.

In this case we deliberately start the three part analysis in 1977, one of the years in which income and expenditure inequality were at their lowest levels. This is represented in the first chart at the top of the previous page and again with 1977 as represented in lime green and 2018/19 in dark blue.

The chart in the middle offers a recent intermediate picture of 1997/98 illustrated in the light green line in contrast to 2018/19 in the dark blue line. This shows an interesting result of the alternative approach to seeking an income inequality analysis from household expenditure rather than personal incomes as it captures a much larger portion of the population living at the lower reaches of income distribution levels and again illustrates the coincidence of the "real" incomes and expenditure of the first 5% of households, shown by the crossover of the light green line for 1997/98 with 2018/19 dark blue line at the left of the middle chart.

Illustrating this point further is the chart at the bottom of the page, again comparing 2007/08 illustrated in the royal blue line with that of 2018/19 in the dark blue line.

Again the theme revealed in the analysis of total expenditure in the previous section, further reveals itself in the HBAI analysis after accounting for housing costs in which the lowest 5% of households are revealed to appear to have not benefited from the huge material advances throughout the period after the end of The Second World War that have been available to the other 95%, albeit in unequal shares across the distribution range of household and similarly illustrated earlier in personal incomes.

The real implications of these trends, visible in the detailed data will be explored in the forthcoming chapters.

> Whilst inequality is spoken of and discussed in vocal and emotive terms by a great many people, it is generally so considered from a base of preference rather than derived from a conscious political position, though usually the opposite in academic and campaigning circles.
>
> Here we see real change through time, but we must be aware that income inequality is greater from the 1980s than it was in the period of most of the 1960s and 1970s, but remains quite stable since 1990. However inequality is actually much lower than before the 1960s.
>
> But we must also be aware that whilst the UK economy was still struggling to recover from the depredations of two economically and socially devastating world wars, it was also a society exhibiting signs of disruption until enterprise was re-invigorated from the 1980s.

Cost of Living

"Oh, God! that bread should be so dear.
And flesh and blood so cheap!"

Thomas Hood:
The Song of the Shirt,
1844

Calculating the "real" value

Readers are aware that the value of money changes, even in their own lifetimes, invariably diminishing. Thus in UK currency terms a pound sterling bought more bread in 2010 than it did in 2019 and significantly so as we go back in time.

For our purpose, the nutritional and life sustaining qualities of bread, in general, may be treated as though not changing in that time (though thanks to the lack of robust legal frameworks and enforcement we know that bread itself was occasionally very seriously adulterated at various times in history).

Thus the concept of inflation and the devaluation of the currency of exchange can be understood accordingly.

Throughout this work the chosen method of accounting for this devaluation of currency, in order to represent the "real" modern equivalent value of earnings, incomes and the cost of purchasing goods and services, is the Consumer Price Index (CPI, developed, maintained and analysed by the ONS and launched in January 1996, including a calculated back series to 1988), but being historically connected to the earlier similar indices calculated by the foremost academics such as Charles Feinstein and Gregory Clark, all using a similar methodology, albeit with more sparse original data sources as we go back in history.

This long term Cost of Living (CLI) and CPI history is made available particularly conveniently in the Bank of England Millennium Database.

An alternative index that most readers might be familiar with is the older Retail Price Index (RPI), introduced at the end of The Second World War in order to inform policies intended to address the plan for efforts to improve social and economic well-being throughout the population. This index uses a different mathematical methodology to compose the aggregate and tends to yield greater values for inflation. Its methodology is not generally used in other similar economies and has recently been deprecated in favour of the previously referenced CPI. It should be noted as well that since the RPI tends to yield greater values for inflation, there are significant implications for those who use this index to guide annual increases for costs and payments. In addition to the work of the above academics in this field, the ONS also published an historical analysis in 2004 that estimated a composite index from 1750, re-using analysis by G. H. Wood, E. H. Phelps Brown & S. V. Hopkins as well as Charles Feinstein. The RPI is also the index still used by the people at MeasuringWorth.

Unfortunately, as with all such mathematical methodologies, informed by policy and ideological intent as much as "rigorous statistical correctness", there are a plethora of other indices that are used for short and long term historical analysis of inflation and currency devaluation.

The most significant of these is again from the ONS and is called the CPIH (see p14), launched in 2013. This extends the cost of living analysis to include "*a measure of the costs associated with owning, maintaining and living in one's own home*", which are not included in the CPI. The earliest calculated values from the ONS for this index are from 1977, though they are normally extended back to 1988 in most historical series.

In practice, for the very long term analysis presented in this work, the CPI and CPIH yield very similar "real" modern equivalent values, unlike the RPI, which tends to alter the view of the effects of long term inflation.

To illustrate the changes in the average value of items purchased by households (the cost of living), the chart on the opposite page represents both the calculated CPI in the green line and the RPI in the red line, using a logarithmic scale to reveal the early years of the 18th century.

Both end in 2019 at an index value of 100 and also start moderately close to each other in 1700 at 0.71 for CPI and 0.66 for RPI (suggesting an approximately 140 to 150 fold devaluation of currency), however they clearly separate in the decades of inflation from the mid 19th century.

Comparing ONS/Measuring Worth RPI to ONS/Bank of England CPI (2019=100)
(GC CoL, ONS RPI from 1947/48, Charles Feinstein CoL, ONS CPI from 1997)

Logarithmic Scale, factor 10, 2019=100

— ONS/ MW RPI — ONS/ BoE CPI

The "real" cost of bread and earnings

Whilst we are all aware that "man cannot live by bread alone", we are equally aware that from the dawn of agricultural society and economics, humans have generally treated bread as a chief staple to sustain them. An example of an exception for many years, thanks to different climate and land productivity, includes the greater use of oats than wheat in Scotland. Similarly much of the Far East makes greater use of rice than wheat. But in England, and in general in the UK, wheat and bread were the basic staple and especially so for the poorest in society.

Since wheat and flour were core trading commodities, and bread a core staple in most of the UK, we have available reliable and invaluable data about prices through time for all of these commodities.

On occasions, academics have substituted wholesale prices of wheat and flour for retail prices of bread, when the latter has been difficult to ascertain, but in fact prices of the three moved inexorably together for at least the first century and a half since 1700, before trading conditions changed from the late 1840s onwards, after the abolition of the corn laws.

Brian Mitchell in his 1988 "*British Historical Statistics*" re-published the data extensively used and previously published by Lord Beveridge. In addition, data published by Nicholas Poynder in 1999 and Gregory Clark in 2003 adds greatly to the picture, but also the ONS has collated a very large range of food prices from 1914, thereby allowing us to look at bread prices over the whole period from 1700 to 2019.

Since we also have a continuous series for average full time earnings available for the same period, we are able to look at both sets of metrics, adjusted using the previously discussed values for the calculated CPI for the same period and then index them to our start year of 1700 and see how the two changed in "real" terms over 320 years.

The chart on the opposite page illustrates the average "real" full time earnings, indexed to 1700 (set to 100) to 2019 in the dark blue line and average "real" price of an 800 gram (approximately 2 lb) unwrapped, unsliced loaf of white bread, again indexed to 1700 (at 100) in the cyan line.

Since, by definition, a significant component of the cost of living index and later Consumer Price Index was bread, along with other foods, plus heating, housing, clothing and many other items available to people in general, as the twentieth century progressed, it is unsurprising that here the index of the "real" price of bread tends to move around the value of 100 from 1700 to 2019.

On average it is just under 102 for the whole period, but does vary significantly over time from as low as only 40% of the "real" average in the era of rationing, to as high as 90% above the long term "real" average in 1709 and also greater than 60% above the long term "real" average several times in the 18th century, during times of severe economic and harvest downturns. All, whilst over the long term, average "real" earnings have apparently grown 16 fold compared to those of the 18th century.

An index of the real value of key household income and expenditure relative to 1700.

Earnings and Bread

(All metrics normalised to "real" current values before indexing.)

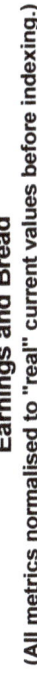

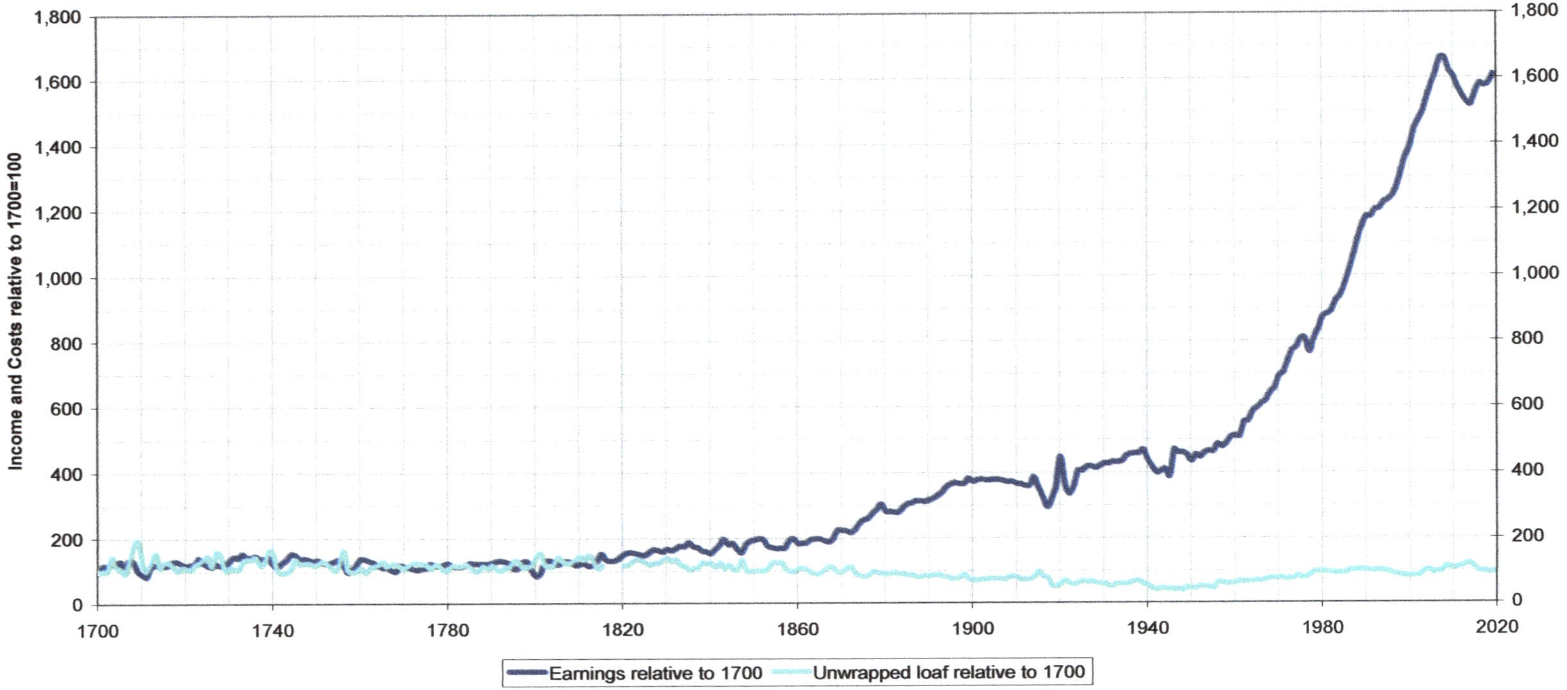

Income and Costs relative to 1700=100

— Earnings relative to 1700 — Unwrapped loaf relative to 1700

The trend of the "real" cost of rent

Thanks to Gregory Clark's work published in 1999, plus the previous work of Charles Feinstein (published in 1988), we have some indication of the cost of housing rental from 1700 to the eve of The Great War.

Clark's estimates are given either as nominal decadal or quinquennial periods, indexed to the period 1820 to 1824. However, by re-indexing housing rent to the 18th century in line with the estimates for earnings and bread given previously, and simply normalising for decadal cost of living accordingly, a strong picture emerges of change through the 19th century.

The chart on the opposite page now shows the "real" overall average earnings in dark blue, plus manual labourers' earnings in pink and agricultural labourers' earnings in green, discussed previously in the third chapter **Earnings and Income**, indexed to values estimated for 1700.

Repeated in the chart is the "real" price of bread indexed to 1700 illustrated in the cyan line. It should be noted that this clearly suggests that the price of bread was declining in real terms for most people, and in fact its point of sustained decline correlates extremely well with the growth of mass importation of wheat and wheat flour from the abolition of The Corn Laws in 1846.

Now also added in the bold purple line are the decadal average housing rental estimates, from Gregory Clark's analysis, which strongly suggests that housing rent and manual labourers' wages kept pace with each other, whilst the price of bread fell. However the overall average earnings including the burgeoning middle classes outperformed the growth of housing rental costs, as well as the cost of bread. Also notable is the implication that agricultural labourers' earnings fell behind average housing rental costs but still improved relative to the cost of bread. It is possible that the agricultural labourers housing rental costs may not have fallen behind in practice, due, at least in part, to the continuation of various tied cottage rental arrangements from earlier centuries.

The overall notable exceptional period seems to be after the end of the Napoleonic Wars to the end of the 1840s when housing rental costs appear to have increased in real terms considerably, and it may be no coincidence therefore that these decades were a period of very great social and economic upheaval as the effects of The Industrial Revolution were felt at their greatest; with the mechanisation of agriculture and accelerating depopulation of the countryside, resulting in "Luddism" (machine breaking), the "Peterloo Massacre", the campaigning of William Cobbett and Henry Hunt amongst many others, the "Swing" riots, the conviction of the Tolpuddle Martyrs and the growth of "Chartism"; the whole period being encapsulated by the modern term "The Hungry 40s".

Also suggested is the long term trend for housing to consume a larger share of peoples' expenditure than food. This is re-affirmed from the 20th century as a sustained change to living costs to which we will return further in the next two chapters.

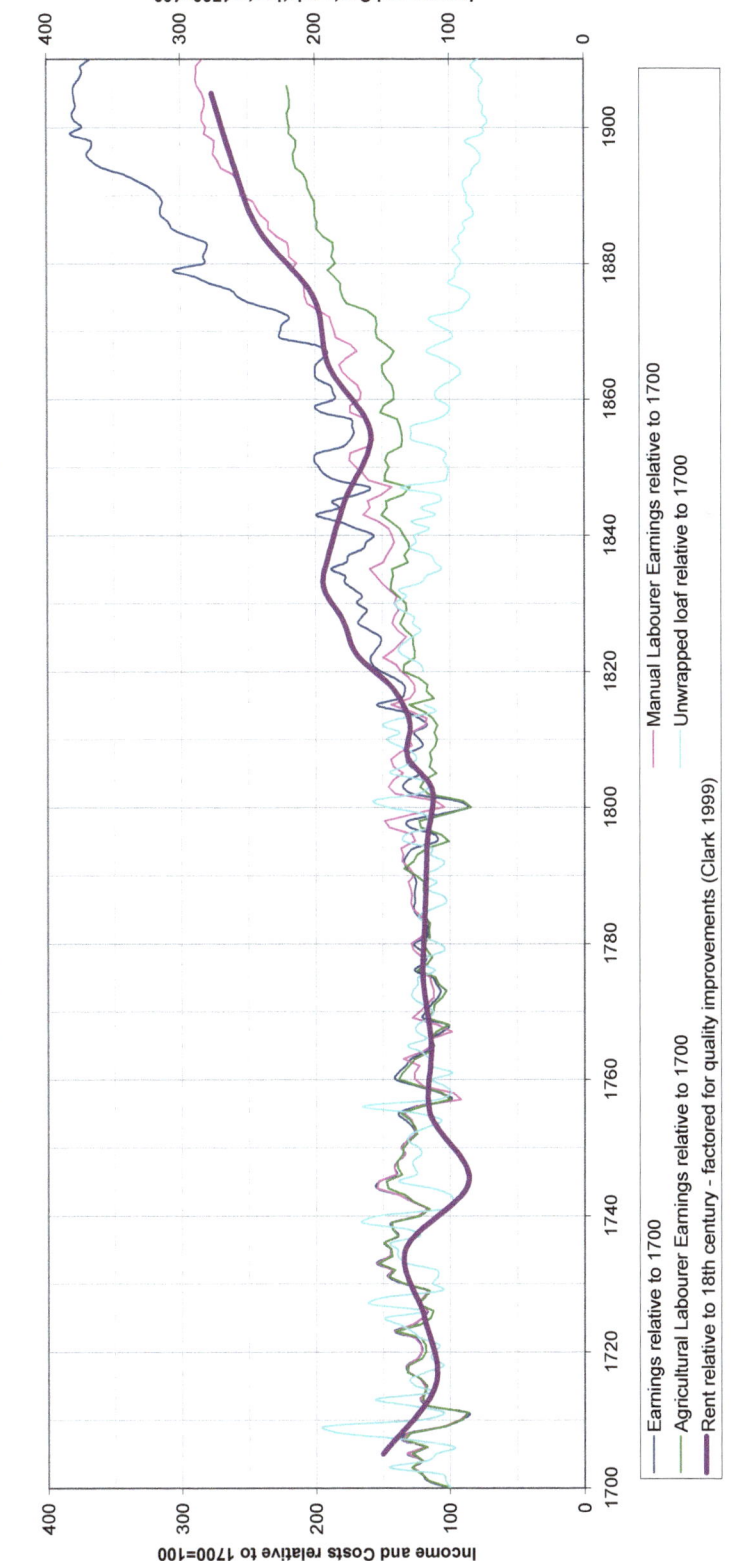

An index of the real value of key household income and expenditure relative to 1700.
Earnings, Bread and Rent
(All metrics normalised to "real" current values before indexing.)

Income and Costs relative to 1700=100

— Earnings relative to 1700
— Agricultural Labourer Earnings relative to 1700
— Rent relative to 18th century - factored for quality improvements (Clark 1999)
— Manual Labourer Earnings relative to 1700
— Unwrapped loaf relative to 1700

The "real" cost of bread and income

Thanks to the work of Charles Feinstein "*National Income Expenditure and Output of the United-Kingdom - 1855-1965*" (published in 1972), we have a calculated estimate of gross disposable income available from 1855.

The data from this analysis is again conveniently made available in the Bank of England Millennium Database, and can be connected with the analysis from the ONS from 1948 to 2019.

Dividing by the population estimates for the period, an average annual disposable income per head of population from the middle of the 19th century to 2019 is derived. Calculating the "real" value from this, again using CPI and indexing it to 1855, along with annual full time earnings and with the cost of bread, as previously, yields a new useful picture of change over the 165 years from 1855 to 2019, this time with disposable income represented as well as full time earnings.

The chart on the opposite page illustrates as before "real" earnings in dark blue and bread in cyan, both relative to their "real" values extant in 1855, but now the "real" disposable income per head of population in orange is available over the time period and yields a strong picture of greater improvement in disposable income per head since the late 1970s and 1980s onwards.

Again the picture that emerges is that the price of bread began its steady fall in "real" terms from the middle of 19th century thanks to growth of free trade with the abolition of The Corn Laws in 1846 and the consequent steady and considerable increase of importation of wheat and wheat flour from that time.

Although not shown here, the figures for the importation of wheat and wheat flour and domestic wheat production, available in Brian Mitchell's 1988 "*British Historical Statistics*", show that importation had grown from almost none before The French Revolutionary Wars to constituting 11% of wheat available in the UK at the end of Napoleonic Wars, then growing to almost 80% of wheat available in the UK on the eve of The Great War. In fact domestic wheat production fell by 50% from its peak in the 1860s to the eve of The Great War.

Contrasting the fall of "real" bread prices from 1855 and their return to almost the same "real" level by the end of the second decade of the 21st century is the very large 13 fold increase in calculated "real" average disposable income per head of population, similar to GDP per head.

Whilst this is a very large increase on average, it does remain important to keep in mind the income inequalities in society.

In real terms though, despite a low of income and earnings inequality in the 1960s and 1970s, we have observed repeatedly, that the data for the period to the end of the 21st century strongly suggests less inequality of income than the past, and thereby also suggest real improvements for all people's financial well-being since the 1850s as well.

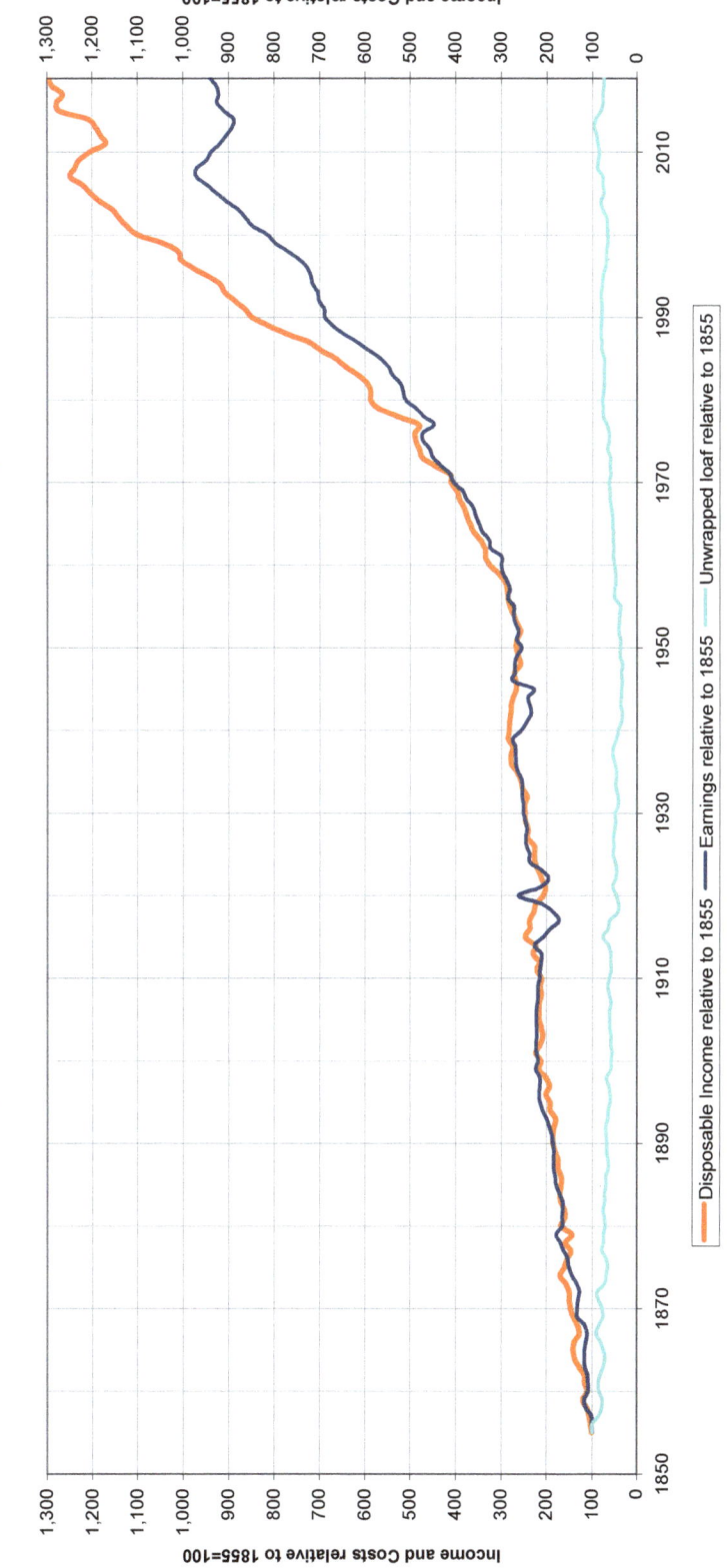

An index of the real value of key household income and expenditure relative to 1855.
Income and Bread
(All metrics normalised to "real" current values before indexing.)

Income and Costs relative to 1855=100

Disposable Income relative to 1855 ——— Earnings relative to 1855 ——— Unwrapped loaf relative to 1855

The "real" cost of food and income

Moving forward to the 20th century on the eve of The Great War to 2019, the data start to point us to the periods of greatest advance in general financial well-being.

The two decades prior to The Great War also start to see the most wide-spread analysis of the breadth and depth of poverty throughout society, thanks to the analysis of Charles Booth, Seebohm Rowntree, Arthur Lyon Bowley and Alexander Burnett Hurst, also aided by the Board of Trade's surveys of the food expenditure of the urban working class in 1904 and the earnings of manual workers in 1906.

Thus by using the data for earnings, disposable income per person and some consistently available food items collated by the ONS from 1914, we are able to extend our analysis slightly beyond bread, incorporating cheese and milk as pointers to relative change in the "real" cost of living, at least for certain staple food items.

The chart on the opposite page, using the same colours as before of orange for disposable income per person, dark blue for earnings, cyan for bread and now bright blue for milk and mid-blue for cheese, illustrate the slight variation of the prices of the three food stuffs over the century, with both bread and cheese clearly being at their cheapest in real terms during the era of rationing, and to the early 21st century milk being a cheaper food commodity than previously, and bread and cheese returning to very close to the same "real" value as one hundred years earlier. However again "real" full-time earnings tend to suggest a four fold gain compared to 1914, whilst average "real" disposable income per person appears to sustain an almost six fold gain compared to 1914.

The overall pattern of change for earnings compared to disposable income per person is maintained during this period as in the previous period, using a start point 60 years earlier, again with the two measures separating from each other from late 1970s onwards with the separation sustained and in fact even continuing to grow further, at least slightly until the mid-1990s.

The reader might see that an element that has been clear from the beginning of the analysis, that is equally obvious in this 105 year analysis, is the effect of the 2008 economic crash.

This can be seen in the right hand sections of all the previous earnings and income representations as dip and slight recovery from 2008 to 2019 in every case.

From these data, this appears to have had a more lasting and widespread effect even than the well known depression of the 1930s. Though we know that unemployment and possible local, even regional consequences of that earlier depression were very severe indeed.

This also points us to the very real perception that is felt by people since 2008 of a general failure to experience continued real improvement in their financial well-being for well over a decade.

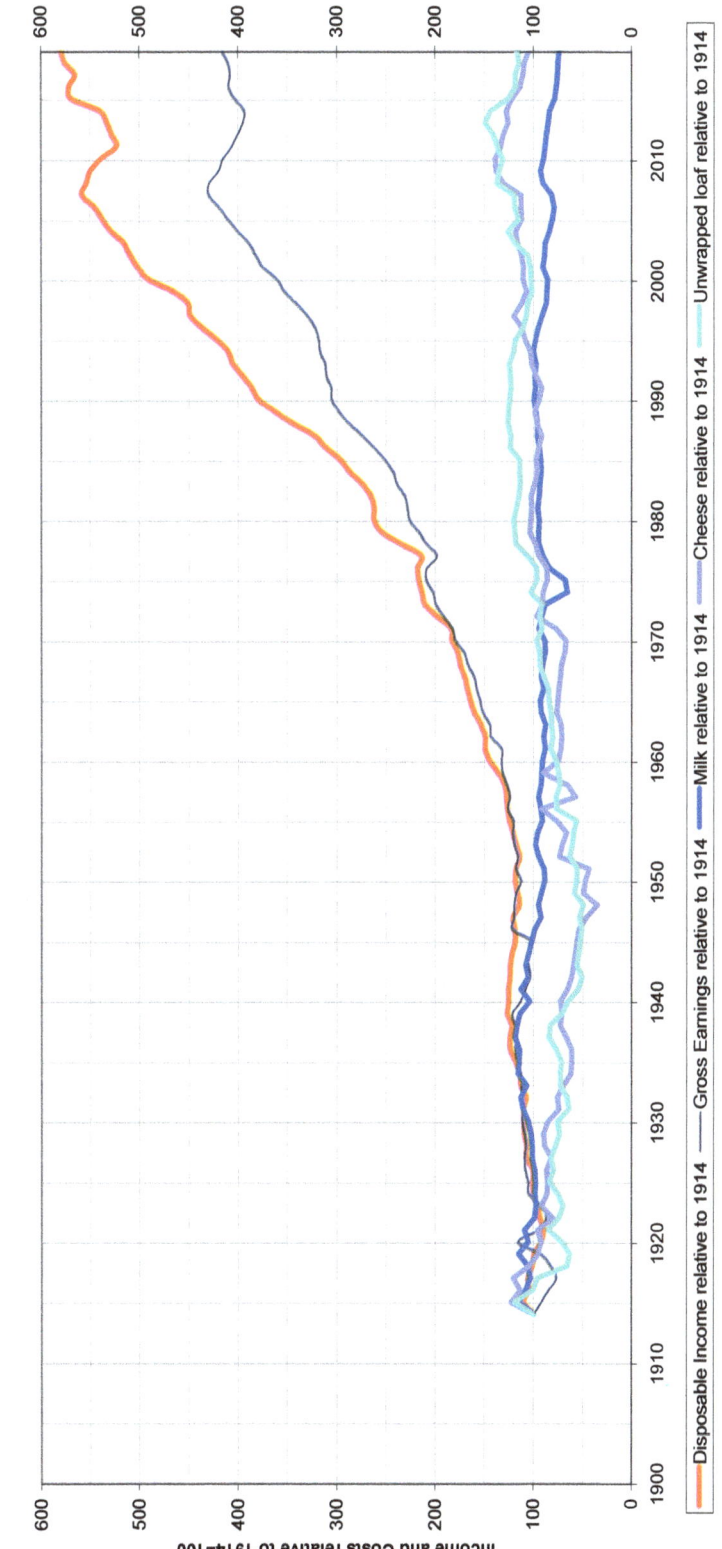

An index of the real value of key household income and expenditure relative to 1914.

Income and Food

(All metrics normalised to "real" current values before indexing.)

Disposable Income relative to 1914 —— Gross Earnings relative to 1914 —— Milk relative to 1914 —— Cheese relative to 1914 —— Unwrapped loaf relative to 1914

Income and Costs relative to 1914=100

The growth of access to motor cars

A secondary pointer to the sustained improvement in general financial well-being for most people from the twentieth century onwards is simply in the form of the access to personal motor transport.

The first indicator of ever-improving affordability of personal motor transport in the UK comes simply from the number of registered private vehicles.

In the chart on the opposite page this is represented in purple, showing the number of cars registered to be allowed on the roads since 1910. The data are from the Department for Transport, and they have given an estimate of approximately 53 thousand private motor vehicles registered or used on the eve of The Great War. Although the numbers noticeably increase between the two wars, it is from the 1950s that numbers increase significantly, as the economy recovers and earnings grow, reaching approximately 32 million private cars in 2019.

A major contribution to the growth of possession of personal motor transport in the years since the end of rationing, particularly, comes from an estimate of the "real" effective price of cars in comparison with average earnings over the same period.

This can be illustrated in the following table using two simple groups of cars with the list price of the car as a percentage of average annual earnings. The left group representing the more economical and the right group the middle range:

1939	Hillman Minx	96%		1939	Rover 12	162%
1959	Mini	93%		1958	Austin A40	131%
1977	Renault 4	90%		1978	Ford Capri 2.0S	123%
2006	Mini Cooper 1.6	62%		1999	Ford Mondeo 1.8GLX	101%
2019	Mini Cooper 1.5	55%		2018	Ford Focus Estate 1.5 TDCi	72%

Of course we have also seen in the first chapter **Population**, that the population of the UK grew significantly over the same decades, as did the number of dwellings and households. As such a third useful indicator is a simple estimate of the average number of registered private motor vehicles per household over the time period.

This is shown in the chart on the opposite page in the lavender line and ranges from fewer than 0.01 cars per household on the eve of The Great War, to 0.15 cars per household just 6 years after The Second World War to 1.12 cars per household on average in 2019.

The growth of average household possession of personal motor transport from 1951 to 2019 is over 7 fold.

Again as with earnings and disposable income the same pattern of slow down is exhibited in the 21st century, though in this case this first appears from 2006, recovering from 2015.

All illustrating a very clear sign of people's preference for access to personal motor transport.

UK registered road vehicles and private vehicles per household

Average private cars per household

Millions Registered

— All vehicles, including commercial — Cars (PLG) — Cars per Dwelling/ Household

The "real" cost of living from 1977

Due to a wider range of data for the costs of different common expenditure items available from the ONS as the 20th century progressed, particularly from the late 1960s through mid-1980s onwards, we are able to broaden the analysis by choosing a useful relatively recent start point. A start point meaningful to many readers of the older generations, is 1977, which corresponds to the living memory of those who are generally now retired by the end of the second decade of the 21st century.

The items chosen are divided into three primary groupings of selected food items, two housing items and two transport items. For each the relative "real" change to full-time earnings and average disposable income per person are also shown in each case as well.

The chart at the top of the opposite page illustrates how "real" disposable income and earnings grew relative to 1977, this time in the darker and lighter orange lines respectively. The selected food items are again represented in the various blue lines, this time including bread, cheese, milk, eggs, shoulder of lamb and carrots. The picture again is of the growth of "real" earnings and income, relative to food items, even indicating disposable income outgrowing food items by as much as two and half fold over the 43 year period.

The chart in the middle of the opposite page contains two indicators of housing costs available to us, namely the average "real" cost of rent from the OECD in the dark green line, and a calculation of the theoretical "real" cost of repaying a new mortgage based upon a fixed methodology in the light green line, both relative to 1977.

The latter assumes 75% loan to value ratio, uses the average reported mortgage interest rates from The Bank of England Millennium Database, and also that reported by the Building Societies Association (BSA), all applied to the reported annual average price of houses. This provides a theoretical annual repayment amount. Note that it is not the average of the actual amounts paid by all of those still re-paying their mortgages in each year, but rather a consistent indicator of the amount a new home buyer might face each year, and as such is a pessimistic indicator only.

It is very clear that both rental costs and theoretical mortgage repayment costs have almost kept pace with "real" disposable income growth, and have even outgrown average earnings. This will be discussed in much more detail in the next chapter.

Finally in the chart at the bottom of the opposite page is a limited view of the running cost of private motor transport in the form of the "real" cost of petrol fuel in the pink lines and diesel fuel in the plum line, again relative to 1977, as well as the growth of "real" earnings and disposable income in the orange lines. This again strongly suggests that by the second half of the 1990s this was growing in "real" cost relative to 1977, being 50% more expensive in 2019 than 1977, but was still outgrown by both "real" earnings and "real" average disposable income per person.

**Index of the real value of key household income and expenditure relative to 1977.
Income and Food**

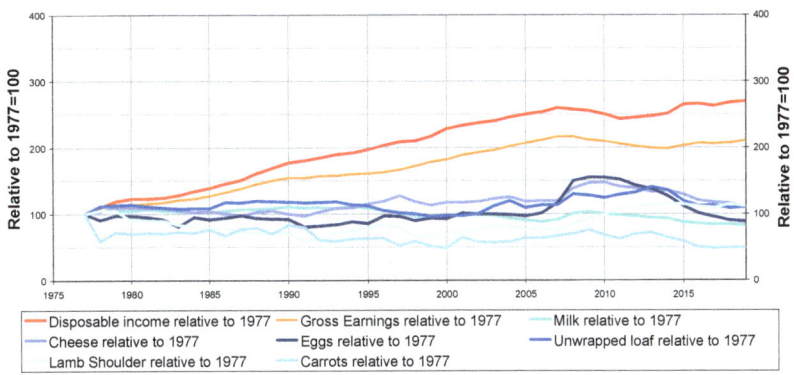

**Index of the real value of key household income and expenditure relative to 1977.
Income and Housing**

**Index of the real value of key household income and expenditure relative to 1977.
Income and Transport**

The "real" cost of living from 1997

Finally we are able to extend the selected data further and shift to a much more recent base comparison year of 1997 to see how the cost of living compared to average earnings and disposable income have changed over these 23 years to 2019.

The picture that emerges is again very, very strong and this time offers an insight into the probable perceptions formed by the younger generation of people who have been subject to the effects of economic change over that time.

In the chart at the top of the opposite page are "real" earnings and average disposable income per person in the orange lines and selected food items in the blue lines. This time it is very clear that both earnings and income have grown to end the period at only 25% higher than in 1997, this time disposable income not outgrowing earnings, but even more noticeable the cost of food items have varied again similarly above and below the central measure of the index. This suggests that income and food are quite close to each other in "real" terms and will be a strong influence in the perception of the younger generation.

In the chart in the middle of the opposite page the costs of housing and heating and lighting are represented, again using relative index of rent and the previously discussed theoretical cost of a new mortgage. This is a very revealing explanation of the substantial "real" increase in costs faced by the younger generations relative to 1997 suggesting that all but rent have significantly outgrown any "real" gain in earnings and disposable income. Clearly the cost of heating and lighting in the form of gas (bright green) and electricity (olive green) have hugely outgrown earnings and incomes by over 50% and 40% respectively, with theoretical mortgage re-payments being 20% higher than in 1997.

In the chart at the bottom of the opposite page are data that represent "real" costs of transport relative to 1997 and again repeating the average earnings and average disposable income per person. In this case we can see rail fares in lavender and petrol and oil in salmon pink have also again outgrown earnings and incomes but the particular huge increase is shown in the cost of insurance and tax for cars since 2009.

This is likely driven by a range of factors including the huge explosion in cost of repairs from comparatively minor collisions due to the very great increase in technical complexity of cars in the 21st century, including multiple safety features. This burden is also skewed heavily towards younger drivers as the ability to acquire a car of considerable performance has become more affordable than in the past, increasing the risks of collisions and the consequences of such collisions. In addition it largely coincides with a range of varying policy decisions by successive governments bent on their ideological fixation with so-called "climate change" and so-called air-pollution. Whilst only a correlation, it is notable that this also corresponds with the aftermath of the 2008 economic crash.

**Index of the real value of key household income and expenditure relative to 1997.
Income and Food**

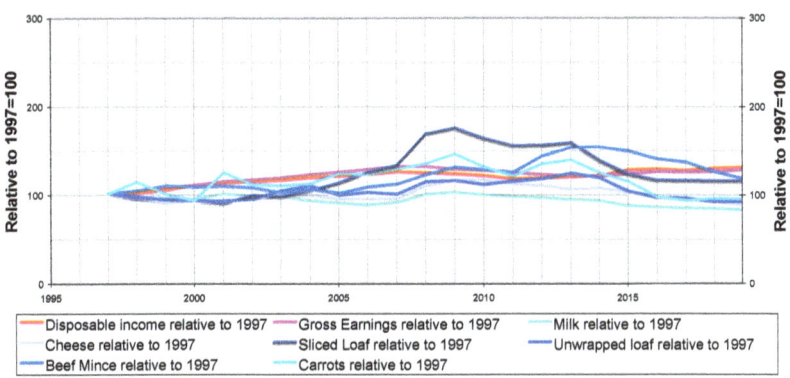

**Index of the real value of key household income and expenditure relative to 1997.
Income and Housing**

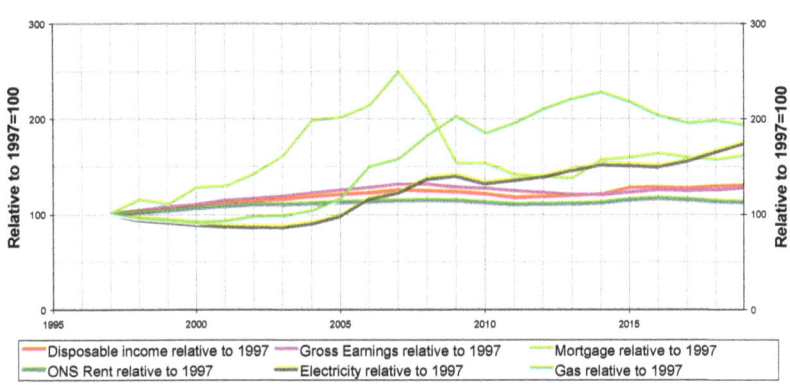

**Index of the real value of key household income and expenditure relative to 1997.
Income and Transport**

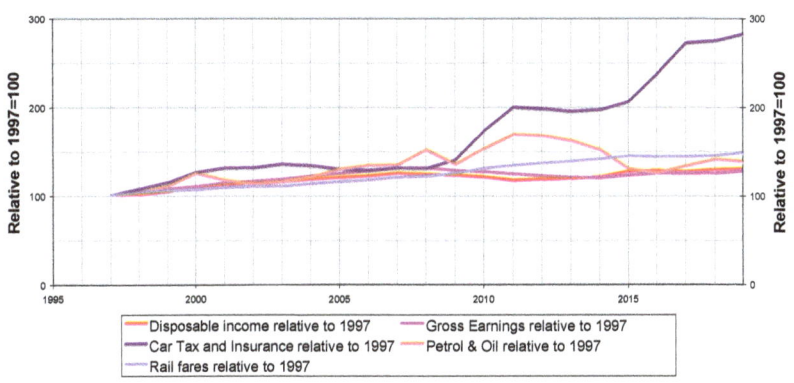

The reality of the cost of living

From this analysis we can see a strong picture of the very long term improvement of material well-being over the period of 320 years from 1700, including real earnings, incomes, and the costs of many of the principal items of everyday life on which people and households spend their money.

However, we do know that hidden within this long term improvement there is significant variability in response to such factors as issues with the harvests, economic crises and war particularly.

Also quite strong in the long term trend is the message that despite the huge economic and social changes wrought by the "Industrial Revolution", its fruits were very slow to "trickle down" to the majority of people; in fact the very people working the hardest, at least physically (and usually in the most dangerous conditions), to bring about the overall economic improvements.

All the indicators so far discussed, both in previous chapters and now incorporating the first look at items of expenditure that constitute "the cost of living", are very consistent in supporting the suggestion of slow improvement, peppered with sometimes severe crises that brought about extreme hardship for great numbers of people.

But in the end the improvements did start to be felt by more and more people and particularly from the twentieth century onwards.

> The problem now is that whilst the real improvements of the first three hundred years have not yet been lost to people, continued improvement seems to have halted for almost two decades to 2019 in all real terms for the vast majority of people.
>
> It must be acknowledged that there are apparently many complex reasons for this halt to progress, but many are due directly to failed policies of the last almost three decades from successive governments mostly driven by narrow ideology and irrational policies that have repeatedly yielded hopelessly failed outcomes for the majority.
>
> Whilst beyond the scope of this work, every social and economic indicator and outcome from the policies of 2020 and 2021, both in the UK and internationally, suggest much, much worse to come.

Housing

"Mid pleasures and palaces though we may roam
Be it ever so humble, there's no place like home"

John Howard Payne:
Clari, The Maid of Milan,
1823

Population, dwellings and occupancy

As a non-nomadic society, certainly since at least the early middle-ages, the population of the UK has needed and, accordingly, built dwellings to house and shelter them from the weather, neighbouring communities and wild animals.

A useful simplistic indicator of at least the availability or theoretical "shortage" of housing for the population of the UK, Great Britain and England is a crude average occupancy rate of people per estimated or enumerated dwelling through the ages. This of course does not offer any indication of the size of the dwellings and even less an indication of the cleanliness and condition of the dwellings. It is only much later from the 20th century that some analysis of these latter characteristics of housing were offered and even later recorded and tracked.

The counts of dwellings have been subject to changes of definition, often leading census enumerators to count in different ways. These anomalies have been analysed by the foremost academic studying the UK's housing, the late Dr. Alan Holmans in his seminal work *"Historical Statistics of Housing in Britain"* (published in 2005). This work offers a comprehensive analysis of most aspects of housing, at least since the first census was taken in 1801 through to 2001. Data for the post-Second World War period is published by the Ministry of Housing, and used here.

Although somewhat less reliable and also a little contentious, the earlier contemporary works of Charles Davenant (1695), Gregory King (1696), Joseph Massie (1755 and 1758), George Chalmers (1782 to 1804) and Patrick Colquhoun (1806 and 1815) do provide useful 18th century estimates of housing and population as well, at least for England.

Although these latter data from pre-census contemporary analysis are somewhat sparse and variable, the population estimates at least are now more reliable thanks to the work of Tony Wrigley and Roger Schofield. In fact these latter estimates generally support some of the early calculated estimates offered by Gregory King from 1696.

From a count of population divided by a count of dwellings it is therefore feasible to represent the crude average rate of occupancy of people per dwelling through time, even if not precise, nor yet accounting for nuances of the distribution of the number of people of different family sizes occupying dwellings. This latter is at least enumerated from 1911 thanks to the census reports from that year.

The chart on the opposite page offers a view of the average calculated occupancy rates firstly for England from 1700 to 1801, from the previously mentioned contemporary analyses, then Great Britain to 2019.

The population of England is represented in the orange dashed line and the estimated number of dwellings, households or families in the light blue dashed line. Dividing population by dwellings yields an average occupancy rate represented in the dashed pink line.

The figures for Great Britain are then represented with population in the mid-grey line, whilst dwellings are represented in the dark blue line. Again dividing population by dwellings yields an average occupancy rate for Great Britain in the red line.

Notable in the trend is a growth of occupancy rates from over 4 per dwelling before the era of The Industrial Revolution through to the period in the immediate aftermath of The Napoleonic Wars of 5.6 per dwelling.

From the 1820s to The Great War the data suggest a steady fall of occupancy rates; after which, thanks to the 1919 Liberal Government's policy of "Homes fit for Heroes", the data suggests a rapid fall of occupancy rates to the 1980s; then a gradually slowing rate of decline from the 1980s until the late-1990s. Rates noticeably slow further from the late-1990s to 2009, before a small increase from 2010, following the 2008 economic crash. Occupancy rates then return to 2.3 people per dwelling in 2019 (a rate also found in several government surveys).

Population, Housing Stock and Occupancy Rates

Number of People per dwelling

Population and Stock (Millions)

Legend: UK Population — GB Population — England Population — GB Dwellings — England Dwellings — GB Occ. Rate — England Occ. Rate

The question of crowding

Returning to the analysis of the size of households and the relative numbers of each size of household, data is readily available for England and Wales from the 1911 census onwards, collated and published in Alan Holman's work, but supplemented from the 2001, 2011 and 2021 censuses, as well as detailed annual analysis from the ONS that also offers an estimate of the distribution and numbers to 2019. In addition an annual set of estimates from 1996 to-date for the whole of the UK is also available from the ONS.

The chart on the opposite page repeats the crude average occupancy rate since 1900 in the red line, this time for England and Wales, but is now supplemented by coloured blocks representing the number of single person (mid-blue), two person (light blue) up to ten or more person (bright pink) households. The latter actually stops being reported after the 1981 census and the figures switch to six and seven or more people households (light pink and salmon pink respectively).

Very clear in the chart is the effective near disappearance of the larger households, of which 7 or more people constituted 16% of households in 1911, whilst census data, and current survey analysis from the ONS, show such households only constitute less than 1% of the households for both England and Wales as well as the UK as a whole in 2019.

Overwhelmingly clear is the huge growth of one and two person households since the start of the twentieth century. In 1911 such households only constituted a little over 5% and 16% respectively of all households, but by 2019 they constituted approximately 29% and slightly over 34% respectively of all households in England and Wales, as well as near identical proportions for the UK as a whole.

In addition three person (bright green) and four person (olive green) households have slightly reduced in constituent share of all households, though less dramatically than larger households, from slightly over 19% and 18% respectively in 1911 to slightly over 15% and 14% respectively in 2019. Again the constituent shares for the UK in 2019 are very similar.

Of particular interest to the claims of a housing "shortage" due to lack of building, and in particular such a shortage being the cause of the house price boom that has afflicted the housing market since the late 1990s; the data reveal a very notable trend both for crude average occupancy rates and distribution of household sizes.

The average crude occupancy rate only stops falling after 2009, although its rate of fall slowed from the late 1990s, but also the household size distribution for the smaller households, particularly single person and two person, only stop increasing from the middle years of the first two decades of the 21st century. Notable is that the three and four person household shares generally remain very stable from 1996, with four person households tending to increase only in the second decade of the 21st century.

Households (million) by Number of People (from Holmans/ONS) and Average Occupancy Rate for England and Wales

Average Occupancy Rate per Dwelling

Households (million) by Number of Residents

Legend: 1 2 3 4 5 6 7 8 9 10 or more E&W Occ. Rate

The age of UK housing stock

Another useful background view of the characteristics of the UK's housing is simply the age of the housing stock.

Data are published regularly for the various nations of the UK, and the recent data re-published by The BRE Trust for the UK is similarly representative of England also derived from the English Housing Survey and published by the Ministry of Housing, Communities and Local Government.

Of course there was very little, if any, house building either during The Great War or The Second World War, and thus the age categories in the chart opposite are set to show similar time span groups available from the data, generally at least after The Great War in near 20 year cohorts.

From this we can see that approximately 21% of the UK's (and England's) housing stock dates from before The Great War. The estimated number of such dwellings for the UK is over 5.8 million, of which approximately 4.9 million are in England. We also know from the analysis of the Lady Day Hearth Tax books for 1688, undertaken by Charles Davenant and published in 1695 (the tables being republished in full by both Sir Frederick Eden and George Chalmers), that the enumerated number of dwellings in England was approximately 1.2 million, though some estimates as low as 1.1 million were suggested by Gregory King.

An unknown number of such properties have no doubt been lost and therefore we might suggest that perhaps 4 to 4.5 million properties from the 18th and 19th century, including also a number from the years before The Great War, are extant in the UK's housing stock at the end of the second decade of the 21st century. The calculated net additional dwellings and the best known counts of building from Brian Mitchell (1988) and Alan Holmans (2005) suggest that in fact over 7 million were added to the stock from 1700 to the eve of The Great War, and thus some 3 million have since been lost due to demolition, war damage and possible other change of use. However, this number of pre-Great War dwellings has not significantly changed over the first two decades of the 21st century according to the Ministry of Housing analysis previously discussed.

The second period of extant housing represented is the two decades between the two major wars and of course covers the first building boom of "Homes fit for Heroes". This is estimated at 15%, or 4.2 million extant dwellings, with building estimates from Mitchell and Holmans estimating almost 4.4 million, therefore suggesting few have been lost.

The groupings thereafter cover the post Second World War house building boom to 1980, largely driven by council housing, constituting 39% of total stock and just over 11 million dwellings, though building completion estimates are slightly lower at approximately 10.5 million.

The last pair of groupings from 1981 to 2019 only constitute 25% of housing stock as of the year of available data for both UK and England, reiterating that the UK does have a generally old stock of housing.

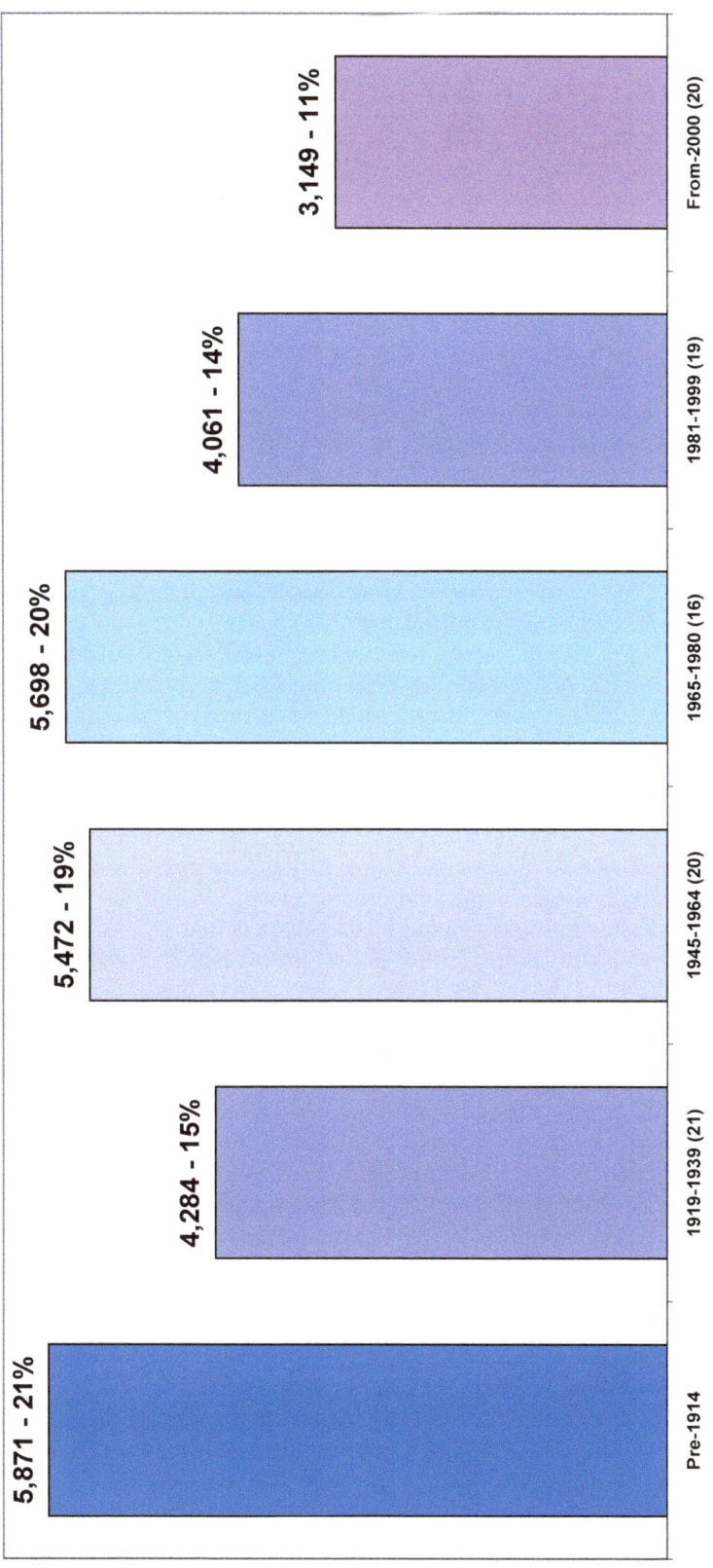

UK dwelling stock by age 2017/18 ('000) - 28.5 million

Pre-1914: 5,871 - 21%

1919-1939 (21): 4,284 - 15%

1945-1964 (20): 5,472 - 19%

1965-1980 (16): 5,698 - 20%

1981-1999 (19): 4,061 - 14%

From-2000 (20): 3,149 - 11%

The rate of building completion

Looking in more detail at the estimates of annual building published by Mitchell in 1988 (previously analysed in Mitchell and Deane 1962), plus the analysis of Holmans published in 2005, both starting in 1852, then from the ONS after The Second World War, yield a well correlated picture of housing with decadal census enumeration of extant dwellings.

The estimates have been crudely extrapolated to the start of the 19th century from the first census taken in 1801 and accordingly at least show a simplistic net additional average annual dwelling count between those census years of 1801 and 1851.

Thus the chart on the opposite page shows both net additional dwellings for the first fifty years of the 19th century, then the annual building completion estimates thereafter.

The funding source for the building completion is represented in the three colours of mid blue for privately funded, salmon pink for local authority funded and instigated, and the olive green for both housing association and those classed as "other" by Mitchell, Holmans and later the ONS and Ministry of Housing.

Clearly visible are the two major phases of Local Authority instigated and funded house building programmes that constituted about 40% of house build between the two world wars, then constituted approximately 50% of total building in the period from the end of The Second World War to the early 1980s. Thereafter the Thatcher Government policy of less reliance on Local Authority, tax-payer funded, house building was introduced. It is notable from that era that housing associations were formed in ever greater numbers to help the least well off to access a potentially decent home at affordable prices.

A factor not represented in this chart is that the building completion estimates and counts do not entirely represent the whole picture of the contribution to available housing in any year or decade.

Particularly important are the number of demolitions that were undertaken in the inter-war years and even more in the decades in the aftermath of The Second World War.

The former was mostly driven by the need to clear old slum dwellings that were no longer deemed fit for habitation and Holmans estimates this amounted to about 290 thousand dwellings. However thanks to both the losses during The Second World from bombing, then demolition of unfit housing to the end of the 20th century, Holmans estimates this to be a total of over 1.6 million dwellings cleared from the housing stock. The sum total estimated at almost 2 million demolished, at least since 1921.

Most were the older 18th and 19th century buildings fallen into extreme disrepair and were generally classed as no longer fit for habitation.

Note also the fall of building rates firstly from the 1989 peak thanks to that economic downturn, then slow rise to the 2007 peak and extreme fall for a decade after the 2008 crash, before recovering again to 2019.

GB House building: permanent dwellings completed (thousands), by funding type (Combined Mitchell and MofH/ONS)

Annual Dwelling Completions (thousands)

Private Enterprise   Housing Associations/Other   Local Authorities   All Dwellings

Post-war net additional housing

Looking now at the available housing and calculating the average net additional housing per year by decade since 1951 shows a picture that is somewhat different to the annual or decadal building completion rates.

In the chart on the opposite page both metrics for the UK are represented in orange bars for the average annual net additional values by decade, whilst average annual building completions are represented in the bright blue bars.

Each decade starts from census year for ten years, with the last of course only covering 2011 to 2019, being the end point of this analysis. As such, average annual values are presented to cater for the uneven last period.

Overwhelmingly clear is that house building completion significantly out-performs net additional dwellings available for the first three decades from 1951 to 1980, in fact by approximately 2 million dwellings according to the published dwelling counts from the decadal census and building completion counts from the Ministry of Housing. This difference is mostly accounted for thanks to demolitions of over 1.6 million given by Holmans.

However following the 1991 to 2000 decade in which the two are similar, the final two decades of the period show net additional dwellings increasing at a greater rate than building completion rates. This latter period is bolstered by a large amount of change of use and a number of conversions of larger buildings, particularly larger pre-Second World War houses converted to blocks of flats. This latter has particularly helped the growth of single occupancy as discussed previously, the growth of which gathers pace from the post Second World War period onwards.

Approaching the trends at a decadal level does however mask the notable falls in building completions that occurred in the wake of the 1989 economic downturn (shown in the chart on the previous page in the dips in total building completions on the right hand end of the chart).

This downturn resulted economically in a large number of home owners being placed in a position that became known as "negative equity", in which their home became valued at a lower level than the amount they actually owed, thanks to their paying high prices before the subsequent crash in prices from 1990 (shown in the next section).

The building rates finally recovered for a short period after the low of 2001 peaking in 2007 before plummeting in the wake of the 2008 crash.

It was this latter crash in building that was not compensated for entirely by change of use and conversions, allied to the effects of mass net-immigration (5 million) and the large increase of population (8.5 million) from 1998 to 2019, that resulted in the increase of the crude average occupancy rate from 2010.

The data suggests the seeds for the modern housing "crisis" lay in the period from mid-1990s to 2007, mostly in fiscal "demand" rather than physical "supply", as the latter gamely tried to keep pace regardless.

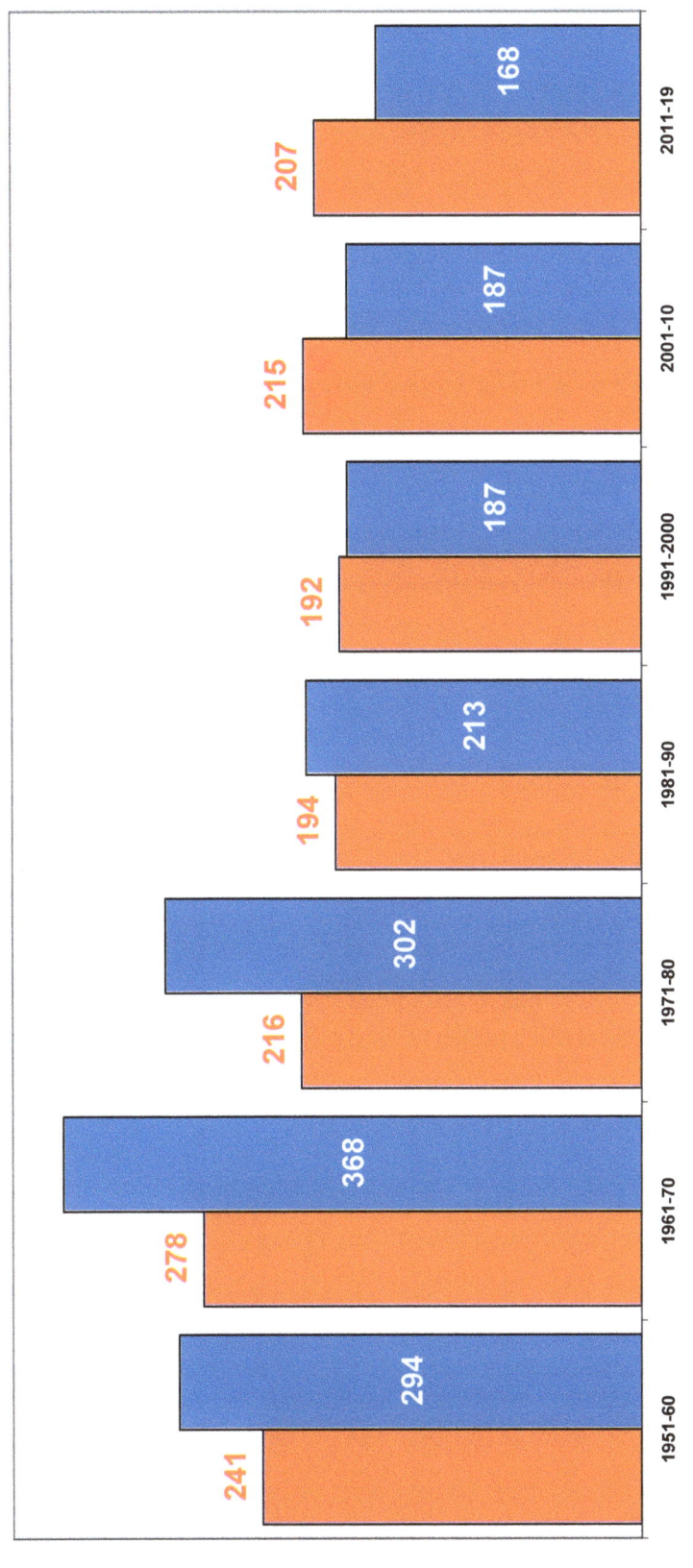

Average annual UK - net additional dwellings and build completions (thousands) by decade - 1951-2019
Total 15.4 million additional dwellings, 205% increase

Decade	net additional dwellings	build completions
1951-60	241	294
1961-70	278	368
1971-80	216	302
1981-90	194	213
1991-2000	192	187
2001-10	215	187
2011-19	207	168

Buying a home of one's own

For the 18th and 19th centuries owner occupation was a rarity and in practice impossible for almost all people in the UK. However it was a growing aspiration for many as time progressed and it was seen as a possibility as income and earning opportunities improved. This at first affected particularly the growing upper middle classes in the 19th century and gradually became a more likely prospect for the lower middle classes, at least from the early 20th century.

To achieve some form of owner occupation there are three primary economic factors that underpin the ability, or otherwise, to take possession of one's own home, rather than rented lodgings.

The first factor is the price of a dwelling, from a small flat to a large mansion. It is this factor that is represented in the chart on the opposite page, from the oldest available estimates and actual data to 2019.

Again we use data collated in the Bank of England Millennium Database, that takes us back to the 1840s, derived mostly from Brian Mitchell's aforementioned 1988 "*British Historical Statistics*". Early estimates of approximate average house prices are offered using building costs, that are more readily recorded for the period to the early 1950s.

This historical data is represented in the dark green from 1845 to 2016, being factored by the prevailing cost of living and CPI, as discussed previously, offering a realistic view of the price of houses in modern currency value terms in 2019.

Data from the 1950s is available from the major building societies, in particular The Nationwide Building Society and The Halifax Bank (formerly a building society). These latter are represented in the chart on the opposite page in the light green and yellow lines respectively.

Both generally correlate well with each other and with the data provided in the Bank of England Millennium Database.

All clearly show a strong pattern of overall growth in real terms but also suggest four large and one small boom of house prices within the overall trend.

The first price boom is in the immediate aftermath of The Second World War, when a very large building boom started and probably caused the boom of prices due to the cost of materials and delays in completion before people could acquire a home of their own. The second large boom, the small boom and third large boom are visible in mid 1970s, late 1970s and then the late 1980s respectively. Common to all four such booms is the subsequent reduction in "real" prices within a year or two.

It is the most recent price boom that started in 1997 that clearly does not reduce back to earlier levels that correspond to earnings, despite even the 2008 crash.

These trends are correlated in relation to the growth of average "real" annual earnings being represented in the dark blue line for the same period.

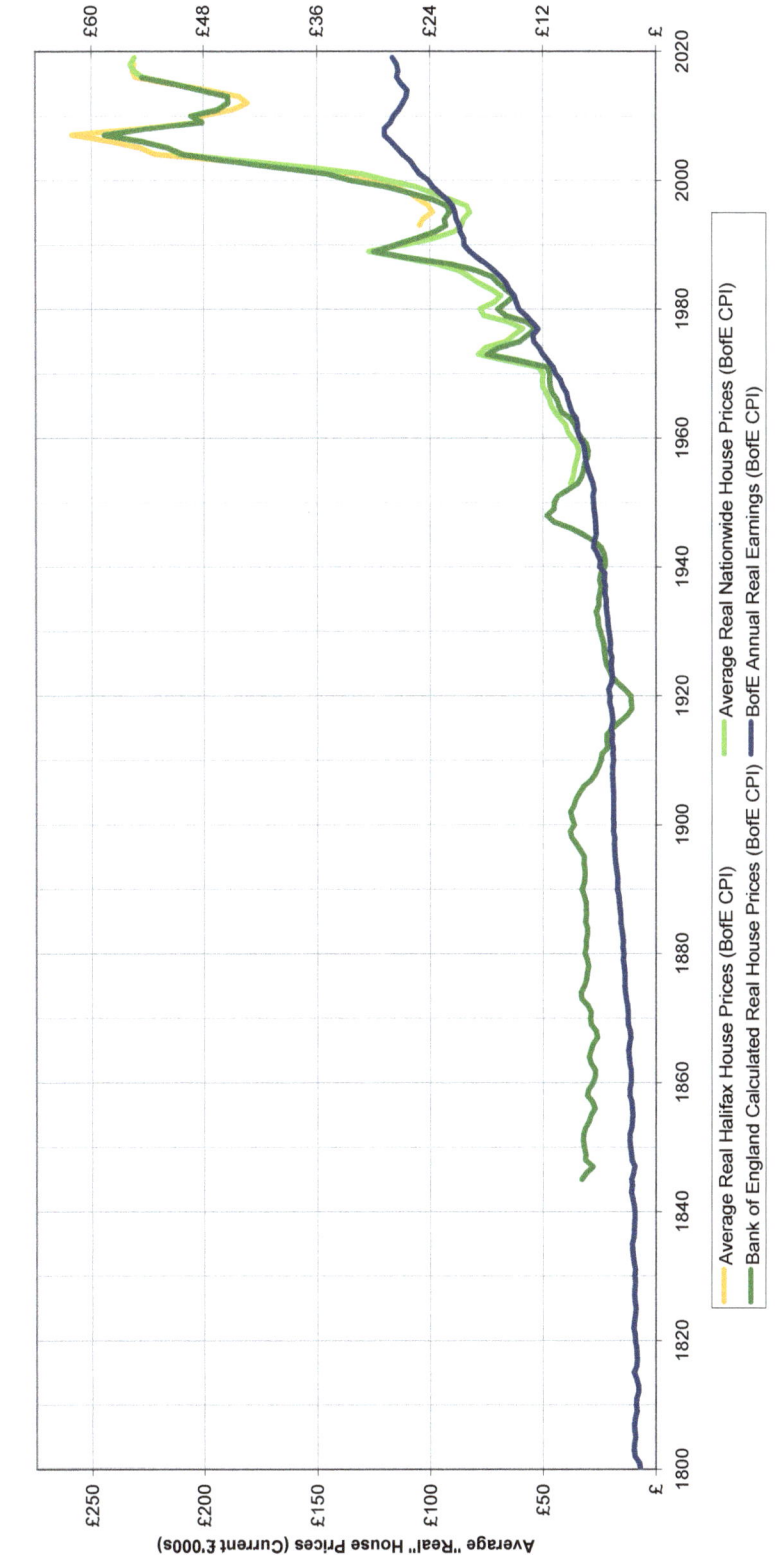

Average "Real" House Prices and Average Annual Real Earnings (Current £'000s)

Average "Real" Annual Earnings (Current £'000s)

Average "Real" House Prices (Current £'000s)

Average Real Halifax House Prices (BofE CPI)
Average Real Nationwide House Prices (BofE CPI)
Bank of England Calculated Real House Prices (BofE CPI)
BofE Annual Real Earnings (BofE CPI)

The ratio of house prices to earnings

The second factor that might make home ownership a possibility for a person looking to acquire their own home is in relation to their earnings.

In the same chart on the previous page the average annual "real" earnings, that were discussed in the third chapter **Earnings and Income**, is represented in dark blue (however, also note the caveats related to inequality measures discussed in the fourth chapter **Income Inequality**).

This again reveals the effect of the 2008 crash on earnings, as is also the effect on house prices, but the overwhelming revelation is the failure of house prices to return to the previously estimated levels in relation to earnings seen from the earlier price booms and reductions.

By simply dividing average house prices by average annual earnings the ratio of the former to the latter is revealed and allows us to see the generally quoted ratio that tended to allow more and more people to take possession of their own home and become owner occupiers.

This long term historical ratio is represented in the chart on the opposite page in the orange line and very clearly shows that ratios of estimated house prices to average earnings were generally between 12 to 1 and 6 to 1 for the period of data available from the mid-1840s to the eve of The Great War.

The first suggestion of a ratio closer to that prevailing for much of the time in the aftermath of The Second World War is apparent only on the very eve of The Great War and the inter-war years.

However we also know that until the end of the 1940s and early 1950s earnings inequality was consistently much greater than since and as such supports the idea that in fact relatively few households were able to buy a home of their own even in this inter-war era of a more favourable house price to earnings ratio.

The real change takes place from the 1950s when the ratio of prices to earnings fell to just 4 to 1, whilst earnings inequality started to fall, enabling more people to become owner occupiers, as we shall see in the next few pages.

Clearly visible in both the orange Bank of England Millennium Database derived ratio and the red Nationwide Building Society derived ratio we can see the first, second, third large booms and small boom as mentioned previously, as they affected this indicator ratio. In each case these all return to, or at least very close to, the vaunted indicator ratio of 4 to 1.

That ratio holds until the late 1990s boom. But despite the effects of the 2008 crash, the indicator ratio soars to approximately 8 to 1, not previously seen since the start of the 20th century, temporarily falling to about 7 to 1 before returning again to approximately 8 to 1 in 2019.

Although only an indicator ratio, in fact this ratio does remain a reasonably useful indicator of the real effects of such house price and earnings disparity even in the very different age of the 21st century.

Ratio of House Prices (Bank of England Index) to MeasuringWorth & Bank of England Annual Average Gross Earnings

Ratio of House Prices to Average Annual Income

Ratio BofE House Price (Re-in) to BofE Annual Income — Ratio Nationwide House Prices to MW Annual Income

The cost of borrowing to buy a home

The third factor that underpins the relative affordability of buying one's own home is centred around the cost of, and the availability of, credit extended to those intending to purchase a property.

The first element of this factor, namely the cost of borrowing, is expressed chiefly in the form of prevailing interest rates available from lenders for house purchase.

Again the Bank of England Millennium Database offers a long term historical analysis of best known mortgage/home-loan interest rates, but this is supplemented since The Second World War by the figures collated by The Building Societies Association (BSA).

The latter data are somewhat more comprehensive but also more complex in that, at least since 1993, the rates of more mortgage options and types of deal are presented, reflecting the ever greater deregulation of the market that started to take place from the late 1960s.

To keep the post-Second World War BSA based estimates as simple as possible, and to ensure a theoretical continuity with the more simplistic collation of data from the Millennium Database, a crude, un-weighted average for the later BSA data is calculated (and cross checked against each type of mortgage deal represented).

The results are presented in the chart on the opposite page in which the lavender line represents the annual average mortgage interest rate collated in the Bank of England Millennium Database, whilst the crude average annual interest rate derived from the Building Societies Association collection is represented in the bright pink line.

The most obvious overall trends are the relative consistency of low interest rates from the mid-1850s to a notable inter-war increase followed by steady fall back to lower rates to the mid-1950s.

Thereafter there is a significant rise of rates, represented in both data sets and again showing extreme spikes of considerable duration in the mid-1970s, again in 1980 and then again in 1990.

These extremely high mortgage interest rates all follow on, usually within one year or so from the previously discussed booms of house prices and are generally closely related to other significant economic disruptions at each time.

The first boom relates to the extreme inflation in the aftermath of the "Barber boom", oil crisis and subsequent IMF borrowing crisis of the mid-1970s. This is followed by the economic downturn and disruption in the aftermath of "The Winter of Discontent" from 1979 to 1982. The third of these is in response to major house price inflation and other disruption from another economic downturn from 1989.

In each case the mortgage interest rates rose in the immediate aftermath of each connected house price boom, then fell back in the subsequent year or two. The interesting exception is from 1991 onwards after which interest rates almost continuously fall to a 2019 all-time-low.

Bank of England and Building Societies Association (BSA) derived annual average Standard Variable Rate Mortgage

Mortgage Interest Rates

BofE Variable Mortgage interest rate CMRAUKA — BSA Average Variable Mortgage Interest Rate

The cost of repaying a mortgage

There is no data readily available that comprehensively analyses all the different amounts paid by all those buying a property with a mortgage, be they owner occupiers or those buying a property as a landlord in order to let it or otherwise for profit or investment.

We must therefore use a generalised indicator of the possible consistent amounts repayable for prospective purchasers using normal actuarial calculators to offer an estimate for each year's average repayment, being derived from the average house price and the average interest rate for a certain type of mortgage.

The chosen type of borrowing used to illustrate this theoretical repayment and its share of the average earnings is based upon a 25 year loan period, where the loan is 75% of the value of the property (at that year's average house price).

Using standard formulae yields a theoretical annual repayment amount which is divided by the average annual earnings for that same year. This yields the theoretical share of individual full time average annual earnings that would need to be used to repay such a mortgage.

The result is plotted in the chart on the opposite page in bright blue and clearly supports the findings from the indicator of the ratio of house price to annual earnings, and suggests that on average, and given the earning inequality before The Second World War for the overwhelming majority of households, the cost of repaying a consistently calculated mortgage was impossible.

In addition even being granted a loan, at the best known prevailing house prices and earnings prevalent before The Second World War was unlikely, and in the 21st century so far, is increasingly difficult.

For the majority the prospect only became realistically possible from the 1950s as some households managed to find ways to raise a deposit, persuade a lending institution (mostly bank or building society) to advance a secured loan and then to be able to maintain employment at improving earnings to afford to repay the loan over the required period.

Thus for the available early data a share of average income between 60% and 40% prevails until the eve of The Great War, then falling below 30% for the interwar years.

It is this inter-war fall that allowed more lower middle class households to acquire their own home in that period.

The pattern of this theoretical indicator again shows a low repayment share of less than 25% of earnings in the 1950s but again sees a steady rise, punctuated by extreme bursts of repayment rates in the three booms as previously discussed.

It is the fourth boom that started in 1997 that is notably different, in that it was driven by house prices, not interest rates and consequent repayment amounts, and is maintained by the policy of collapsing interest rates from the Bank of England and lenders shown on the previous page.

Percentage of Average Annual Real Earnings spent on Mortgage Repayments for new Mortgage

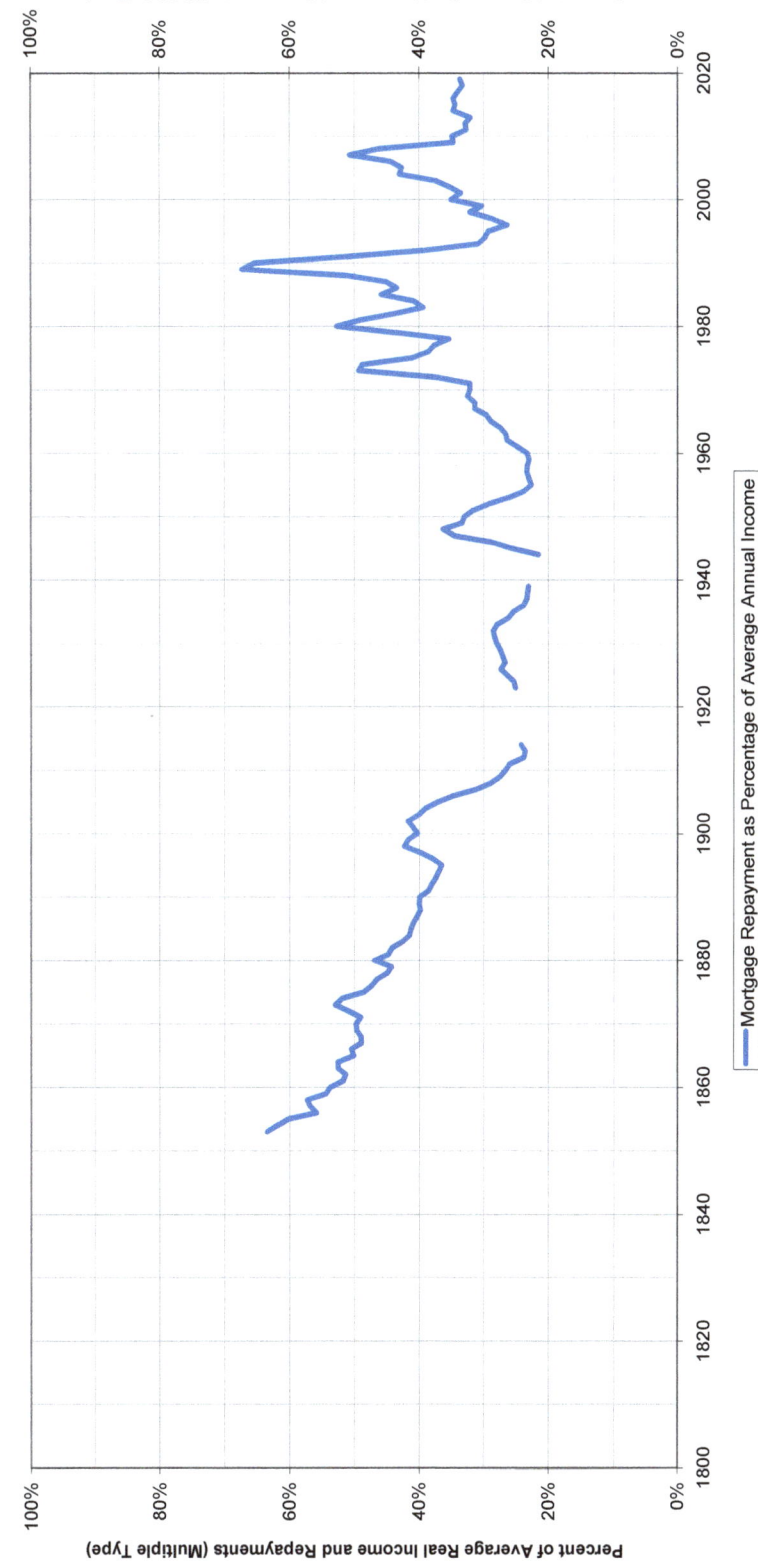

Percent of Average Real Income and Repayments (Multiple Type)

——— Mortgage Repayment as Percentage of Average Annual Income

Housing tenure from 1900

It is well understood and accepted that few households or people owned their own property before The Great War. In fact there was also little social housing either, as might be categorised by today's standards.

There was some effectively "subsidised" housing in the form of low rent rural cottages, usually tied to farm labouring, but this was often only a small compensation for such low wage rates throughout the 18th and 19th centuries for rural labourers, as has been discussed previously in the third, fourth and fifth chapters.

The earliest known estimate for the share of owner occupation tenure, on the eve of The Great War in 1914, was repeated in Ministry of Housing and ONS figures, having been re-quoted in the 1991 report "*English House Condition Survey*" from the Department for the Environment. However, Alan Holmans traced the origins of this estimate and suggests it is long repeated and is first documented as an estimate in the Department for the Environment's 1977 analysis published in "*Housing Policy Technical Volume*" in Table I.23. (Even then subject to its own caveat in Chapter 1, paragraph 91 of that document, though not available to this author).

This estimate is of approximately 10% being owner occupied on the eve of The Great War, rising to 23% at the end of The Great War in 1918.

These estimates are represented in the chart on the opposite page in the mid-grey line on the left, and particularly the two points marked by the mid-grey squares.

A tentative alternative might be possible, being derived instead from the analysis of wealth owned by various shares of the population as calculated by Facundo Alvaredo, the late Anthony Atkinson and Salvatore Morelli in their 2017 paper "*Top wealth shares in the UK over more than a century*" and applied to housing owner occupation. This is represented in the very light grey line on the left covering the decade or so before The Great War. This simple alternative estimate suggests this figure might have been as high as 14%, but is also speculative.

Essentially the data suggest that between 85% and 90% of all homes were privately rented at this point in time and no doubt more in the previous two centuries. This estimate is represented in the space between the grey lines and the dark blue line.

The character of renting changed for many in the aftermath of The Great War thanks to the policy of council house building that continued until the early 1980s. This is represented accordingly in the chart firstly in the gap between the blue line and the red line, then with the addition of housing association homes from the later 1970s in that between the blue and green lines.

Superimposed on the chart is an estimate of the share of people who own their homes outright, derived from English figures and represented in the bright cyan line, but also mathematically extrapolated back to 1900, interestingly coinciding with the calculated 14% as mentioned above.

Percentage of Housing Occupancy by Tenure for Great Britain

Percentage of dwellings

Legend:
- Own Outright
- Owner Occupied (estimate based on P90 wealth)
- Owner Occupied
- Privately rented
- Housing Association
- Local Authority

Owning plus buying with a mortgage

Exploring the growth of owner occupation from the 1960s to 2019 in more depth, including a correlation between the estimates for Great Britain versus those purely for England, further reveals very strong patterns over these six decades.

In the chart on the opposite page we represent the share of housing that is owner occupied for Great Britain as before in the mid-grey line. Correlated behind it is the sum total of the share of all owner occupation for England represented in the bright cyan line.

However by reversing the previous order from the superimposition of the England share of outright ownership subtracted from the English total share for owner occupation, allows us to plot the share of housing occupation driven by those buying their own home with a mortgage shown in the bright green line.

These two representations strikingly reveal two very significant changes in the market from the 1990s onwards.

The first is that the peak of the share of households buying with a mortgage (43%) takes place between 1992 and 1995, gradually falling thereafter until suffering a significant fall from 2000, gathering more pace from 2005 until a new low in 2017 (29%), not seen since the early 1970s.

The second significant change is the resultant effect on total share of owner occupation. From the previous tenure analysis, we can clearly see that the share of own outright from the English analysis clearly grows continuously, almost unchecked save for brief slow downs in the same years as before. Thus the effect of the peak and subsequent reduction in the owner occupiers buying with a mortgage is finally seen in the peak of total share of owner occupation apparently from the year 2000 in England, and from the year 2002 in Great Britain as a whole (69% to 70%), then falling significantly from 2005, reaching a low in 2016 (62%).

Both tenure shares of the housing market do make small recoveries thereafter, but the effect remains limited at the end of the second decade of the 21st century at 64% as owner occupiers.

Those households not able to become owner occupiers with a mortgage, revealed in this analysis, are mostly realistically offered the option of private renting with a few also able to take advantage of the availability of housing association homes.

Within the private rental market a notable new phenomenon started to appear from the mid-1990s that actually formed a very large engine of the house price boom and consequent shift from buying with a mortgage to renting a home. That was the new "Buy to Let" which as a distinct and defined mortgage product first appeared in 1996, though some individuals were buying additional properties by means of standard loans previously. By freeing capital from existing properties to secure loans for subsequent properties these new landlords drove the house price boom, thanks to the explosion of ready credit from the mid-1990s until 2008.

Percentage Housing Stock by Tenure for England and GB
Buying with Mortgage falls from mid-1990's, owner occupation falls from 2002
Rental becomes the only option for up to 5 million households

Percentage of Owner Occupied dwellings

England buy with mortgage — plus Own Outright — GB Owner Occupied

The real lost decades

Thanks to these notable phenomena in the housing market from the 1990s and the significant consequences for younger generations; and the considerable social and political disruption they have caused, it is worth exploring the possible effects in the form of a simple counter-factual exercise of "*what might have been*", but for these changes.

As such a simplistic extrapolation of continued growth of share of owner occupation has been attempted based upon the comparatively stable rate of growth from 1970 to 1990. It should be noted that the rate in the 1980s was actually slightly greater than the 1970s thanks chiefly to the ability of council tenants to buy their council properties at reduced prices, introduced that decade.

This counterfactual estimate is presented in the chart on the opposite page and the projection suggests that in fact as many as 4.5 million more households might have been owner occupiers by 2019 than is actually the case.

Both the actual own-outright and total share of owner occupied are again represented in the light cyan line and the mid-grey line respectively, as before. A simple theoretical extrapolation derived from the 1970 to 1990 trend, but allowed to peak in 2015, yields a theoretical owner occupation share of 80%, instead of the actual rate of 64%, representing in 2019 22.7 million potential owner occupying households as against 18.2 million actual owner occupying households accordingly.

The resulting residual 20% of the households as assigned to the rental market is actually simply arbitrarily divided equally between private rental and "social" rental, the latter made up of remaining local authority housing and housing association for illustration purposes.

Whilst being entirely theoretical, the growth of owner occupation seen in the chart that covers the period from the start of the 20th century does strongly suggest the possibility that in fact this simple extrapolation is entirely in keeping with the 70 year trend from 1920 to 1990, and there is no reason not to believe that within the limitation of the affordability of housing and people's earnings it might not have continued, at least to the arbitrary limit of 80% of the housing market applied here.

This speculation on top of 70 years of actual growth, of course runs entirely counter to the narrative speculated by others in the public discourse that what the UK needs is more social rented housing.

70 years of growth of owner occupation, the purchase of their home by large numbers of council tenants in the 1980s, albeit at effectively subsidised prices, in fact as their rental costs were also subsidised, tends to suggest that until the house **price** "crisis", brought about since the late 1990s, it is in fact highly probable that the 4.5 million speculative owner occupation shortfall do not seek social rented homes, but rather owner occupation, if only housing were allowed to be affordable in the typical ratios prevalent from most of the 1950s to the mid-1990s, at 4/1 to 5/1.

Housing Stock by Tenure (Percentage of Stock) from Great Britain
Strong forecast (1970-1990) of latent desire for owner occupation rather than rental
Latent (lost) desire for owner occupation up to 4.5 million households

Legend: Own Outright — Owner Occupied (Actual) — Owner Occupied (Latent) — Privately rented — Privately rented (Latent) — Social

Fiscal driver of house price "crisis"

Whilst there were falls in building rates from 1990 onwards, combined with a huge growth of net immigration from 1998 that were due to new policies of the Blair government, these effects are not such that crude occupancy rates per dwelling actually rose until 2010. Though the annual rate of reduction in crude occupancy rates did slow during this time.

In addition there is no major decline in the share of single or two person households. Even the ONS estimate of average household size does not reach its lowest rate until the period 2002 to 2012 followed by a rise again in 2019 to the level of 2001. However, the English Household Survey does indicate an increase in rates of *over-crowding* (as defined by the survey, based upon the *bedroom standard*) for private rental households from 1997 onwards and for social rental households from 2004 onwards.

All approaches to the various data, of population, immigration, net natural replacement rates, dwellings, households, building completion and net annual changes (including change of use and conversion) all tend to suggest that a "shortage" of housing supply, due to a lack of building, was not a primary driver of the house **price** boom that started in 1997.

As with the previous booms of the mid-1970s, late-1970s and late-1980s the primary driver is again fiscal failure and economic disruption.

The key difference for the boom from 1997 is that the driver is firstly due to the flood of very readily available credit in the market from the early to mid-1990s. That flood gathered pace over the next decade and a half, with such ultimately disastrous offerings such as 125% mortgages (as a percentage of purchase price), all combined with the reactive policy of repeatedly reducing interest rates from the mid-1990s, that thereby fuelled further demand thanks to relatively "cheap" repayments.

The credit flood facet of the house **price** "crisis" was in fact an international market phenomenon and the whole period might reasonably be described as a period of "irrational exuberance", a term coined by Alan Greenspan, head of the Federal Reserve in the USA.

The failure to attempt to manage the overheating of house prices, even with such a crude tool as the increase of interest rates was another policy choice of the Bank of England, Treasury and government of the time.

Only secondarily is the 1997 government's mass immigration policy, and resultant population boom from that immigration and birth rates among new immigrants, an aggravating factor to the house **price** "crisis".

The end result was the international crash and credit squeeze of 2008 that halted the social and economic progress that had benefited the population of the UK for 300 years to the turn of the century, albeit with severe interruptions along the way.

Though far from alone in suffering the consequences, the UK was exceptionally badly affected by the 2008 crash thanks to repeated local policy and fiscal failures throughout the period from the mid-1990s.

Poverty

"All the arguments which are brought to represent
poverty as no evil, show it to be evidently a great evil.
You never find people labouring to convince you that
you may live very happily upon a plentiful fortune"

James Boswell:
The Life of Samuel Johnson,
1791

Poverty, relative and real

Unquestionably the most controversial and emotionally charged topic related to socio-economic well-being, and in turn anything that might by some means be truly measurable, is the question of poverty.

There are many and various accounts and descriptions of life in poverty that are available to us from time immemorial and also throughout the period we are discussing from 1700 to 2019.

In the foreword we have outlined various definitions of poverty that have either been historically prevalent or have in recent decades gained more currency.

To attempt to represent the core results from the use of the most common modern definition of relative *"poverty"*, we open with calculated measures from the best known reliable data available.

Relative *"poverty"*, personal income

The first set of representations available to us of relative *"poverty"* are derived from the data previously discussed in the fourth chapter **Income Inequality**, and are again presented here using personal income distribution from four contemporary sources.

The best and most reliable early data available dates back to the analysis by Robert Dudley Baxter for 1867, as enhanced thanks to detailed work by Peter Lindert (see the fourth chapter **Income Inequality**).

In the chart at the top of the opposite page we show the representation of the data from the contemporary analysis of Baxter for 1867 in the red line. Keep in mind the data for 1867 is factored for inflation to 2019, using our reliable measures of the Cost of Living Index (CLI) and Consumer Price Index (CPI), discussed in detail in the fifth chapter **Cost of Living**.

Again we also represent the data derived from the HMRC analysis of personal incomes before tax for 2018/19 in the blue line, but extended to estimate the range of incomes including those not liable for tax.

Now we have added a simple calculation of the value of 60% of the median for each series, represented in the large orange dot and blue dot for the same years respectively. These are plotted to the same distribution to reveal the percentage of the income recipients who would be estimated to be in relative *"poverty"* according to this commonly used modern definition, for those whose income falls below these values.

This first chart suggests that in 1867 approximately 22% of personal income recipients fell below the theoretical relative *"poverty"* line of 60% of median income, whilst in 2018/19 over 25% of personal income recipients fell below this same theoretical line.

Interestingly the very clear pattern that emerges again is both the very extreme inequality of the whole data set for 1867, but that the portion below the upper quartile is notably less unequal.

In the chart in the middle of the opposite page, we move forward to 1911, just three years before The Great War. Using the data from the Inland Revenue (see the fourth chapter **Income Inequality**) presented in the pink line, factored for CLI/CPI, again annotated with a large pink dot for 60% of median income relative *"poverty"* line, we see the data now suggests that 17.5% of recipients of personal income fell below this relative *"poverty"* line, again against over 25% in 2018/19.

In the chart at the bottom of the opposite page we show the data from the Inland Revenue for 1949 in the brown line, again factored for CLI/CPI, and again against the extended data for 2018/19.

This time the data for 1949 suggests that over 26% of people in receipt of personal income fell below this theoretical relative *"poverty"* line against over 25% in 2018/19.

This personal income data distribution analysis suggests that this definition of relative *"poverty"* tends to produce incongruous results, in which fewer were in relative *"poverty"* in 1867 and 1911 than 2018/19!

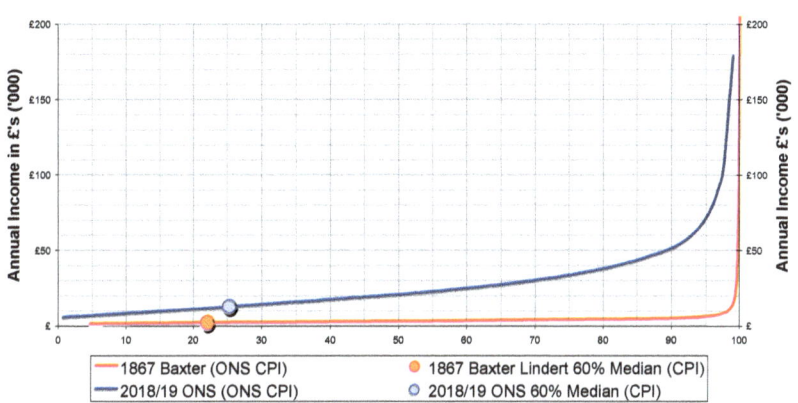

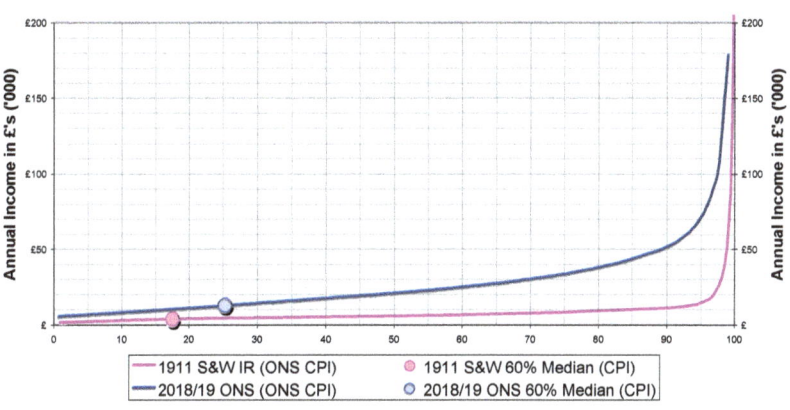

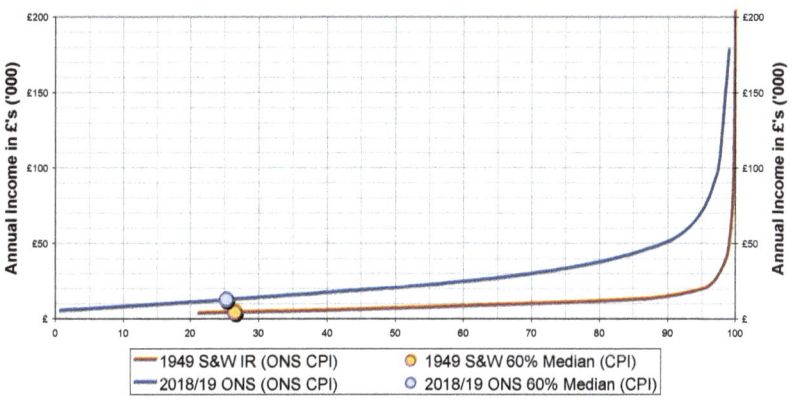

Relative *"poverty"*, disposable income

The second set of data that we now use to illustrate the results of this modern definition of relative *"poverty"* cover the near-60 year period from 1961 to 2018/19.

In addition we switch to the data processed by the ONS and IFS for equivalised household disposable income and expenditure, as calculated using the Households Below Average Income (HBAI) methodology and after housing costs (AHC) have been accounted for.

This combined set of analytical methodologies allows us to be as rigorously comprehensive in catering for all forms of taxation and re-distributive benefit allocation, but also to cater for the known effects of the increasing real costs of housing that disproportionately disadvantage the least well-off.

In the chart at the top of the opposite page we represent the analysis for the year 1961 in the dark green line in comparison with the year 2018/19 in the dark blue line. Again both are cast in terms of 2019 "real" values using the CPI measure of inflation.

As with personal incomes previously, we represent the 60% of median income in the light green and blue dots respectively.

This yields a measure of those household's disposable income after housing costs that fell below the theoretical relative *"poverty"* line in 1961 of approximately 13%, whilst those in 2018/19 constituted approximately 22.5% of all households.

In the chart in the middle of the next page we jump forward to a comparison of households in 1977 in the bright green line, the year generally thought to represent the time of least inequality, against the year 2018/19 in the dark blue line. Again factored to "real" 2019 values using the CPI.

The two dots representing the shares of households at which the 60% of median theoretical relative *"poverty"* line fall, are again the bright green and blue dots respectively. This yields approximately the same percentage for 1977 as 1961, at 13% of households.

In the chart at the bottom of the opposite page we jump forward to a comparison of 1997/98 in light green to 2018/19 in dark blue. Again factored to "real" 2019 values using the CPI.

The two dots representing the shares of households at which the 60% of median theoretical relative *"poverty"* line fall, are again the light green and blue dots respectively. These yield a different percentage for 1997/98 of approximately 24% of households falling below the theoretical relative *"poverty"* line in 1997/98, slightly higher than 2018/19 at 22.5%.

The best conclusion as to the meaning of this measure that clearly emerges is that it is certainly a valuable *indicator of inclusion/participation* in the benefits of the economy for the bottom half of income recipients, but is in fact a measure of lower median inequality, and does not represent a measure of **real** poverty.

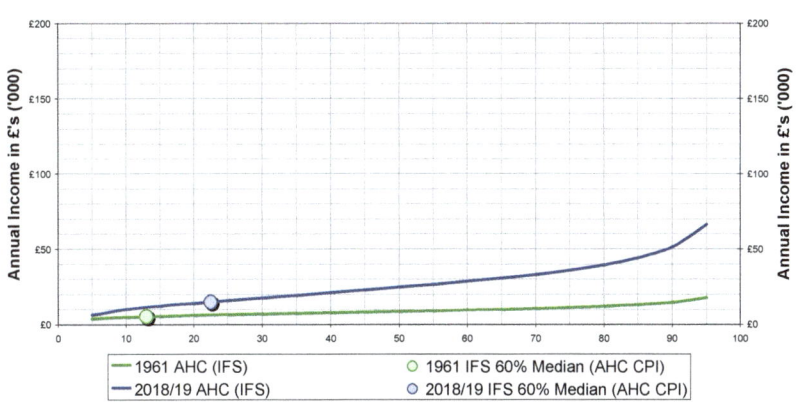

"Real" (IFS CPI) equivalised household disposable income distribution (AHC)

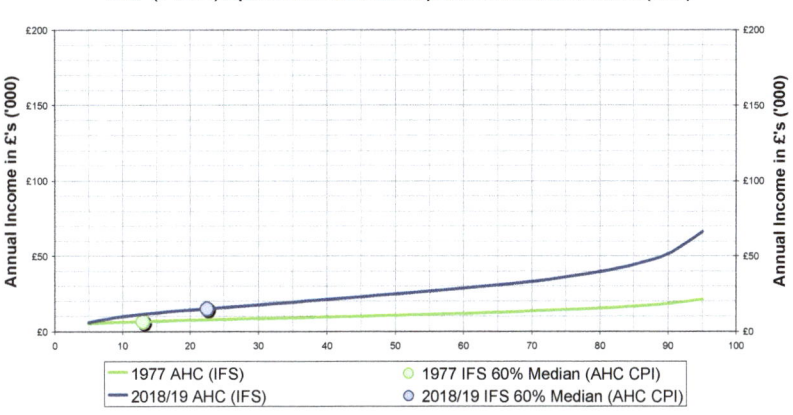

"Real" (IFS CPI) equivalised household disposable income distribution (AHC)

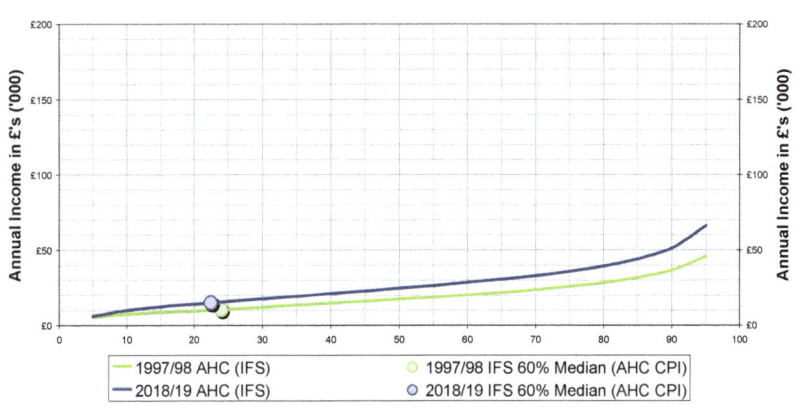

"Real" (IFS CPI) equivalised household disposable income distribution (AHC)

Real (CPI) *"poverty"* and housing

The reality is that until very recently the vast majority of people throughout history had a generally consistent idea of what poverty truly means and were desperate to avoid slipping into a state of such poverty.

Of course, poverty has been seen in various ways, but is fundamentally seen as something real and something that is injurious to life, health, longevity, well-being and happiness by most people.

Thankfully in the modern era, at least the last three to four decades in the UK, most people's only brush with such real poverty has been through reading or encountering the writings of authors such as Charles Dickens, Elizabeth Gaskell or Thomas Hardy.

Unfortunately some people do still live at or close to the levels at which real hardship and poverty threatens their lives, and have continued to do so despite the otherwise widespread improvements seen since the end of The Second World War.

It is this gulf between misuse of language in public discourse and the reality of some people's lives that has caused a clear view of this reality to be lost; thanks firstly to the mistaken hubris of the 1950s when even Seebohm Rowntree concluded that poverty had all but disappeared, then the shift of the meaning of the word poverty, promoted heavily since then, particularly by Professor Peter Townsend, that conflates the idea of *exclusion from participation in society's benefits* with poverty.

This did result in improved focus from governments and all sectors of society, but all have repeatedly failed to spot the real poverty persisting, even if retreating from major prevalence, throughout modern society.

The chart on the opposite page illustrates the progress for the vast majority of people for almost 60 years from 1961 to 2018/19. This again uses the same data from the analysis by the IFS and ONS for household expenditure after housing costs, as derived from the Family Expenditure Surveys etc. (FES/EFS/LCFS plus FRS/HBAI/ETB).

With each decade (or near decade) represented in each distribution curve from the first 5% to top 95%, the picture that emerges very clearly is that between 90% and 95% of people over this 60 years have experienced real and mostly substantial improvements in their standard of living, as measured by their total expenditure after accounting for housing costs.

This is demonstrated by the fact that each distribution curve rises higher and higher up the chart, particularly after 1977 (the bright green line), reaching a high point in 2018/19 (the dark blue line).

However very noticeable, and therefore highlighted by the red circle on the left of the chart, are the least well off 5% to 7% who have benefited to a much lesser degree, if at all, since 1961 or at least 1977.

Note the jump from 1961 (dark green) to 1968 (olive green), but little change then to 1977 (bright green), thereafter continuous improvement each decade for the 90% or more.

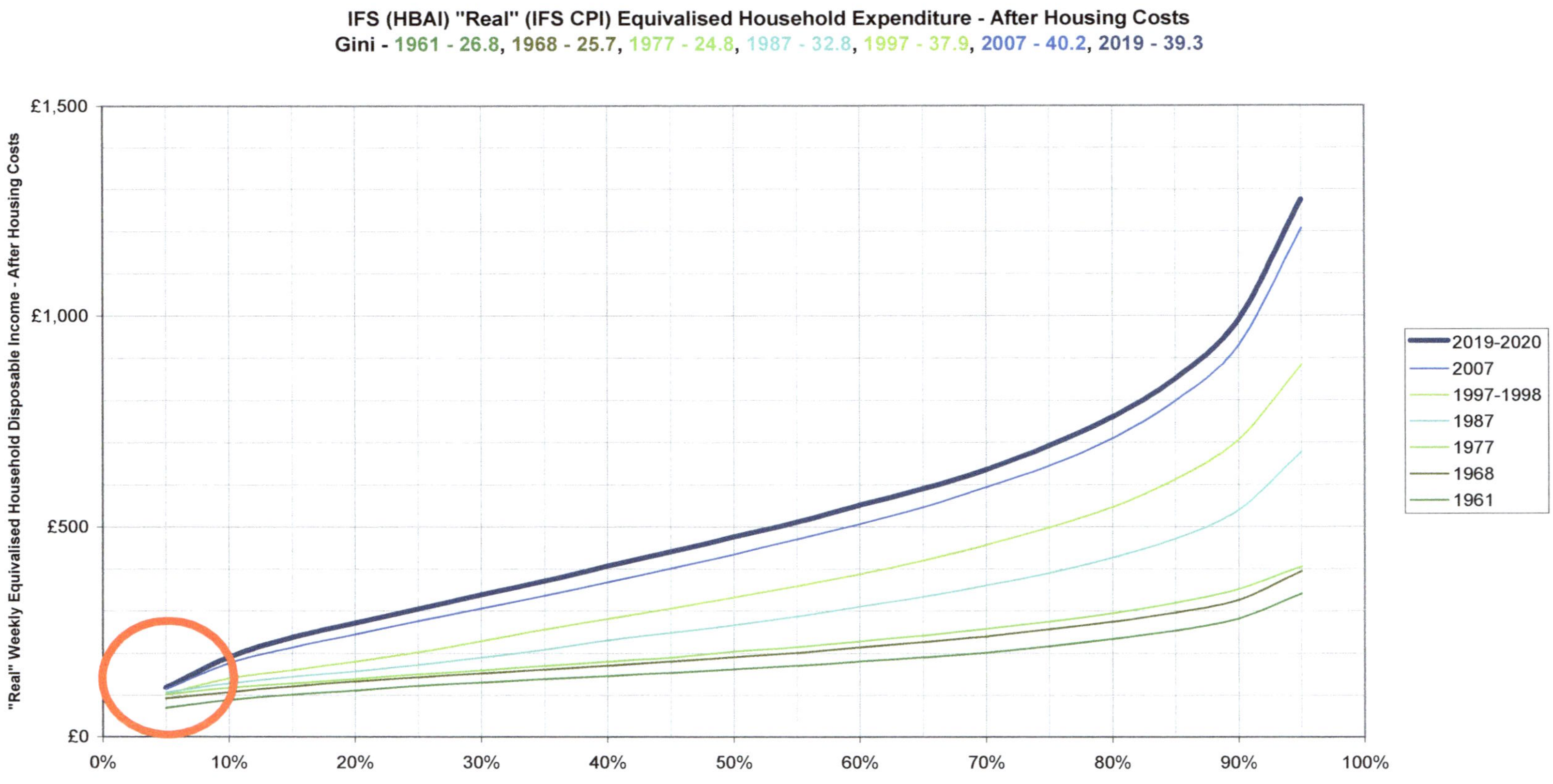

IFS (HBAI) "Real" (IFS CPI) Equivalalised Household Expenditure - After Housing Costs
Gini - 1961 - 26.8, 1968 - 25.7, 1977 - 24.8, 1987 - 32.8, 1997 - 37.9, 2007 - 40.2, 2019 - 39.3

Legend:
- 2019-2020
- 2007
- 1997-1998
- 1987
- 1977
- 1968
- 1961

Y-axis: "Real" Weekly Equivalised Household Disposable Income - After Housing Costs (£0, £500, £1,000, £1,500)

X-axis: 0% to 100%

Real (CPI) *"poverty"* and food

Notable in this alternative approach is the focus on the biological "essentials" of living as a general marker of real poverty.

This is centred around the concept of *"absolute" poverty*, and itself is expressed in a multitude of ways from the dollar-a-day standard for the poorest people of the world to the measures now discussed here.

Many debates have taken place about the meaning of poverty and the modern generally accepted view is that "relative" participation (or non-participation) is promoted as a better definition.

However this shows every sign of being politically motivated and the resultant term of *"relative poverty"* is then almost always abbreviated to just *"poverty"* which in turn confuses most people who know something of the reality of poverty in the past and the reality of poverty still prevalent in much of the world in the 21st century.

In turn this causes widespread misunderstanding and ignorance about the real progress that has been made throughout the world since the end of The Second World War; and accordingly causes governments, charities, aid bodies and in fact the tax-paying and voting public to lose focus on the real needs of people, and the malaise of compassion fatigue and disbelief as a result of this public narrative becoming stronger.

This is clearly the classic "Peter and the Wolf" syndrome and has proven to be ever more harmful in the developed and developing world.

A second approach to discover if the pattern previously discussed in relation to housing costs holds from an alternative perspective is to look this time at total expenditure in relation to food expenditure.

Using the same data as before (FES, EFS and LCFS, but not using the HBAI methodology), this time calculated not in relation to housing costs, but indexed to food expenditure, and now incorporating the 1953/54 detailed study at the end of the period of rationing, reveals a very similar pattern again, but with a notable difference.

Represented in the orange line is the average distribution of food expenditure from the least well off households on the left to most well off on the right, each indexed to the median. This tends to show that food expenditure does increase over the distribution considerably, but significantly less so than total expenditure.

The improvements maintain a similar pattern of growth between 1953/54 (the teal line) and 1961 (the dark green line), then again jumping by 1968 (olive green) over the whole range, but then only lifting very slightly to 1977 (bright green).

Interestingly the greatest jump is to the levels of 1987 (the aqua line) with the growth clustering quite closely thereafter to 2018/19 (the dark blue line), again showing the same pattern for the least well off 5% to 7% of households. In addition, this tends to also re-affirm that housing supersedes food as the most costly element of household expenditure in the substantial growth decades from after The Second World War.

Equivalalised Total Expenditure and Food plus Housing, indexed to median food expenditure for 65 years

Real "*poverty*" in the 18ᵗʰ century

By one means or another it remains very valuable to illustrate change of the possible prevalence of poverty over time as best as we are able.

Even though the term "*absolute*" is used in relation to measurement of the expenditure on essentials, or biological "*needs*", in fact even definitions of such "*needs*" change over time as more is learnt particularly about nutrition and consequential health effects for example of poor housing, lack of heating and so on.

When we search back into the first century of the period covered herewith, any available data measures of such living conditions and expenditure by households are very sparse and very limited. From a modern perspective this is seemingly very strange, but of course also coincides with the later centuries of an era in which for many poverty, destitution and hardship was overwhelmingly thought to be an evil that was largely the "fault" of those on whom it was visited. This being expressed in religious tones, as a punishment from God, and not viewed with quite the same sense of compassion and zeal as in later centuries.

The best markers we have available from any contemporary analysis, extends to four works. The first two from social and economic campaigners, Jacob Vanderlint in 1734 in his book "*Money Answers All Things*" and the previously discussed Joseph Massie in his composite work of 1758 that was primarily titled "*A Plan For The Establishment of Charity Houses*", but importantly for our purposes also included "*A New System Of Policy For Relieving, Employing and Ordering The Poor*".

Both authors offered estimates of probable expenditure patterns of various household types, Jacob Vanderlint two types, and Joseph Massie one type. These are far from definitive, but their resultant primary expenditures, as estimated by the authors, are presented in the table on the opposite page, in the columns for the 1730s and 1750s. They tend to show that the "average" families were estimated to be spending 50% and 54% respectively of their incomes on food (the orange boxes), and 17% and 10% respectively on their housing (the lavender boxes).

The first real measured analysis of those we can clearly distinguish as living mostly in poverty is derived from the extensive work of two campaigners at the end of the 18ᵗʰ century just before and just at the outbreak of the French Revolutionary Wars.

These are the works of The Reverend David Davies in "*The Case of Labourers in Husbandry, Stated and Considered*" (published in 1795) and Sir Frederick Eden published in three volumes in "*The State of the Poor, or An History of the Labouring Classes in England*" (published in 1797).

A simple summary of their findings is represented in the two columns for the 1780s and 1790s respectively as poor families were found to be spending 72% of their total expenditure on food (the bright pink boxes) and 10% and 9% respectively on housing (in the lavender boxes), reiterating how expensive food was for those in poverty in the past.

Simple "example" analysis of Household Expenditure patterns by Social Commentators in the 18th Century

	1700	1710	1720	1730	1740	1750	1760	1770	1780	1790
Analysis by:				Clark (2001 & 2005), JRC (2021)		JRC (2021)			Horrell (1996), Griffin (2018), JRC (2021)	Horrell (1996), Griffin (2018), JRC (2021)
Contemporary source:				Vanderlint (1734)		Massie (1758)			Davies (1794)	Eden (1796)
"Middling" — Food				18%						
"Middling" — Household				20%						
"Average" — Food				50%		54%				
"Average" — Household				17%		10%				
Labourers, "The Poor", 1st Quartile — Food									72%	72%
Labourers, "The Poor", 1st Quartile — Household									10%	9%
Decade:	1700	1710	1720	1730	1740	1750	1760	1770	1780	1790

Real *"poverty"* in the 19th century

Data for the 19th century becomes more extensive, but still does not match modern standards required of survey analysis.

Sarah Horrell in *"Home Demand and British Industrialisation"* (published in 1996) has offered a very useful analysis of much of the early data, including that available to the middle of the 19th century, also including the Davies and Eden data discussed previously.

Further, the data from Davies and Eden is later analysed by Ian Gazeley and Nicola Verdon in *"The first poverty line Davies' and Eden's investigation of rural poverty in the late 18th-century England"* (published in 2014). This work investigates if the Davies and Eden analysis helps to identify the prevalence of poverty in any way comparable to at least the later Victorian analyses; from the analysis by school boards to identify which children should be eligible for the remittance of school fees after the 1870 Education Act, plus that of Charles Booth for London poor in 1886 (published 1889-1891) and Seebohm Rowntree for York poor in 1899 (published in 1901).

These data and analyses have been usefully extended in further depth by Emma Griffin in her paper *"Diets, Hunger and Living Standards During the British Industrial Revolution"* (published in 2018).

Thus a composite from these primary sources is used in the table on the opposite page and tends to suggest that there may have been some minimal improvement over the course of the 19th century, especially in relation to similar groups of families that had been previously analysed by Davies and Eden in the later years of the 18th century.

Thus the estimates offered by David Chadwick in his article for the Quarterly Journal of the Statistical Society *"On the Rate of Wages in Manchester and Salford, and the Manufacturing Districts of Lancashire, 1839-59"* (published in 1860) in his capacity as Treasurer of the Borough of Salford are of particular value here.

Although not well identified in any real distribution of incomes and expenditures, an apparent pattern emerges from Chadwick's analysis indicating that as a share of total expenditure, food expenditure might possibly have fallen to less than 70%, whilst housing has risen to 17% or more. This data must be viewed with caution though as there is an indication that Chadwick's examples are perhaps not as poor in real or relative terms as the samples from their various correspondents used 70 years previously by Davies and Eden.

Again very cautiously, the other data for those in groupings or "classes" that might loosely be termed "Average" or "Middling" derived from Ellic Howe for 1810, the anonymous author of *"A New System of Practical Domestic Economy"* for the 1820s, and that from James Knowles, editor of *"The Nineteenth Century: A Monthly Review"* for 1888, all suggest similarity with the equivalent estimates for the 18th century. Thus the measures all suggest some comparability for measures of real poverty.

Simple "example" analysis of Household Expenditure patterns by Social Commentators in the 19th Century

Analysis by:			1800	1810	1820	1830	1840	1850	1860	1870	1880	1890
		Analysis refs:		Horrell (1996), Griffin (2018)	Inglis (1971), Burnett (1989), JRC (2021)		Hayward (1926), Burnett (1969)					
Contemporary source:				Howe etc.	Anon. (1825)		Chadwick (1860)				Knowles ed. (1888)	
"Middling"	Food				33%		33%				22%	
	Household				14%		21%				21%	
"Average"	Food			56%	52%						50%	
	Household			19%	15%						23%	
Labourers, "The Poor", 1st Quartile	Food					66%	63%	62%				
	Household					17%	18%	18%				
Decade:			1800	1810	1820	1830	1840	1850	1860	1870	1880	1890

Real *"poverty"* before World War 2

The analysis from Charles Booth does not quite break down expenditure in this manner and has not therefore been included, but that for Seebohm Rowntree is provided in the table on the next page for the first years of the twentieth century, even though the study mostly took place in 1899.

The analysis of Rowntree's study is then supplemented by the 1904 Board of Trade survey of urban working class communities and particularly their expenditure on food, followed by the study by Arthur Lyon Bowley and Alexander Robert Burnett Hurst in 1912 of working class families in five major English towns.

There has been much debate about so-called poverty lines, extensively summarised for the 20th century analyses in Ian Gazeley's 2003 book *"Poverty in Britain, 1900-1965"*; here we look instead again at the shares of total expenditure on food and housing, as previously.

For the decade before The Great War a further suggestion of the shift from food to housing appears in the data for those who are least well-off, represented in the bottom row. This shows itself in the gradual reduction of the shares spent on food over the 120 years from 72% to 61% or 59%. However the counter effect shows itself from the apparent increase of housing expenditure as a share of total expenditure from 10% to 27%.

Note adding the two together yields an overall apparent fall in living standards for the least well-off from the 1780s to the first decade of the 20th century in which food and housing apparently consumed 82% of total expenditure rising to 88% of total expenditure.

However this must be considered with extreme caution as we cannot be at all sure that the relative position of the households studied or data collected are truly directly comparable over time.

Nevertheless this provides a useful, if flawed, pointer to possible changes over time. It also highlights a very useful way of mathematically identifying a household that is likely to be struggling and either actually living in hardship or poverty in some measurable "real" sense or very likely to be at extreme risk of being plunged into real hardship or poverty, and even destitution (see **Foreword** for definitions used).

A new change in fortunes finally appears to be seen in data from a seminal Board of Trade study of labouring families, both urban and rural, undertaken in the years 1937 and 1938. Note this also coincides with a very detailed analysis of personal incomes and tax liabilities by the Inland Revenue in 1938, the results of which correlate well with the patterns that are found in the labourers household expenditure study.

Clearly emerging from the analysis of the extant data for this time is the suggestion that, despite the continued presence of the effects of the depression of the 1930s, working-class household share of expenditure on bare essentials of food (47%) and housing (24%) declined as a share of total expenditure and much more is expended on leisure pastimes.

Simple "example" analysis of Household Expenditure patterns by Social Commentators in the 20th Century, + surveys

		1900	1905	1910	1915	1920	1925	1930	1935	1940	1945
Analysis by:		Bowley (1900), Burnett (1969), Feinstein (1991)	Gazeley & Newell (2003)	Bowley (1912)					Gazeley & Newell (2003), Scott & Walker (2003)		
Contemporary source:		Rowntree (1901)	1904 Board of Trade Survey						1937/38 Ministry of Labour Survey		
"Middling"	Food	22%									
	Household	21%									
"Average"	Food	48%							40%		
	Household	13%							20%		
Labourers, "The Poor", 1st Quartile	Food	59%	61%	61%					47%		
	Household	27%		27%					24%		
Half Decade:		1900	1905	1910	1915	1920	1925	1930	1935	1940	1945

Real *"poverty"* after World War 2

In 1953/54, and thereafter annually from 1961, the government, thanks to various departments, have undertaken detailed surveys of household expenditure and composition that allow us to finally draw a substantially more reliable picture of expenditure patterns for effectively all households over income ranges. There is known to be some under-representation of the very poorest and very richest and the ONS (and preceding responsible bodies) have attempted to compensate as best as possible for this under-representation. It is for this very reason that the ONS/IFS analysis using the aforementioned HBAI methodology generally only report between the fifth percentile and ninety fifth percentile.

Using the data from 1953/54 to 2018/19 we are able to report mean, median and even 1st decile shares of expenditure on food and housing with confidence and accordingly see the patterns of change for these three statistical groups of households in a like table.

As was discussed in the third chapter **Earnings and Income**, the process known as equivalisation is applied in order to achieve the closest representation of like-for-like according to the age composition of each household, in order to best assess their "real" material well-being from household income and thereby household expenditure patterns.

The table on the next page, again using colourisation of blocks consistent with the three previous tables, but also with the percentages found for each group in each year, shows the continuing trend of real improvement since the near end of rationing after The Second World War.

For the mean household in 1953/54 total expenditure on food and housing emerges as 49% of total expenditure whilst by 2018/19 this has fallen to 40% of total expenditure.

For the median household these shares fell from 52% in 1953/54 to 48% in 2018/19.

The progress becomes more certain however in so far as the estimated position of the households surveyed in the previous 170 years, fell closer to the lower quartile (20% to 25%) of households than the first decile we are reporting here for the post Second World War survey analysis.

Thus using the first quartile to attempt to draw an alternative consistent parallel since The Second World War with historical data yields an estimated share of total expenditure for food and housing for 1953/54 of 59% falling to 53% by 2018/19 (see the subsequent table).

If we then compare these shares with the total figures for the previous 170 years, back to the earliest analysis for the 1780s, we see that this apparently ranged between 82% and 87% from various surveys, down to 71% for 1937/38 for something similar to the first quartile.

Most tellingly though are the shares for the first decile, or 10%, of households that are the least well off. Their total share spent on food and housing fell from 68% in 1953/54 to 58% in 2018/19. Reemphasising that measurably real progress has been made for almost all.

Analysis of food and housing (inc. fuel & power) from government surveys since the Second World War for 65 years

		Gazeley & Newell (2003)	JRC from OPCS/ONS UKDA posted data (2021)				IFS Derived Variables - RPI Categories, (UKDA study 8583, September 2020)			JRC RPI Categories from ONS UKDA posted data (2021)	
Analysis by:											
Contemporary source:		1953/54 Ministry of Labour Survey	1961 OPCS FES	1968 OPCS FES	1976 OPCS FES	1977 OPCS FES	1987 OPCS FES	1997/98 ONS FES	2007 ONS EFS	2017/18 ONS LCFS	2018/19 ONS LCFS
Mean	Food	33%	30%	26%	25%	24%	19%	17%	15%	16%	15%
	Household	14%	17%	20%	22%	22%	24%	23%	27%	25%	25%
Median	Food	38%	35%	31%	30%	28%	23%	20%	20%	19%	18%
	Household	14%	19%	21%	20%	25%	27%	25%	27%	29%	30%
1st Decile	Food	46%	43%	38%	39%	37%	35%	30%	28%	27%	25%
	Household	22%	28%	31%	30%	33%	26%	26%	30%	32%	33%
Year:		1953/54	1961	1968	1976	1977	1987	1997/98	2007	2017/18	2018/19

Real *"poverty"* in detail

Examining the shares of household expenditure on food and housing in more detail for the whole available expenditure distribution from all the best conducted surveys from 1937/38 to 2018/19 reveals the pattern of improvement very well (noting that "housing" here includes such items as rent and mortgage as well as fuel and lighting).

To visually show the pattern, threshold based colourisation is used to reveal the changes using the simplest green through to red and even bright pink, akin to the colours of traffic lights, but otherwise eye catching.

The thresholds were chosen centred around the values identified in the data, rather than starting from initial arbitrary numbers. However the levels are intentionally also set to correspond to the best data available for the centuries before The Great War as well.

One particular adjustment was needed for the data from the survey for 1937/38 since that was targeted only at labourers' households as mentioned previously. For this period data patterns were assessed against the conveniently available breakdown of the 1938 personal income analysis which is reported by Ainsworth and Scott and Walker, plus the analysis of types of households by job description from the 1931 census data. As a result the 1937/38 labourers' household expenditure survey is estimated to be representative of perhaps 80% of households in the UK at the time and thus the distribution is calculated from 0% to 80% only.

Thus in the table on the opposite page we have data from 1937/38 to 2018/19, all colourised to consistent thresholds to offer a suggested gradual trend, effectively near decadal, for the households in the UK.

The dark green coloured blocks represent those households in each survey's distribution who are spending less than 48% of their total expenditure on food, rent/mortgage and fuel and lighting. The olive green represents those spending between 48% and less than 60% on food and housing. This threshold of spending 60% or more of total expenditure on food and housing is used as the key threshold to highlight change over the decades and the pattern that emerges is very clear in the reducing prevalence of firstly these amber blocks.

Even more significant is the disappearance of the orange blocks (68% or greater but less than 73%) and red blocks (73% or greater but less than 78%) by the mid-1980s.

This suggests possible continuity with the best available data for the previous 170 years through the bright pink blocks, representing the first 2% to 5% of households who spend in excess of 78% of their total expenditure on just food and housing. These disappear before 1961.

Reflecting on those identified in the studies from the 1780s to 1912 from which we might estimate that up to 20% (or even 25%) of households spent such shares just on food and housing, our confidence in the measurable reality of progress becomes high as we see these bright pink and red, and even orange blocks disappear before the mid-1980s.

Profiles of share of Total Household Expenditure for Food, Housing plus Fuel & Power for 80 years

Percentile	1937-1938	1953-1954	1961	1968	1976	1977	1987	1997-1998	2007	2017-2018	2018-2019
98%		33%	19%	27%	30%	28%	24%	23%	28%	20%	23%
95%		31%	32%	34%	34%	35%	34%	30%	33%	29%	27%
90%		35%	38%	36%	37%	37%	36%	32%	36%	33%	31%
85%		39%	42%	40%	40%	38%	38%	35%	37%	36%	35%
80%	39%	41%	44%	42%	42%	41%	38%	37%	39%	36%	38%
75%	52%	44%	45%	44%	43%	42%	42%	39%	41%	40%	40%
70%	56%	45%	46%	44%	44%	45%	43%	39%	43%	41%	42%
65%	58%	47%	49%	47%	45%	46%	43%	40%	43%	43%	42%
60%	62%	48%	49%	48%	48%	47%	44%	41%	44%	43%	45%
55%	61%	49%	53%	50%	48%	48%	47%	42%	45%	45%	45%
50%	65%	50%	52%	50%	51%	51%	48%	44%	47%	46%	48%
45%	66%	52%	54%	52%	50%	52%	50%	45%	46%	48%	49%
40%	67%	53%	56%	55%	53%	53%	52%	47%	48%	50%	52%
35%	67%	54%	56%	56%	55%	55%	52%	48%	49%	50%	52%
30%	71%	55%	58%	58%	56%	57%	54%	48%	50%	52%	54%
25%	71%	57%	61%	59%	58%	59%	55%	50%	52%	54%	53%
20%	70%	59%	63%	61%	60%	60%	56%	51%	53%	55%	55%
15%	74%	61%	65%	63%	63%	64%	58%	54%	54%	58%	56%
10%	75%	64%	68%	65%	64%	67%	60%	55%	56%	59%	58%
5%	80%	68%	71%	69%	69%	70%	63%	59%	58%	61%	62%
2%	81%	74%	77%	73%	72%	72%	64%	65%	61%	65%	62%

Legend

- Greater than 78%
- Greater than 73%
- Greater than 68%
- Greater than 60%
- Greater than 48%
- Less than 48%

By extending this analysis of the essential categories of spending that are considered to be the means of supporting human biological "*needs*", we incorporate the expenditure on clothing in the overall pattern from 1937/38 to 2018/19.

By adding clothing the thresholds must all be adjusted upwards accordingly, in this case just 2% of total expenditure being added to each threshold.

Again adjusting the distribution represented for the 1937/38 survey as previously described, the pattern that emerges is, if anything, even more emphatically obvious in the steady decline of the percentage of households finding themselves spending more than 62% of their total expenditure on food, housing (rent/mortgage), fuel and lighting and clothing.

Those falling into the bright pink, red and orange groupings are generally similar as before, when not including clothing, but this time data does suggest a greater share of households, in each decade before the 1980s, that fall into the amber groupings, suggesting greater risk of real hardship or poverty using such an independent and consistent indicator.

Another indicator that emerges in the data, as processed by decade at least, is that the prevalence of those exceeding both food and housing threshold of greater than 60% of total expenditure and also the food, housing and clothing threshold of greater than 62% of total expenditure, both fall to their lowest share of households in the mid to late-1990s (actually found to be the year 1999/2000), rising thereafter to the mid-2000s and remaining there to our last year of analysis of 2018/19.

It is notable as well that this trend of reduced shares is present throughout the whole distribution range from bottom to top when the column for 1997/98 data is compared at each distribution with its adjacent mid-decades of 1987 and 2007.

It is quite likely that this is the case due to the enormous house price inflation that started from about 1997, as discussed in the previous two chapters. The effect of this on real expenditure patterns seems to show accordingly in these data as well as mean cost of living and of course house price and mortgage repayment indicators, as well as rental costs.

This all re-emphasises the same patterns visible in average earnings, average incomes, average household disposable incomes and of course average house price trends, resulting from the failure to constrain these house price trends and prevent the economic crash that occurred in 2008.

For explanation and final observational note, two consecutive years are presented in both 1976-1977 followed by 2017/18-2018/19. These are included since the data for the first pair of consecutive years, during the height of the extreme inflation and IMF crisis, accordingly confirms that the pattern during that crisis was very consistent. The second pair is due to the fact that the data for 2018/19 was calculated by the author from raw data and is thence compared to the data analysis calculated by the IFS up to 2017/18, again showing reasonable consistency.

Profiles of share of Total Household Expenditure for Food, Housing, Fuel & Power, plus Clothing for 80 years

Percentile	1937-1938	1953-1954	1961	1968	1976	1977	1987	1997-1998	2007	2017-2018	2018-2019
98%		43%	26%	37%	40%	36%	29%	30%	31%	23%	26%
95%		48%	46%	44%	42%	45%	41%	37%	37%	33%	30%
90%		53%	53%	47%	46%	47%	44%	39%	40%	37%	35%
85%		54%	55%	51%	49%	47%	46%	42%	42%	40%	39%
80%	62%	56%	55%	52%	51%	50%	46%	44%	45%	41%	42%
75%	67%	57%	58%	54%	52%	51%	50%	45%	45%	45%	44%
70%	67%	59%	57%	53%	53%	54%	51%	46%	47%	45%	46%
65%	70%	60%	58%	55%	54%	54%	49%	46%	47%	47%	47%
60%	71%	61%	59%	57%	56%	55%	52%	47%	48%	48%	49%
55%	69%	62%	61%	58%	55%	58%	54%	48%	50%	50%	49%
50%	73%	63%	60%	59%	58%	58%	54%	50%	51%	50%	50%
45%	72%	63%	63%	60%	60%	60%	56%	51%	53%	52%	53%
40%	74%	65%	62%	63%	61%	62%	58%	52%	54%	54%	55%
35%	73%	65%	65%	64%	62%	63%	57%	53%	55%	53%	55%
30%	75%	67%	66%	65%	63%	64%	60%	55%	57%	56%	57%
25%	77%	68%	68%	67%	66%	66%	61%	55%	57%	57%	57%
20%	75%	69%	70%	68%	68%	68%	63%	58%	58%	59%	58%
15%	77%	71%	72%	69%	68%	71%	64%	59%	60%	61%	59%
10%	79%	74%	75%	72%	72%	73%	65%	59%	61%	62%	61%
5%	84%	79%	79%	76%	74%	75%	65%	61%	64%	63%	64%
2%	85%	82%	77%	78%	78%	79%	67%	66%	65%	67%	64%

Legend

Decade	1937-1938	1953-1954	1961	1968	1976	1977	1987	1997-1998	2007	2017-2018	2018-2019
Legend	Greater than 80%	Greater than 75%	Greater than 70%	Greater than 62%	Greater than 50%	Less than 50%					

Consumer durables and *"poverty"*

Continuing with the results of the surveys from the period after the end of The Second World War, the ONS and previously the Department for Employment and Productivity's *"British Labour Statistics"*, both *"Historical Abstract 1886-1968"* and subsequent year books to 1976, have published analysis of the prevalence of access to various consumer durables as shares of households from 1959 to 2018/19.

Selecting some of the most valuable and interestingly technical durables over those years, and showing the ever growing shares having possession of, or access to, these durables strongly suggests exactly the same rapid retreat of the prevalence of real poverty since the 1950s (and accordingly all previous centuries).

In the chart at the top of the opposite page the shares of households with access to at least one motor car or small van (the bright blue line) has increased from just 24% in 1959 to 79% in 2018/19. It is useful to compare this with the rapid growth of the average number of cars per household from the fifth chapter **Cost of Living**.

A factor that is not revealed in the latter calculation is that there has been a notable increase in the number of multi-car households over that period as well. The 21% of households without access to a car include many such living particularly in London, though must inevitably include a share of people who are not able to drive for health reasons, but must also include a portion unable to afford access to a car at all.

Two of the greatest boons to well-being and health are shown in the form of possession of a washing machine (in the dark green line) and availability of central heating in the home (in the light green line).

Access to a washing machine has increased from 34% of households in 1959 to 98% in 2018/19, whilst the prevalence of central heating has increased enormously from just 7% of households in 1964 to 97% of households in 2018/19. Both of these (along with the prevalence of the fridge and later freezer) have been amongst the greatest improvements in domestic well-being by means of ensuring labour saving and effective cleanliness of clothing, warmth and reduced dampness of housing and of course preservation of food to improve access to affordable diets. These are amongst the greatest contributions to the reduction in death rates and consequent improvements in life expectancy since the end of The Second World War, along with access to ever improving health interventions.

Technological developments are represented in the middle and bottom charts in the growth in access to household telephones (pink line) from just 22% in 1964, peaking at 95% in 1998/99, then falling to just 83% in 2018/19. It is notable that this reduction in landline based telephones correlates with the growth of access to mobile (microwave cellular) telephony (lavender line), rising from just 16% in 1996/97 to 96% in 2018/19. Other related technologies of note are the rise of ownership of home computers (violet line) and internet connection (plum line).

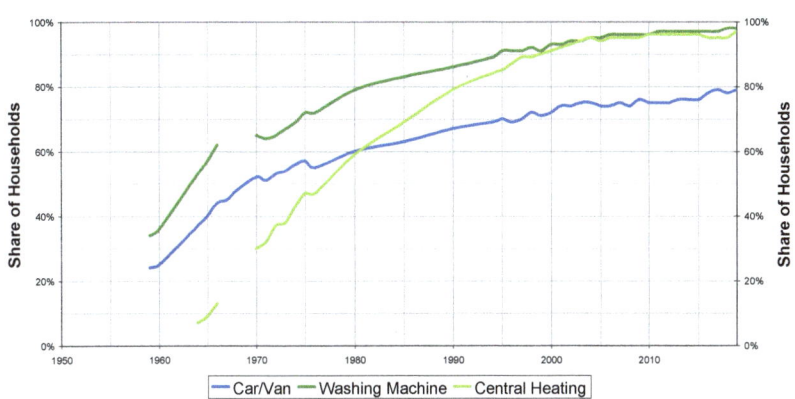

Share of households with access to/possession of consumer durables

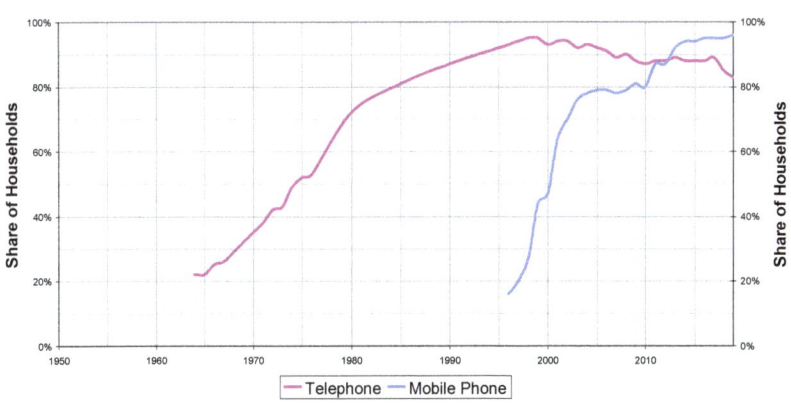

Share of households with access to/possession of consumer durables

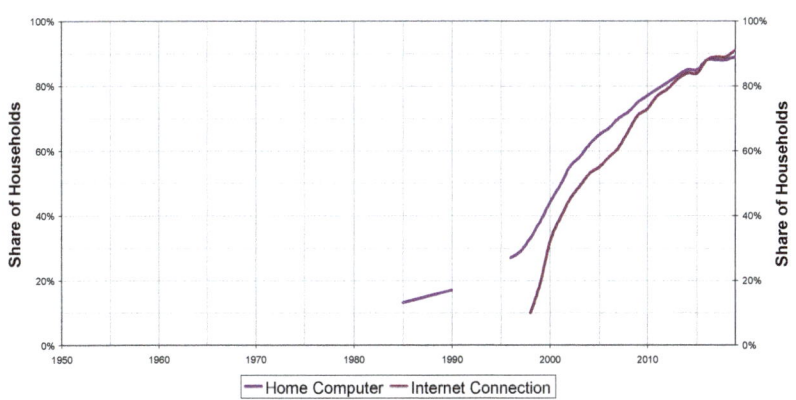

Share of households with access to/possession of consumer durables

157

Access to home computers is recorded as rising from just 13% in 1985 reaching 89% in 2018/19, but the rapid spread of home internet (mostly using broadband technologies and later fibre) has grown from just 10% in 1998 to 91% in 2018/19.

It is worth reflecting that this meteoric growth of such technology has then led to greater reliance on such technology, including for schooling for children which has then placed a requirement on all households with children to provide access for those children.

Overall from these growths in availability and access to these life enhancing durables and technology we also see a shift in perception of "*need*" and "*entitlement*", becoming, at least informally, seen by more and more people as indispensable for a fulfilled life and metamorphosing into a form of "*human right*", thus stressing their absence as in some way an indicator of a life lived in "*poverty*".

Even a cursory knowledge of life in the past in the UK or life for billions of people in the world beyond the UK does rather force a check on such beliefs when the data about the reality of peoples lives and even more hauntingly the qualitative descriptions available (and historical photographs) are studied.

The repeated misuse of the term "*poverty*" (as lazily abbreviated from the inappropriate term "*relative poverty*") about the conditions of life for many in the UK at the end of the second decade of the 21st century has distorted understanding about this very important and emotive subject.

Even the expenditure facts about those living within the first quartile of household income distribution, at least to the first decile, is a telling indicator of both profound ignorance of all the evidence, quantitative and qualitative, of significant improvement, being amply re-emphasized by the widespread access to household durables and modern technologies.

This misuse of language and ignoring of evidence, that we see over and over again in the modern era, has in fact moved focus away from identifying and truly finding ways to help the thankfully reducing share of households in real need.

Interestingly the studies from the foremost charity concerned with poverty, The Rowntree Foundation, particularly the recent reports by Fitzpatrick et al. (2016) and (2018) entitled "*Destitution in the UK*" powerfully describe their findings from extensive studies of those they found who at some point in 2015 and 2017 respectively "*could not afford to buy the bare essentials that we all need to eat, stay warm and dry, and keep clean*". They estimated this afflicts over 1.5 million people (including more than 365 thousand children).

It is interesting to reflect that this represents some 2.2 percent of the UK population, which itself is revealed strongly in all the data analysis discussed in this chapter, and thereby tends to support the possibility of using this method to help identify the prevalence of people living in such dire straits and its persistence, that needs forthright honesty to tackle it; but also supports the notion of the retreat of **real** poverty none-the-less.

Air Quality

"this most excellent canopy, the air, look you,
this brave o'erhanging firmament, this
majestical roof fretted with golden fire, why,
it appears no other thing to me but a foul and
pestilent congregation of vapours."

William Shakespeare:
Hamlet (act 2, scene 2),
1601

The air that we breathe

Scientific investigation, over the very centuries we are reporting in this work, have discovered the molecular components of the air that we, and all other living things, breathe or imbibe. Also in the process science has slowly identified the many and various polluting poisons, in both nature and as a result of human activity, that seriously undermine human health (and other life forms into the bargain).

Here we focus just upon the best known such polluting poisons that are emitted by human activity into the air only (thus not land or water). Sadly actual measures of these pollutants are only available from 1970.

As explained in the foreword this does not include Carbon Dioxide (CO_2) as it is not injurious to the health of air breathing life forms in any real sense and therefore scientifically and according to dictionary definitions of the word "*pollution*" is not such a compound of danger or risk to life and health in the way that pollutants are known to be.

Whilst we do not have any useful historical measures of real pollutants before 1970, we do know at least from qualitative accounts, that for several hundred years large cities, such as London, suffered extremely bad pollution of all forms, including terrible air quality, with many other cities and conurbations deteriorating from the age of the Industrial Revolution onwards.

All culminated in the terrible decades of smog and severe respiratory health effects of the 1950s and 1960s, resulting in large numbers of deaths and driving the Clean Air Acts of 1956, 1968, 1993 and 2010.

In particular the Clean Air Act of 1968 was followed by the establishment of ever more detailed and comprehensive monitoring of air quality and the multitude of pollutants that might befoul it.

Pollutants monitored and reported

The Department for Environment, Food and Rural Affairs (DEFRA), the Department for Business, Energy and Industrial Strategy (BEIS) and Imperial College London, monitor, analyse, collate and report all of the known emissions and pollutant concentrations for the UK, major cities and regions, and multiple locations throughout London (the latter registering more than 270 such locations, 133 of which are active in 2022).

All reports and data are publicly available and data fully downloadable from government web-sites for DEFRA, the BEIS National Atmospheric Emissions Inventory (NAEI) web-site and the LondonAir Imperial College web-site.

As such, annual UK emissions of the principal air-quality impacting pollutants and particulates are represented in the charts on the next page.

The chart at the top of the next page reports measured pollutants that in general are not reported in as much depth, particularly by DEFRA, as they are not seen as the major contributors to health risks in 2019. They all exhibit significant reductions since measurement began in 1970 and notably none are greatly influenced by road transport by 2019.

The chart in the middle of the next page, represents emissions of Sulphur Dioxide (dark green), Non-Methane Volatile Organic Compounds (NMVOC) (violet) and Ammonia (dark red). Sulphur Dioxide shows a significant 97% reduction since 1970, thanks to the phasing out of most uses of coal, particularly coal power stations, various industrial uses and even home coal burning. NMVOCs show a 70% reduction from 1990, mostly from coal mining, unspent hydrocarbons, formerly road transport and other fuel evaporation, amongst other sources. Ammonia emissions, almost exclusively from farming and food production, show only very small reductions since earliest available data from 1980. Again none of these pollutants are greatly influenced by road transport by 2019.

Other Air Pollutant Emissions Trend

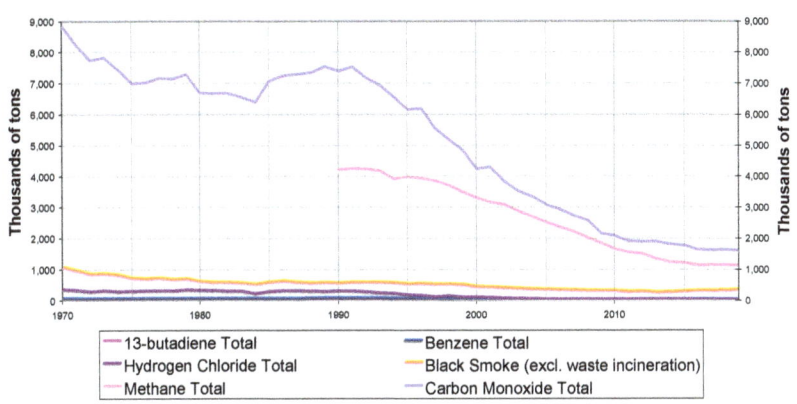

- 13-butadiene Total
- Hydrogen Chloride Total
- Methane Total
- Benzene Total
- Black Smoke (excl. waste incineration)
- Carbon Monoxide Total

UK trend in weight of atmospheric pollutants (Defra)

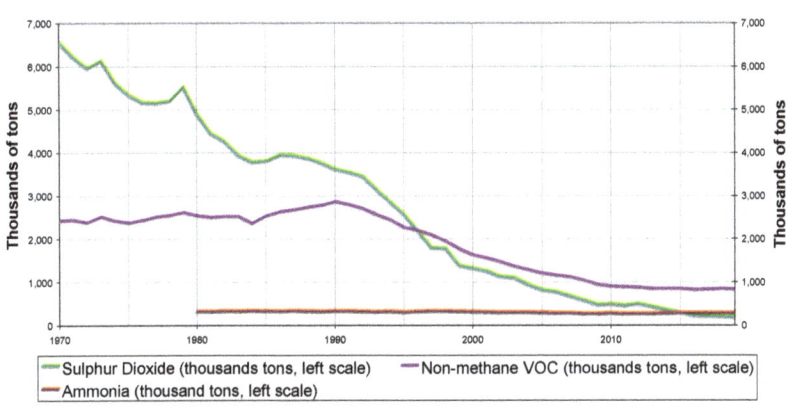

- Sulphur Dioxide (thousands tons, left scale)
- Non-methane VOC (thousands tons, left scale)
- Ammonia (thousand tons, left scale)

UK trend in weight of atmospheric pollutants (Defra/BEIS(NAEI))
(Road use (NOx as NO2 - 33%, 31% Diesel), (PM10 - 12%, 2.5% Fuel) and (PM2.5 - 12%, 4.0% Fuel))

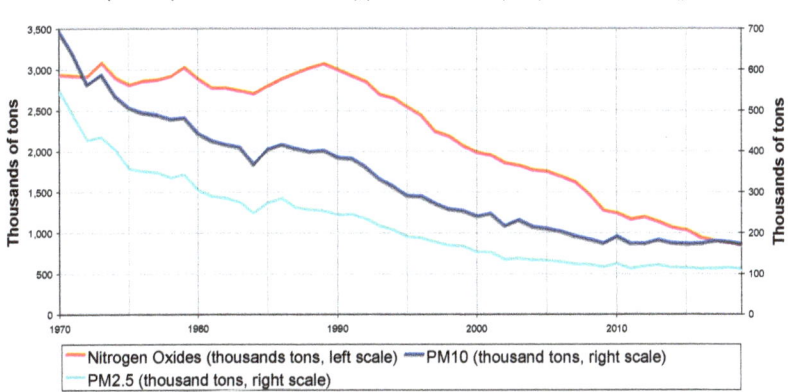

- Nitrogen Oxides (thousands tons, left scale)
- PM10 (thousand tons, right scale)
- PM2.5 (thousand tons, right scale)

161

The chart at the bottom of the previous page represents emissions of Nitrogen Oxides (NO_x) expressed as Nitrogen Dioxide (NO_2) in the red line, plus sub-10 micron particulates in the dark blue line, of which the even smaller sub-2.5 micron particulates are represented in the cyan line.

These latter are the air quality pollutants known to be both significantly injurious to health, and since they are quite heavily influenced by road transport, receive the greatest focus in the public discourse on air quality and levels of modern atmospheric pollution.

All three exhibit very large reductions over the measurement period available. Nitrogen Oxides emissions having fallen by 73% since its peak in 1989, sub-10 micron particulate emissions having fallen by 75% since 1970 and sub-2.5 micron emissions having fallen by 80% since 1970. The relationship between the sub-10 micron and sub-2.5 micron particulates shows that the fall of the sub-10 micron particulates is driven significantly by the fall in sub-2.5 micron particulates, with emissions of particulates of between 2.5 and 10 microns falling by 57% over the period.

These are used as the primary platform to demonise and campaign against the use of road transport in general and private car ownership in particular. These have therefore been subject since at least the start of the 21st century to very detailed analysis of the injurious health effects of the presence of Nitrogen Dioxide and sub-2.5 micron particulates in the atmosphere.

It is therefore important to understand the measured emissions and concentrations of these pollutants in much more detail and to understand the best known estimates of the contributors to the falling emissions and concentrations found in the atmosphere through these 50 years.

Nitrogen Dioxide and road transport

Thanks to the analyses by BEIS, and made available from the NAEI, we are able to see an estimate of the contribution to the emissions of NO_x expressed as NO_2 from road transport, including types of fuel burnt by internal combustion engines.

In the chart on the next page the total emissions of such Nitrogen Oxides from all sources from 1970 to 2019 is represented again in the red line clearly showing the fall from the peak of 1989.

The contribution made by all road transport is represented in the pink line and shows significant growth from 1970 to 1989, falling then to 2019.

By the end of the second decade of the 21st century road transport was contributing 33% of the emissions of Nitrogen Oxides and thus can be seen correctly as a major contributor.

In addition thanks to the detailed NAEI analysis, almost all of this contribution is made by DERV/diesel fuel burning internal combustion engines, 31% points (the teal line) of the 33%. It is useful however to think of this latter figure in relation to the growth of ownership of diesel-powered cars, which will be touched upon in coming pages.

UK trend in weight of atmospheric pollutants (Defra/BEIS(NAEI))
(Road use contribution (NOx as NO2 - 33%, 31% Diesel))

Thousands of tons

— Nitrogen Oxides (thousands tons, left scale) — UK Road Use NOx (as NO2) Tonnage (K) — UK Road Use Diesel NOx (as NO2) Tonnage (K)

Particulates and road transport

Of even greater importance to health effects for people, particularly those living in large cities and especially when living close to major busy roads, is the contribution of road transport to total particulate emissions.

It was the report of 2010 *"The Mortality Effects of Long-Term Exposure to Particulate Air Pollution in the United Kingdom"* from a committee of the Health Protection Agency, called the Committee on Effects of Air Pollutants (COMEAP), set up in 1992, that raised the awareness of the health risks of particulates by estimating the long-term effects on health and longevity caused by sub-2.5 micron particulates in the atmosphere.

As such, sub-10 micron and sub-2.5 micron emissions are represented in the chart on the opposite page in the dark blue and cyan lines respectively as before, but now with the addition of their contributions from road transport derived from the NAEI database. Sub-10 micron particulates are represented in the royal blue line whilst emissions of sub-2.5 micron particulates are represented in the aqua line.

Whilst the overall reduction since 1970 has been very large indeed, 75% and 80% respectively, the reduction of contribution from road transport to emissions of sub-2.5 micron particulates has been smaller since its peak in 1996 of just 63% and a very small reduction of just 18% compared to 1970.

Of note is that in 2019 the NAEI estimated that road transport contributed 12% to total emissions of both sub-10 micron particulates and sub-2.5 micron particulates.

It is also of very special interest that, since the COMEAP report focuses entirely on the long term health effects of sub-2.5 micron particulates, as these are known to be the greatest risk to human health, combined with the overwhelming public discourse demonising particularly DERV/diesel fuel internal combustion engine powered road transport, that in fact only 4% of total emissions of sub-2.5 micron particulates are contributed by the combustion of DERV/diesel fuel in road vehicles.

Almost all of the other 8% of the road transport contribution to total emissions of sub-2.5 micron particulates is caused by brake wear, tyre wear and road abrasion, plus a very small contribution from the burning of petrol in internal combustion engines.

It is also useful to note that the DERV/diesel contribution to total emissions of sub-2.5 micron particulates at its peak in 1996 was almost 15.3%, falling to just 4% in 2019 (from 27 kilotonnes to just 4 kilotonnes in 2019, an 85% reduction); this fall despite a near six-fold increase of the number of registered DERV/diesel fuel powered passenger cars (from 2.2 million to 15.8 million), and a 70% increase in consumption of DERV/diesel fuel by road vehicles over the same quarter century.

This suggests very effective improvements in DERV/diesel fuel technology over the quarter century, being real measured, and is not affected by behaviour such as various emissions scandals.

UK trend in weight of atmospheric pollutants (Defra/BEIS(NAEI))
(Road use contribution (PM10 - 12%, 2.5% Fuel) and (PM2.5 - 12%, 4.0% Fuel))

Thousands of tons

PM10 (thousand tons, right scale)   PM2.5 (thousand tons, right scale)   UK Road Use PM10 Tonnage (K)
UK Road Use PM2.5 Tonnage (K)

Concentration of atmospheric NO₂

The next stage in the risk to human life and health from air pollutant emissions is their concentration in the atmosphere that people are breathing.

DEFRA report such figures for the principal pollutants for the UK as a whole, as well as various locations throughout the UK.

In the chart on the next page we are showing both the NAEI recorded road transport emissions of NO_x as NO_2 for the UK in the pink line, and that component from the burning of DERV/diesel fuel from internal combustion engines in the teal green line.

The period is now limited to just the first two decades of the 21st century as most of the measures of concentration of pollutants in the atmosphere do not stretch back as far as the emissions calculations and this allows us to correlate the two at this national level.

Thus in the chart on the opposite page we can also see the DEFRA reported concentration of NO_2 in the atmosphere, expressed as micrograms per cubic metre, as for both the average for the major roadsides throughout the UK from the various monitoring points, in the dark blue line, plus the average urban background concentration in the mid-blue line.

The urban background is quoted, since approximately 83% of England's population live in urban settings, and is used as a core policy driver by DEFRA and government accordingly.

In addition the chart represents two target thresholds or guidelines derived from the World Health Organisation (WHO) and enshrined in law in the UK in 2010 in the *"Air Quality Standards Regulation"*. Accordingly the legal limit of the annual mean concentration of NO_2 in the atmosphere is 40 micro-grams per cubic metre (in the bright green line) and the hourly mean guideline is 200 micro-grams per cubic metre (in the red line), but that there should be no more than 18 hours that exceed this hourly guideline per year.

Clear from the chart is the trend of reducing emissions from road transport (pink line) that falls over time, and even an eventual reduction of emissions from the combustion of DERV/diesel fuel (the teal green) line that falls from 2007. Also clearly the average countrywide roadside concentrations (dark blue line) and the urban background concentrations (mid-blue line) fall continuously since 2000.

Notable is the fall of the average roadside concentration, meeting the 2010 imposed legal limit by 2013, and then continuing to fall in the subsequent years. Also notable is the fact that at least the average urban background concentration (and though not shown here, the average rural background concentration) for the UK have always been below the 2010 imposed annual limit, even before the law came into force.

This does not mean that there are no locations that do not regularly exceed these NO_2 limits and this will be explored soon accordingly.

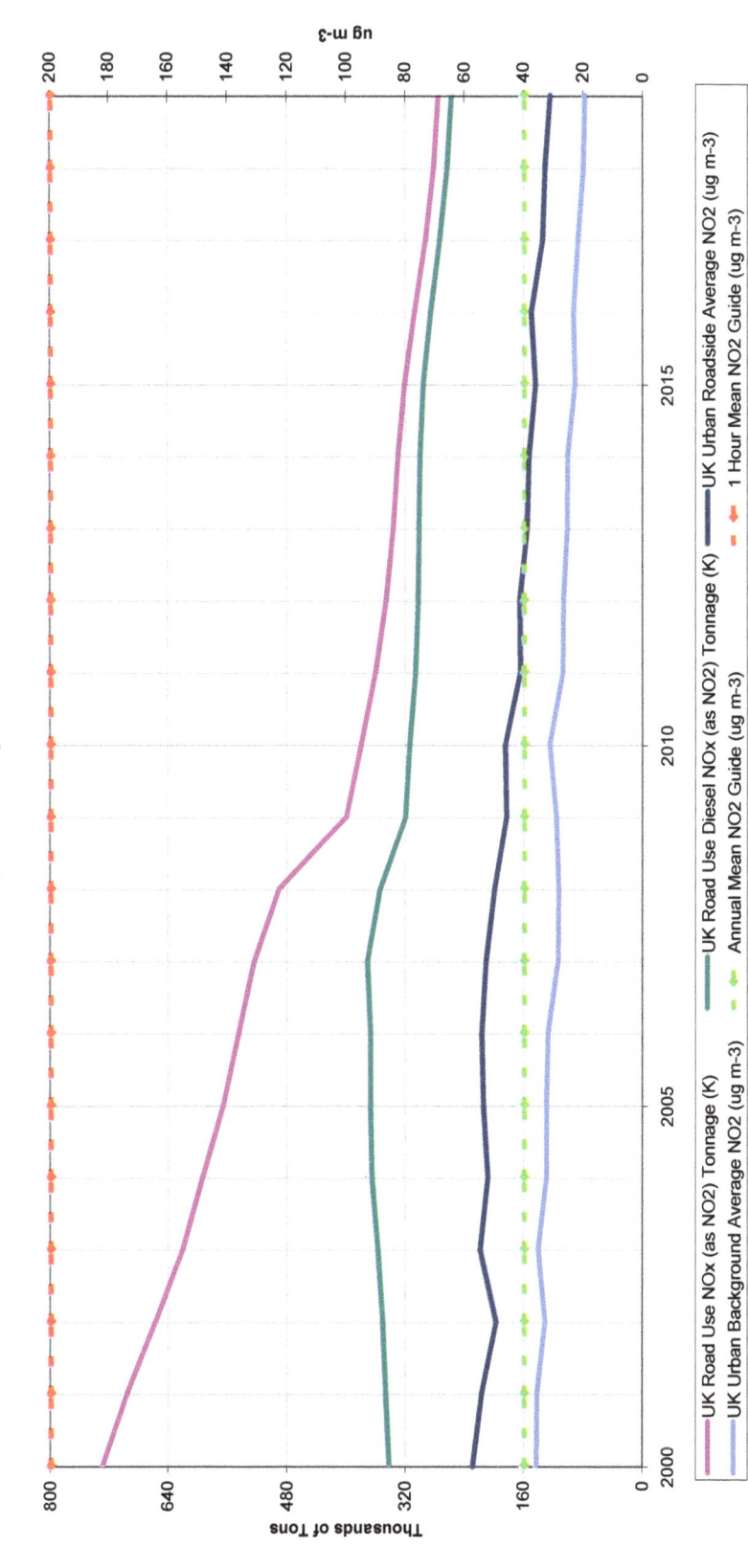

UK recent nitrous-oxide (NOx) & nitrogen dioxide (NO2) air pollutants

ug m-3

Thousands of Tons

UK Road Use NOx (as NO2) Tonnage (K)
UK Road Use Diesel NOx (as NO2) Tonnage (K)
UK Urban Roadside Average NO2 (ug m-3)
1 Hour Mean NO2 Guide (ug m-3)
UK Urban Background Average NO2 (ug m-3)
Annual Mean NO2 Guide (ug m-3)

Concentration of atmospheric PM$_{2.5}$

Frustratingly the measurement of the concentrations of sub-2.5 micron particulates only started to be recorded from 2009, so in the chart on the opposite page we represent again the decline of emissions from road transport in the aqua line and the contribution from all fuel combustion from road transport in the light blue line.

Again the concentrations of sub-2.5 micron particulates, measured as micro-grams per cubic metre, is represented as the average at the UK roadside in the dark blue line, and the average for the UK urban background in the mid-blue line.

It is very important to understand that the guideline references for sub-2.5 micron particulates are cast in a different way in this case.

The 2010 "*Air Quality Standards Regulation*" requires that the annual mean concentration should not exceed 25 micro-grams per cubic metre and is represented in the red line, however this is reduced, in terms of a target, to 10 micro-grams per cubic metre (from the WHO guideline) and is represented in the green line. Note that the legal limit is then used as a reference for hourly mean concentrations as well.

These limits have been constrained in practice as strong targets since it is known how threatening sub-2.5 micron particulates are to human health.

From the data for the UK as a whole, again a clear picture emerges that emissions both from road transport and combustion of fuel from road transport have fallen significantly since the year 2000 to 2019 (50% and almost 80% respectively). Also clear is the 35% fall of the measured concentrations of sub-2.5 micron particulates at the UK roadside by 2019 from the 2011 peak. Also clear is the 25% fall of the measured concentrations of these same particulates within the UK urban background.

Although not shown here for the purposes of brevity the measurement of the concentrations of the sub-10 micron particulates, which does extend back to before the year 2000, and of which sub-2.5 micron particulates form the majority, also shows the same pattern of decline over the whole period of 20 years in terms of both emissions and concentrations. We can therefore be reasonably confident that had concentrations of sub-2.5 micron particulates been monitored and recorded before 2009 they almost certainly would have shown the same pattern of steady fall as both their emissions and the concentrations of sub-10 micron particulates show accordingly.

Also notable due to the slightly different definitions of legal limit from the 2010 Act and the use of the 10 micro-gram per cubic metre as an aggressive target we can see that in practice, nationally, the UK-wide urban roadside and urban background concentrations have, at least since measurements began, never exceeded the legal limit enforced in full from 2015, however they only met the more aggressive target in 2019.

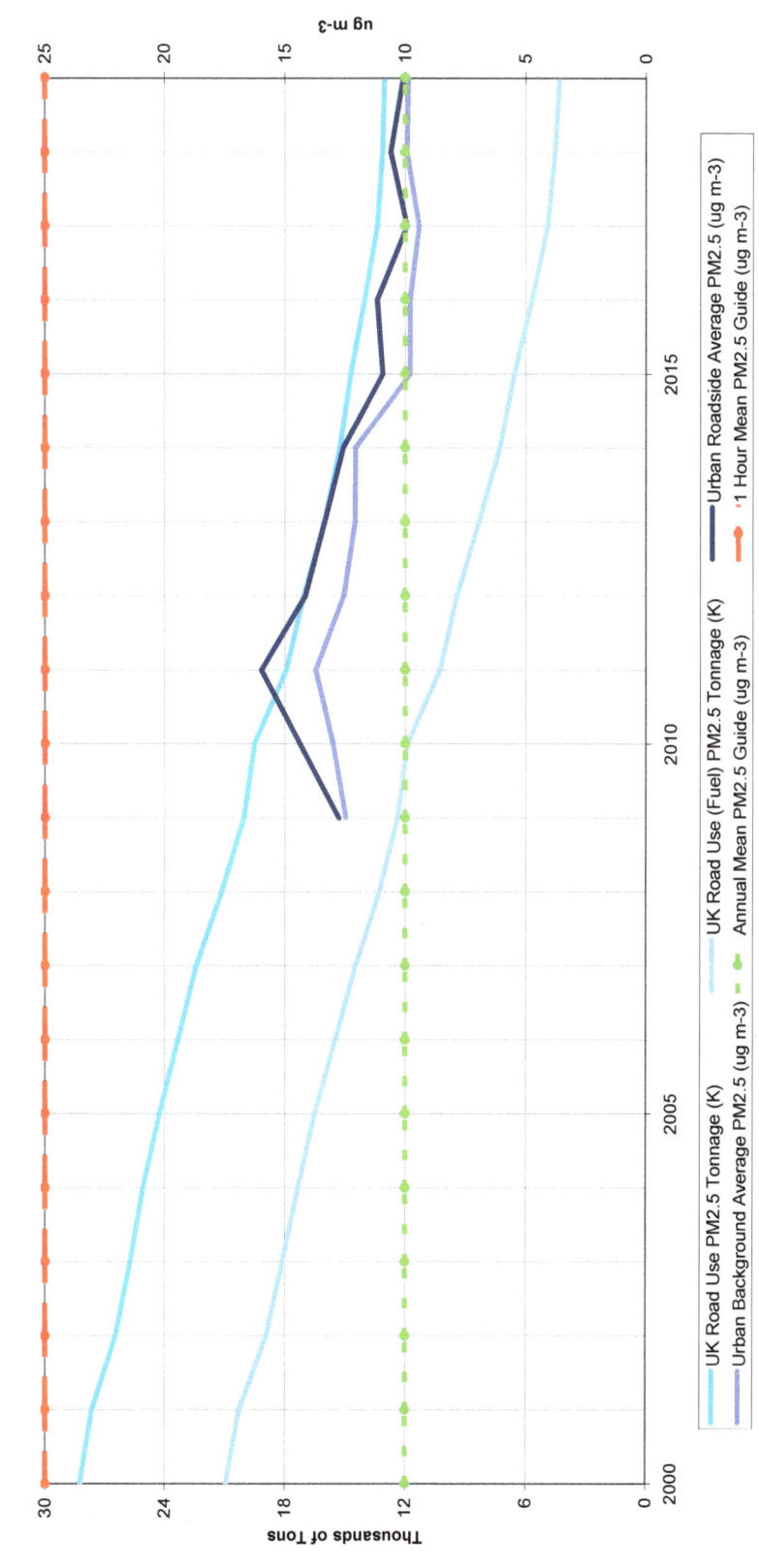

UK, London recent particulates (PM2.5) air pollutants

ug m-3

Thousands of Tons

UK Road Use PM2.5 Tonnage (K)
Urban Background Average PM2.5 (ug m-3)
UK Road Use (Fuel) PM2.5 Tonnage (K)
Annual Mean PM2.5 Guide (ug m-3)
Urban Roadside Average PM2.5 (ug m-3)
'1 Hour Mean PM2.5 Guide (ug m-3)

NO₂ concentrations in London

We now focus in more detail on the concentrations of NO$_2$ in London, this city being known to experience the worst effects of all regions and conurbations of the UK. Thanks to the very detailed monitoring available, plus useful, albeit abbreviated, analysis by The Mayor's Office, we are able to see a very similar though less extreme pattern of gradual reduction even in London.

In the chart on the opposite page, The Mayor's Office analysis is represented in half-yearly averages for the London mean background concentrations in the dark orange line from 2008, and the London mean roadside in the light orange line from 2008.

Note that whilst clearly showing a steady if unspectacular fall to the first half of 2019, the whole dataset was abbreviated to just July 2019 and has not been updated since, for reasons unknown.

From extraction of data for six selected locations from available monitoring sites throughout London, but ensuring that some of the worst roads are included, data from these selections is represented in the dark yellow line from the year 2000 to 2019. Since data before 2008 become more sparse, even for these selected locations, we must be accordingly cautious about that representation.

Note, for NO$_2$, the monitoring station data for the roads and locations selected are: *Westminster – Marylebone Road, MY1; City of London – Walbrook Wharf, CT6; Wandsworth – Putney High Street, WA7; Croydon – Norbury, CR5; Ealing – Horn Lane, EA8; Hackney – Old Street, HK6.*

Note the first three are in fact amongst the worst roadside locations for concentrations of NO$_2$ in London and in turn the UK as a whole.

Quite clear in the trend over time, is the same steady and slightly greater fall, at least from 2008 for this selection of 6 locations used here and represented in the yellow line.

However this selection is clearly notably worse than the overall London roadside average calculated by The Mayor's Office and represented in the light orange line. It is also fortunately not abbreviated to July 2019 and as such covers to the very end of that year.

In so far as it does extend fully to the end of 2019, it very strongly suggests a further significant fall in the second half of the year 2019, that we can only guess what might be reproduced in geographically broader analysis for London from The Mayor's Office, if it were to have been brought up to date by them.

As such we can be confident that whilst there are clearly several roadside and possibly even other locations that might still breach the annual average legal limit (as represented in the green line), even still in 2019, the data strongly suggest that the overall mean was not actually breaching the legal limit by the end of 2019, and in fact mean London background has not been breaching the newly imposed June 2010 legal limit from the middle of 2011 onwards.

London NO2 Concentration (selected roads) plus Mayor's Office all roadside and background mean - Half-yearly

Legend: Average NO2 (Basket of 6) — London Mean Roadside — London Mean Background — Annual Mean Guide — 1 Hour Mean

PM$_{2.5}$ concentrations in London

Now we focus on the even greater risk to human health in the form of sub-2.5 micron particulate concentrations in London. We can clearly see, in the chart on the opposite page, derived from the data sources of The Mayor's Office analysis from 2008 and abbreviated to July 2019, the London mean background of sub-2.5 micron concentration of particulates, represented in half-yearly intervals, in the dark orange line, and London mean roadside concentrations represented in the light orange line.

From extraction of data for seven locations from available monitoring sites throughout London, but ensuring that some of the worst roads are included, data from these selections is represented in the dark yellow line from the year 2006 to 2019. Since data before 2008 become more sparse, even for these selected locations, we must be accordingly cautious about that representation.

Note, for PM$_{2.5}$, the monitoring station data for the roads and locations selected are: *Westminster – Marylebone Road FDMS, MY7; City of London – Farringdon Street, CT2; Camden – Euston Road, CD9; Tower Hamlets – Blackwall, TH4; Greenwich – Eltham, GR4; Greenwich – Plumstead High Street, GN3; Haringey – Haringey Town Hall, HG1.*

Three significant characteristics are very clear from both the trends and from the variation by half year.

Firstly the selection of seven specific locations, happens to produce an almost identical average as the mean London roadside values calculated by The Mayor's Office.

Secondly there is a very large variation between winter and summer almost every year from 2008 to 2019, in which winter concentrations of sub-2.5 micron particulates are noticeably much higher than summer (generally 5 micro-grams per cubic metre higher in winter than summer).

Thirdly the general trend clearly shows a steady and continuous fall in concentrations for the reliably monitored period from 2008 to 2018 yielding a 25% fall in concentration of sub-2.5 micron particulates at the mean London roadside and an estimated 30% fall in concentrations for the mean London background, based upon the consistency of trends.

Since the selected seven locations trend in all other respects to almost mirror The Mayor's Office abbreviated mean London roadside trend to the end of 2018, we can confidently accept that the trend to the end of 2019 is probably consistent with the previous 11 years, thereby suggesting that the fall was even greater to the end of 2019, as per the drop at the far right of the yellow line in the chart.

Note again that whilst the annual mean legal limit is actually represented in the red line, and shows that even before the new legal limit of 25 micro-grams per cubic metre came into force on 1st January 2015 both London roadside and mean background did not breach this limit throughout the whole measured period, we can see that they still exceed the WHO recommended guideline by 2019.

London PM2.5 concentration (selected roads) plus Mayor's Office all roadside and background mean - Half-yearly

Average PM2.5 (Basket of Seven) — London Mean Roadside — London Mean Background — Annual Mean Guide — 1 Hour Mean

NO₂ in the Marylebone Road

Deliberately focussing in yet more detail on just one of the worst roads in London and the UK as a whole, namely the Marylebone Road, yields a very useful picture of the trends in the atmospheric concentration of NO_2 over the period of data available for that monitoring station.

In the chart at the top of the next page we can see the annual mean trend for the Marylebone Road represented in the pink line, whilst the previously calculated annual mean trend for the selection of six locations is again represented in the yellow line.

Whilst again being cautious about the mean for the selected six roads before 2008, due to a dearth of data from some locations, that for the Marylebone Road is actually over 97% complete at the hourly level, as extracted, thus we can be confident of the findings of the overall annual trend.

From this we can see that whilst the annual mean concentration of NO_2 in the Marylebone Road did continuously breach the 2010 imposed legal limit, it did nonetheless steadily and significantly fall by 45% from its 2008 peak to 2019.

This time a special analysis has been performed for each year's hourly data for the Marylebone Road to try to assess both what percentage of each year's hourly available data measures exceeded the legal limit of 200 micro-grams per cubic metre, and thence how many days within each year at least one hour exceeded that same limit.

The latter is represented in the chart in the middle of the opposite page and represented in the red line, with each year's count of days shown as the value against each data point. In addition DEFRA's own analysis is added in the orange line from 2010, the latter being barely visible as the two methods have yielded almost the same number of days in which one or more hours exceeded the hourly legal limit.

Very useful in the extended analysis represented in the red line is the peak year in which 177 days, in 2008, had at least one hour that exceeded the hourly limit defined in the Act that was later imposed from June 2010.

Additionally very striking is that in 2019 no hours on any day in the Marylebone Road exceeded the 2010 imposed legal limit.

By then delving deeper into the data we can see what proportion of each year's hourly mean measures exceeded the hourly limit as imposed from June 2010.

In the chart at the bottom of the opposite page this is represented as percentage of hours each year in the red line and again with the value for each year shown at each point.

Quite clear is the peak year of 2005 in which almost 10% of the year for every hour the concentrations of NO_2 were greater than 200 micro-grams per cubic metre.

But also very clear is the large drop after 2010, then steady fall from 2013 to no hour exceeding the legal limit in 2019.

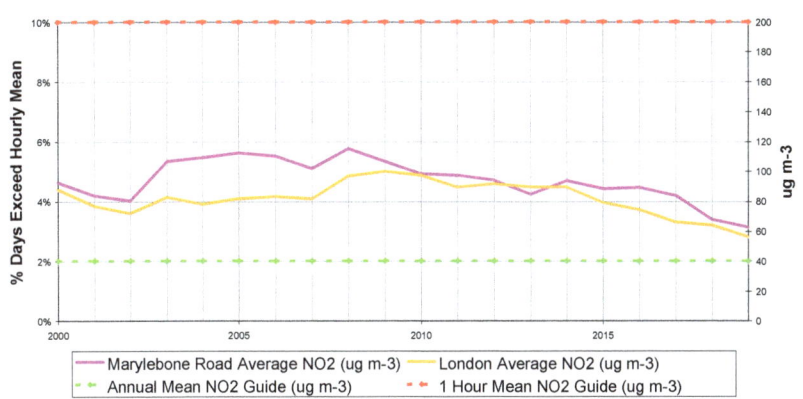

London concentration of NO2 with WHO NO₂ guidelines

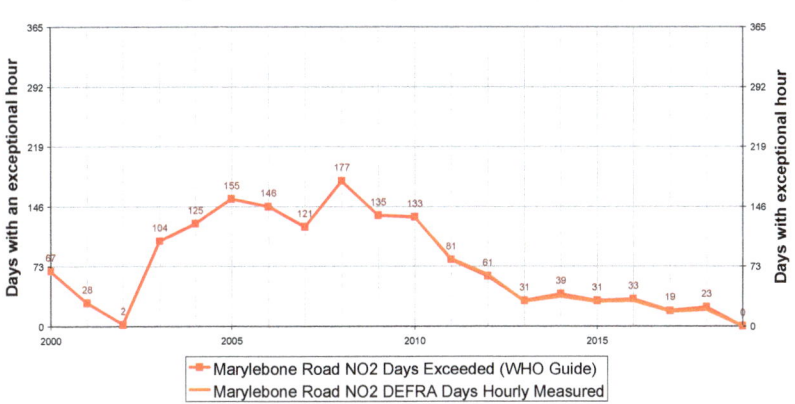

Number of days in which measured exceptional hour of NO₂ occurred (LAQ/Kings)

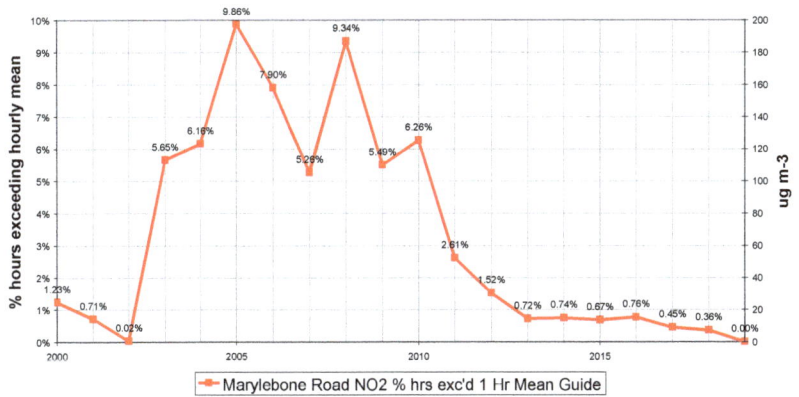

Marylebone Road, London % of hours per annum exceeding WHO NO₂ guidelines

PM$_{2.5}$ in the Marylebone Road

Again deliberately focussing on the Marylebone Road in much more detail we are able to see how the concentrations of sub-2.5 micron particulates for the atmosphere around this road compares, at least, to the selection of seven locations throughout London, which we have seen previously compare well with the analysis from The Mayor's Office for overall mean London roadside concentrations.

In the chart at the top of the opposite page again we can see the trend for the annual mean concentrations from the earliest available data during 2009 for Marylebone Road represented in the pink line, compared to the previously discussed calculated annual average for the selection of seven different locations represented in the yellow line.

Clearly the Marylebone road exhibits a much higher annual average concentration throughout the period but also tends to show a stronger 40% decline from the peak of 2011, in which it almost breached the legal limit defined in the 2010 Act (though not imposed at 25 micro-grams per cubic metre until 1st January 2015).

Because no hourly mean is actually imposed in the 2010 Act, instead an hourly trigger of 50 micro-grams per cubic metre is used as a threshold to count the hours, and in turn days that have hourly exceptions to this trigger value are calculated.

Accordingly by processing the data downloaded from the LondonAir Imperial College database for the Marylebone Road and applying this 50 micro-grams per cubic metre to that hourly measured data, yields both the number of days in each year available and also the percentage of the available hourly measures for each year that exceeded this trigger.

Note that data for the year 2009 is incomplete, only yielding just over 60% of the measures that might have been available for the whole year, had monitoring been in-place for the whole year, only yielding data from the 1st May that year onwards.

In the chart in the middle of the opposite page, the cyan line shows that the peak number of days in which at least one hour exceeded the trigger was in 2011, 70 days, falling to 19 days in 2018, but rising again in 2019 to 25 days. This is compared to the DEFRA quoted days in the teal green line which exhibits a similar pattern, though counts of days exceeding their own internal trigger (68 micro-grams) are lower.

In the chart at the bottom of the opposite page, again using the 50 micro-grams per cubic metre trigger, yields a percentage of the measured hours each year and again re-iterates the same pattern, yielding a fall from the 2011 peak of 5.6% of the measured hours of the year exceeding the trigger, to the low of 2018 in which marginally over 1% exceeded, then a small rise to almost 1.8% of the hours in the year 2019 exceeding the 50 micro-gram per cubic metre trigger.

All measures again then show valuable improvement and by setting aggressive targets, help to incentivise even greater gains.

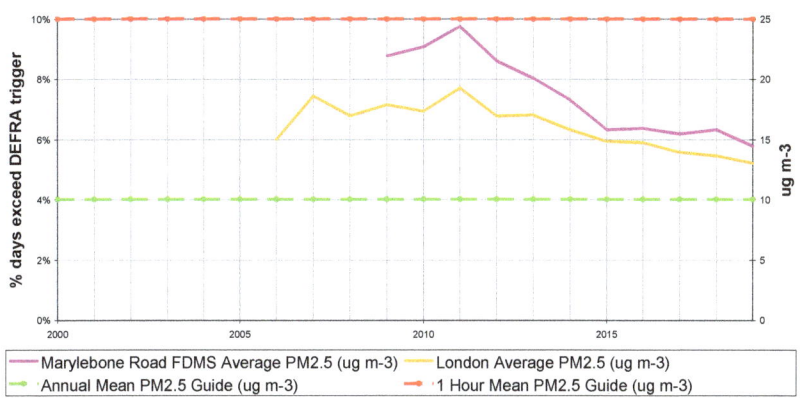

London concentration of PM2.5 with DEFRA PM2.5 trigger

- Marylebone Road FDMS Average PM2.5 (ug m-3)
- London Average PM2.5 (ug m-3)
- Annual Mean PM2.5 Guide (ug m-3)
- 1 Hour Mean PM2.5 Guide (ug m-3)

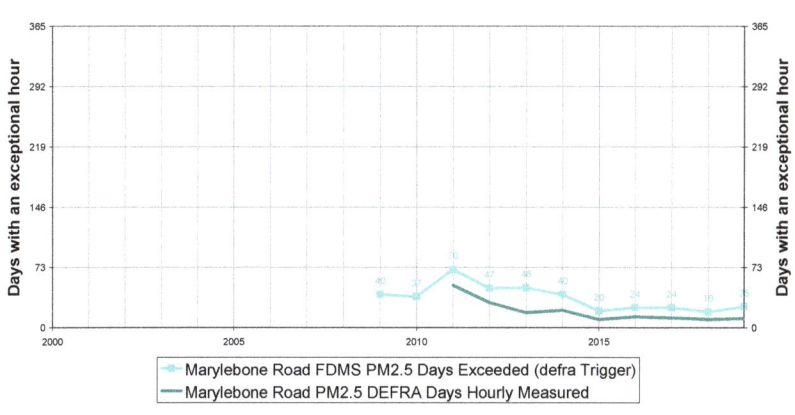

Days in which a measured exceptional hour of PM2.5 occurred (LAQ/Kings)

- Marylebone Road FDMS PM2.5 Days Exceeded (defra Trigger)
- Marylebone Road PM2.5 DEFRA Days Hourly Measured

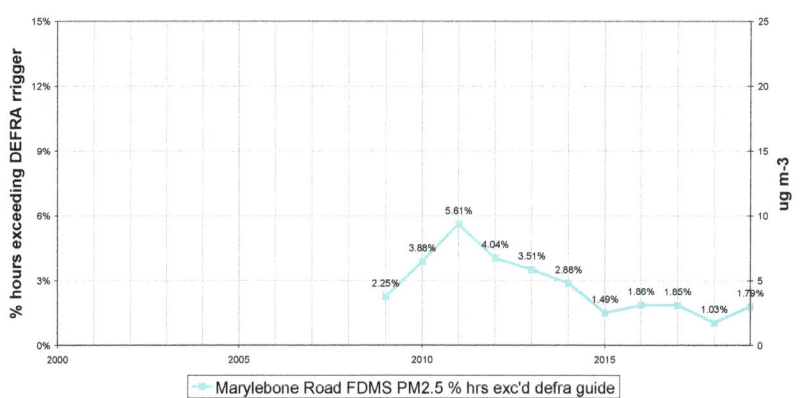

Marylebone Road & London % of hours per annum exceeding DEFRA PM2.5 trigger

- Marylebone Road FDMS PM2.5 % hrs exc'd defra guide

177

An unintended experiment

Although this work is not intended to cover any statistical trends beyond 2019, due to the enormous disruption caused by the spread of the Coronavirus (SARS-CoV-2/Covid-19) pandemic and the consequent precipitate worldwide governmental reaction to that pandemic, it completely unintentionally imposed a useful experiment in the potential effects of removing most road transport from the roads, including London.

By using the best available measures for the relative volumes of road traffic movement from both the Department for Transport (DFT), for relative movement of all transport compared to the norm before the end of March 2020, and Transport for London (TfL) in the form of congestion charging statistics for 2020, we are able to take a view of the correlated changes this might have wrought to the concentrations of NO_2, sub-10 micron particulates and sub-2.5 micron particulates in the same selected locations in London, as used for the previous 2 decades analysis.

The charts on the opposite page present this data correlated by time from the 1st January 2020 to 30th September 2020.

In each chart the nationwide percentage of use of personal cars relative to the expected norm for that time of year, obtained from the DFT, is represented in the bright blue line, as a calculated 7 day moving average (along with its daily average in the light blue dashed line).

Also represented in each chart is a simple analysis of the available monthly congestion charging road traffic volumes for London in the dark blue line, where each month is simply related to the volumes of vehicle movements in the congestion zone counted during January and February 2020. Unfortunately no movement counts are recorded for April as congestion charging was suspended due to the government imposed restrictions on the economy and traffic movement for that month.

By correlating these road transport traffic movements (note also the 85% reduction in TfL bus movements as well as the 70% reduction in private car movements nationally) we can see the relative changes in NO_2 concentrations in the chart at the top of the page, then concentrations of sub-10 micron particulates in the chart in the middle of the next page and finally sub-2.5 micron particulates in the chart at the bottom of the page.

The picture that emerges tends to suggest that NO_2 concentrations (represented in the top chart as a monthly average in the orange line) did gradually fall from the levels in the middle of March, of approximately 47 micro-grams per cubic metre, to a low of 31 per cubic metre in early May, a 34% fall. This suggests a greater road transport contribution to concentrations in London than would be suggested nationwide which should yield a 23% fall, using the NAEI road transport contribution share.

For both sub-10 micron particulate concentrations and sub-2.5 micron particulate concentrations, represented respectively in the middle and bottom charts on the next page, the picture appears to be radically different however, to that of NO_2.

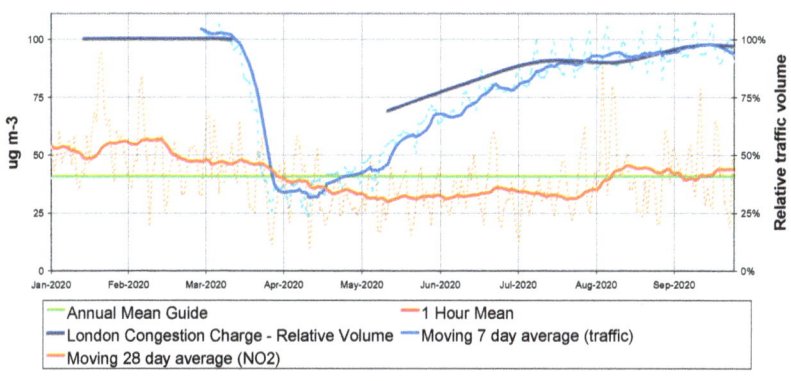

London (selected roads) Daily NO₂ concentration January 2020 to August 2020 correlated to Coronavirus restrictions motor vehicle usage

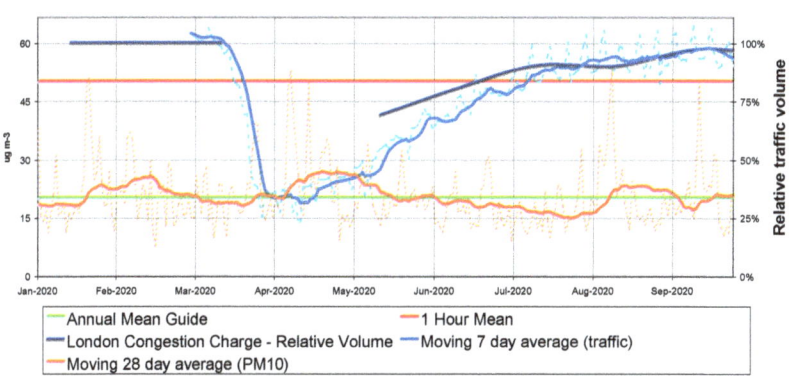

London (selected roads) Daily PM10 concentration January 2020 to August 2020 correlated to Coronavirus restrictions motor vehicle usage

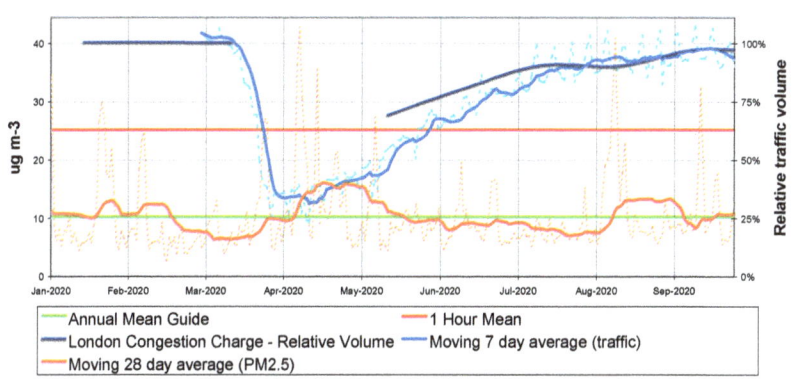

London (selected roads) Daily PM2.5 concentration January 2020 to August 2020 correlated to Coronavirus restrictions motor vehicle usage

Using exactly the same time-based correlation, neither sets of data for particulates show a fall in concentrations from the time of the start of shutdown of the economy and related traffic movements from 23rd March onwards.

In fact in both charts on the previous page in the 28 day moving averages in dark orange (and the corresponding daily averages in the light orange dashed line), a very strong series of very high peaks are clearly visible (and present for every monitored location for both measures) throughout April to early May, followed later by August peaks as well.

This tends to suggest that other, non-road transport factors, may be the largest contribution to the concentrations of particulates, at least in London locations. Both are also clearly short lived in the atmosphere, unlike those for NO_2.

Whilst the cause of these contributions are not known for certain, they clearly overwhelm any contribution from road transport, as suggested by the greatest fall in road transport at a time of the greatest rise in particulate concentrations.

Once again, as with the claims, or more correctly the tone, of the public discourse for; a lack of building and consequent physical housing shortage; the persistent, and almost growing presence of *poverty* in modern Britain (almost never qualified as *relative "poverty"*), we can clearly see that the tone of reporting and discussion, at all levels in the public discourse regarding air-quality and pollution levels, is again found to be somewhat exaggerated in real terms, when actual trends and measurements are used and understood.

It cannot be denied that current levels of pollutants in the atmosphere are damaging to the health of a number of people and particularly so in locations of the highest concentration of such pollutants, including places in London.

But it is an unfortunate fact that these effects actually tend to impact those at greatest risk due to their exceptional underlying vulnerability, when suffering significant serious respiratory health issues. Sometimes these are well diagnosed, but occasionally they may not be, making these latter people even more vulnerable due to the lack of diagnosis of their vulnerability.

As with all such issues, rational and factually informed balance is a far better guide to action and reaction than uninformed emotion or panic. This is amply illustrated by the enormous consequences of the damage wrought to the economies of the world, and near certain long term loss of life outcomes, due to the reactions to the 2020-2021 pandemic.

The consequences of the benefits of the progress over the last 320 years can be seen for all in these key measures, including air-quality improvements when we look in more detail at life-expectancy over time, as we shall in the next and final chapter.

Life Expectancy

"To-morrow, and to-morrow, and to-morrow,
Creeps in this petty pace from day to day,
To the last syllable of recorded time;
And all our yesterdays have lighted fools
The way to dusty death. Out, out, brief candle!
Life's but a walking shadow, a poor player
That struts and frets his hour upon the stage
And then is heard no more."

William Shakespeare:
Macbeth (act 5, scene 5),
1606

What is meant by "Life Expectancy"?

The online Encyclopaedia Britannica defines "Life Expectancy" (authored by Judith Marie Bezy) as an: *"estimate of the average number of additional years that a person of a given age can expect to live. The most common measure of life expectancy is life expectancy at birth. Life expectancy is a **hypothetical** measure. It assumes that the age-specific death rates for the year in question will apply throughout the lifetime of individuals born in that year. The estimate, in effect, projects the age-specific mortality (death) rates for a given period over the entire lifetime of the population born (or alive) during that time".*

In truth therefore, for our purposes, it is not meaningful to focus on the word *"expectancy"* as though it really is a *"projection"* that might be applied to those born or still living in any given year.

The simple *"assumption"* in the methodology that the life longevity outcomes for those who have died in a given year will apply in the future is clearly weak when we examine the data for the past. As such we will instead treat it rather as an historical indicator of life longevity outcomes rather than an *"expectancy"* or *"projection"*.

Caveat emptor

The reader should be aware that this final chapter is in most respects the most complex and also the most specific analysis of the best available data about the life longevity outcomes for the people of the United Kingdom, as published in both the UK and internationally.

In order to illustrate some trends over the periods concerned, a limited statistically *"incorrect"* (un-weighted) analysis of data released from Rashid et al. *"Life expectancy and risk of death in 6791 communities in England from 2002 to 2019"* has been performed, as strictly necessary.

The visual representations in the charts remain consistent with the otherwise most rigorous thoroughly complete analyses available. This does not mean that all the precise numbers from these secondary analyses are correct in themselves, but only serve to illustrate trends in general that represent the real life longevity outcomes that have been experienced by the people of the United Kingdom over the period from 1700 to 2019.

Life expectancy for 320 years (HMD)

By connecting the analysis of life expectancy from the work of Tony Wrigley and Roger Schofield for England, as discussed, with the more extensive data available since the establishment of central registration of births, deaths and marriages from 1837 for the UK and England and Wales (found in the Human Mortality Database, HMD), we are able to show the overall trend of increasing life expectancy from 1700 to 2019.

The presentation style of the chart itself, on the opposite page, is here replicated from that published by "Our World in Data" (OWID) authored by Max Roser, as it comprehensively illustrates many aspects of the improvements over these centuries in a single chart.

The continuous gains of life expectancy at birth from the middle of the 18th century are clearly seen in the dark red and bright red lines. Equally clearly visible are the dramatic effects of both The Great War (plus "Spanish Influenza") and The Second World War, in the fall of life expectancy at those times. Also shown from the 1840s are the annual changes that significantly affect the calculated life expectancy by age range. Another improvement that can be seen is the impact of infant and child mortality as we move from expectancy at birth (bright red) to expectancy at age 80 (in dark blue), all falling dramatically over time.

Finally notable on the right hand side of the chart is a slowing of the rate of improvement in the second decade of the 21st century, and we shall discuss this issue in much more detail for the remainder of this chapter.

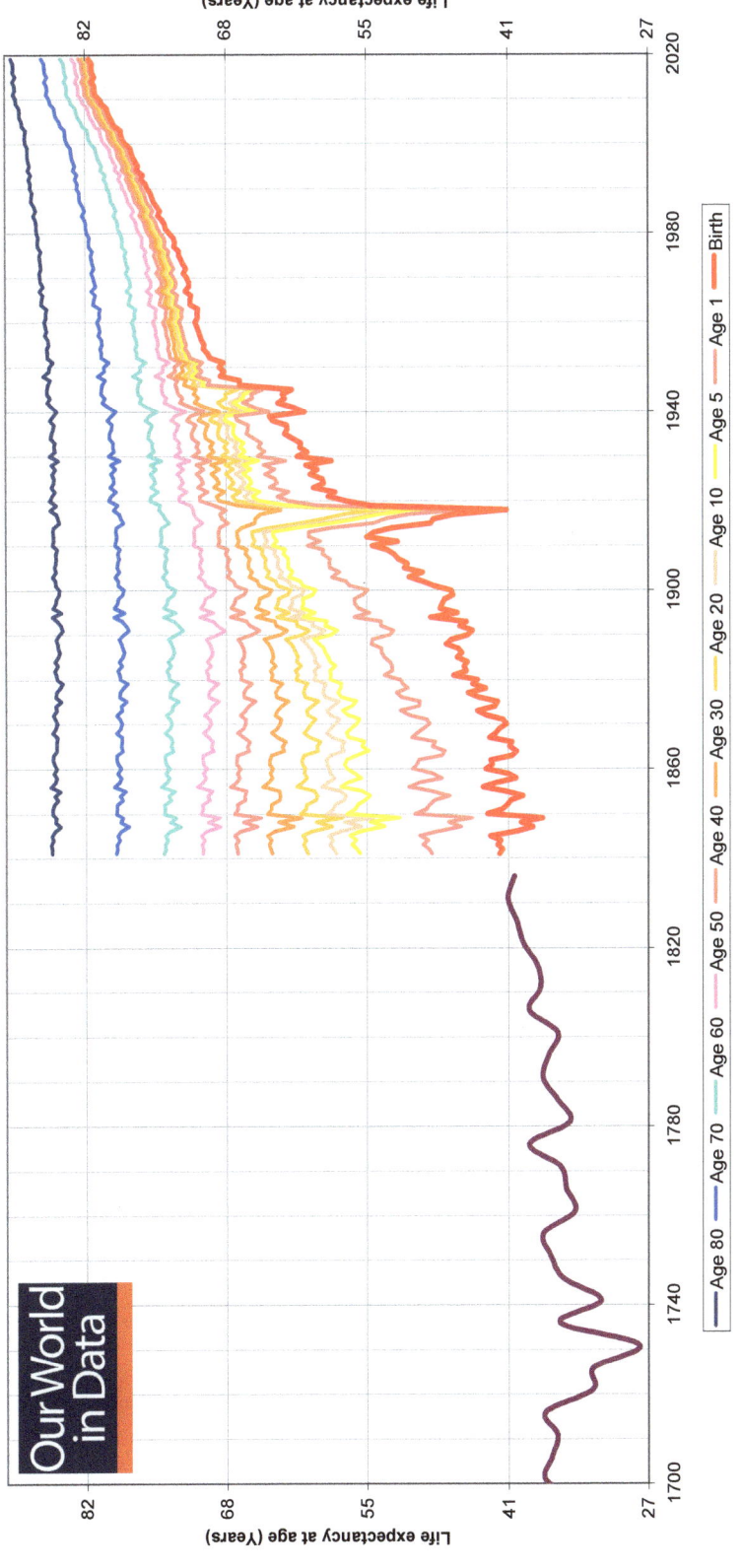

Life Expectancy at Decadal Age for England (Wrigley & Schofield before 1840) & England & Wales (ONS/Human Mortality Database after Max Roser)

Life expectancy at age (Years)

Age 80 — Age 70 — Age 60 — Age 50 — Age 40 — Age 30 — Age 20 — Age 10 — Age 5 — Age 1 — Birth

Our World in Data

Life Expectancy by sex and age (ONS)

The slowing of the rate of improvement of life expectancy in most of the second decade of the 21st century has been the subject of many analyses by multiple organisations and has resulted in several influences on the public discourse of the socio-economic conditions of the life of the population of the United Kingdom.

The general tone of that discourse has noticeably been to strongly lay the responsibility for this slowing of the rate of improvement at the door of the policy of "*austerity*"; introduced from 2010 by the Cameron/Clegg government, then sustained in the Cameron government from 2015, then the May government from 2016, until the October budget of 2018 when the then Chancellor of the Exchequer, Philip Hammond, announced that "*the era of austerity is finally coming to an end*".

It is possible, that in keeping with all the preceding findings, that this has again been ideologically and partisan-politically motivated and thus, as with those subjects of analysis, documented in the previous chapters, this demands deeper investigation to affirm or question those claims.

Starting with the analysis produced by the ONS of all of the deaths each year for the whole of the UK, published in the Single Year Life Tables from 1980 to 2020 from birth to age 100, we are able to reproduce the trends of the first two decades of the 21st century, now split between males and females, but again for decadal ages.

These are by single year and therefore are not officially classed as part of the National Statistics, as only the continuous three year "smoothed" analysis is classed as part of National Statistics; but they do reveal a great deal, including pointing to specific annual characteristics of death patterns and consequent life expectancy outcomes.

In the charts on the opposite page, these trends are shown, again using the same colours as for the previous very long term total population outcome from the data collated in the "Human Mortality Database" and as presented by "Our World in Data".

It is from this analysis that we can see the relative differences between life expectancy for males and females. Using the same axis ranges for both it can be clearly seen that females consistently fare better than males.

Again clearly visible in these two charts are the impact of the slowing of the rate of improvement of life expectancy for both males and females, and notably for all age ranges, from 2011 to 2018.

Also visible is a particular year in which life expectancy falls for all age ranges and both males and females in 2015.

At first view, the period 2011-2018 fits with the bulk of the period of the policy of "*austerity*" and the stricter control of public expenditure, and thus initially suggests the argument might possibly have some merit.

Of note is the uplift between 2018 and 2019 that points to a return to a similar rate of annual improvement more prevalent for most years between 2000 and 2011.

UK Life Expectancy (ONS Life Tables) by age for Males

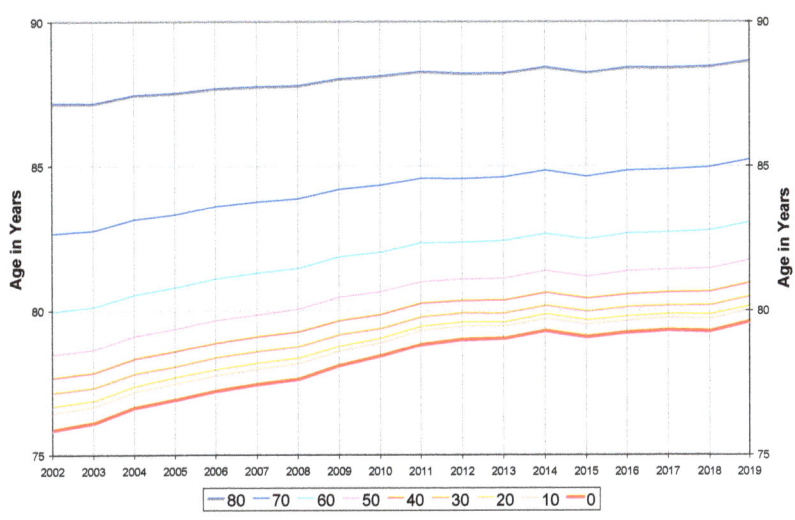

UK Life Expectancy (ONS Life Tables) by age for Females

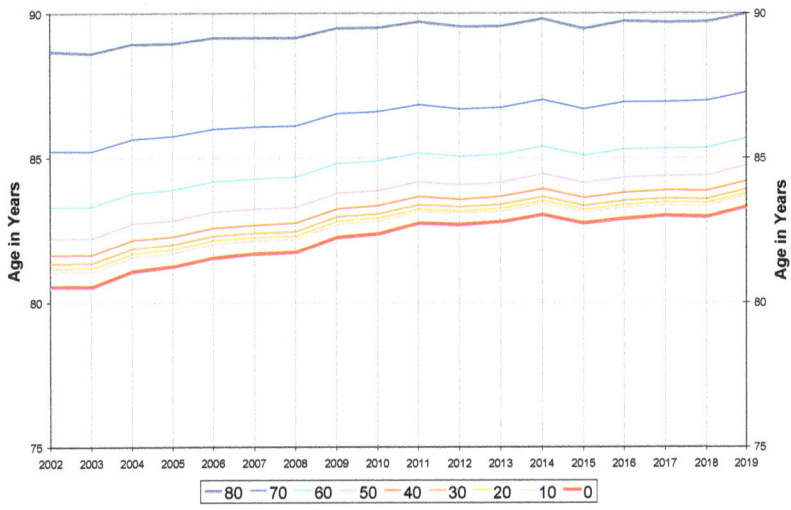

UK nations (ONS)

Having seen that the slowing of the rate of improvement of life expectancy is largely consistent for all age ranges and even for both males and females, we now look in more detail at the same single year life tables both for the UK and the constituent nations, again for both males and females, but this time only for life expectancy at birth.

In the chart at the top of the next page we show the trend for the population of the UK from the year 2000 to 2019 for females in the pink line, males in the blue line, both from the ONS single year life tables; also with the composite for all people in the red line from the Human Mortality Database, showing its correspondence with ONS Life Tables.

This clearly shows that all three are consistent in the slowing from 2011 to 2018, complete with obvious individual years in which visible falls in life expectancy have occurred. This latter is now more obvious for 2003, 2008, 2010, 2012 and 2015, due to the tighter scale.

It is actually for this reason that the *"consecutive 3 year"* National life tables are produced and classed as "National Statistics" to both smooth individual annual variance and ensure that a coherent long term picture of trends are made available. The ONS describes this as: *"Each life table is based on the population estimates and deaths by date of registration data for a period of 3 consecutive years"*.

Still continuing with the annual life table analysis, we are now able to look in more detail at the life expectancy outcomes at birth for the populations of each constituent nation for both males and females, as well as repeating the UK total aggregate life expectancy for all males and females as in the first chart.

Thus the middle chart shows the UK aggregate life expectancy at birth for all males in the dark blue line, as previously, but now we can see the same for all English males in the orange line, which sits consistently above that for the UK, whilst that for Welsh males in the cyan line and that for Northern Irish males in the olive green line sit below but close to the total for all UK males, and cross-over each other, suggesting generally similar but slightly varying annual outcomes over the 20 year period.

Most striking of all though is the consistently lower outcomes for Scottish males represented in the bright blue line, and in particular the significant but limited falls in 2007, then the very notable fall in 2015 until 2018, before the slight recovery in 2019.

The chart at the bottom of the page shows the same trends for females, in which the total for all UK females is again represented in the pink line, with the outcome for English females represented in the orange line and again generally similar patterns visible in the representation of Welsh and Northern Irish life expectancy outcomes for females.

A very similar pattern of life expectancy outcomes is again visible for Scottish females in the bright blue line and also clearly shows a similar pattern of falling expectation from 2015 to 2018, and a tiny gain in 2019.

UK Life Expectancy (ONS Tables and Human Mortality Database)

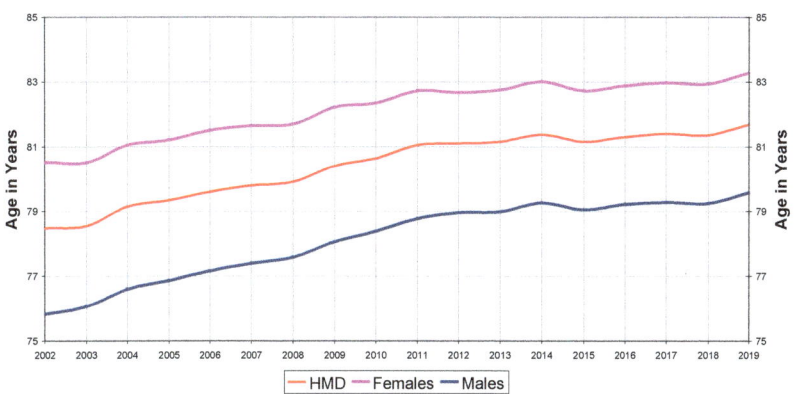

UK Life Expectancy (ONS Life Tables, 2002-2019) - Males

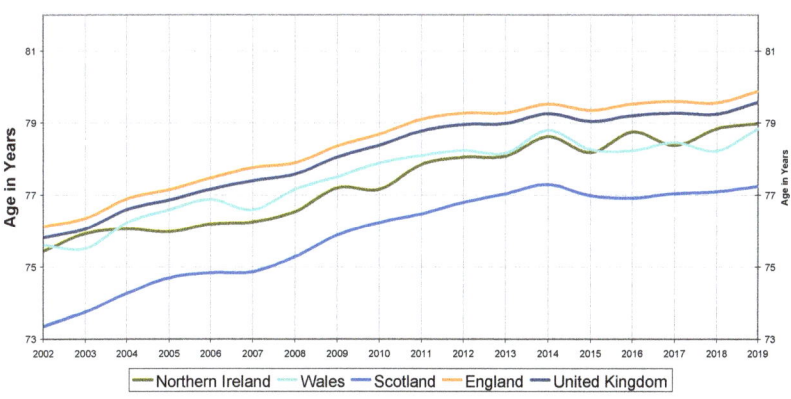

UK Life Expectancy (ONS Life Tables, 2002-2019) - Females

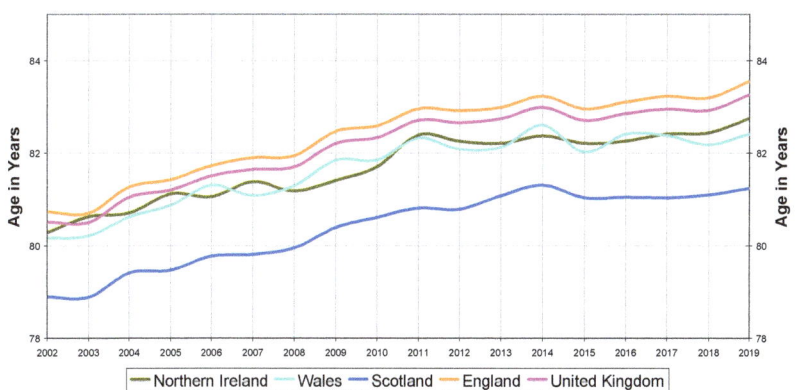

187

English regions (ONS)

Focussing now on the English and English regional life expectancy outcomes over the period of concern, we switch to the *"consecutive 3 year"* life tables, as the single year analysis is not readily available for English regions.

The chart at the top of the opposite page emphatically shows the smoothed trend of the slowing of the rate of increase in life expectancy very well. Again English female life expectancy is represented in the pink line, whilst that for English males in the dark blue line.

Again it also shows the gradual return to an increased rate of growth at the end of the period, mostly caused by the increase in 2019, seen previously for the UK and nations.

Over the period there is a slight visible narrowing of the gap between females and males.

Of particular note, at least for females, there is an indication that a weakening of the rate of increase is even visible from the *"consecutive 3 year"* period 2009-2011.

The middle and bottom charts on the opposite page represent the analysis of the *"consecutive 3 year"* life expectancy outcomes by English region for males and females respectively.

In population size these are closer to the populations of the constituent nations and might therefore be slightly more comparable accordingly.

The regions are quite diverse in geography, climate and social and economic characteristics and as such greater granularity of outcome becomes more visible.

The overwhelming picture that emerges from this English regional analysis is that the greatest improvement and most limited slowing of rate of improvement in life expectancy is clearly visible for male and female Londoners, represented in the very dark green line.

For the *"consecutive 3 year"* period 2001-2003 Londoners experienced a life expectancy notably lower than the South East, East of England and South West regions (and also East Midlands for males). By the period 2017-2019 both males and females experienced a life expectancy outcome greater than all other regions and constituent nations.

Also notable through the whole 18 *"consecutive 3 year"* periods represented, all nine English regions experience a slowing of the rate of increase of life expectancy for both males and females. Within these over-arching consistent trends however, is a notable reduction in life expectancy for males and females in the North East region from approximately 2011-2013, akin to that for the population of Scotland.

Visible, even for females in South West and East of England regions, are small reductions from the *"consecutive 3 year"* periods from 2013-2015 to 2015-2017.

These latter falls in life expectancy are mostly heavily influenced by the significant single year fall in 2015.

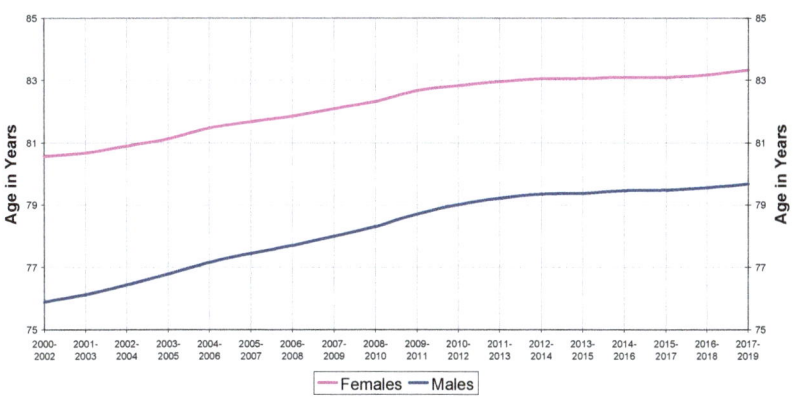

England Life Expectancy (ONS Life Tables, 2000-2002 to 2017-2019)

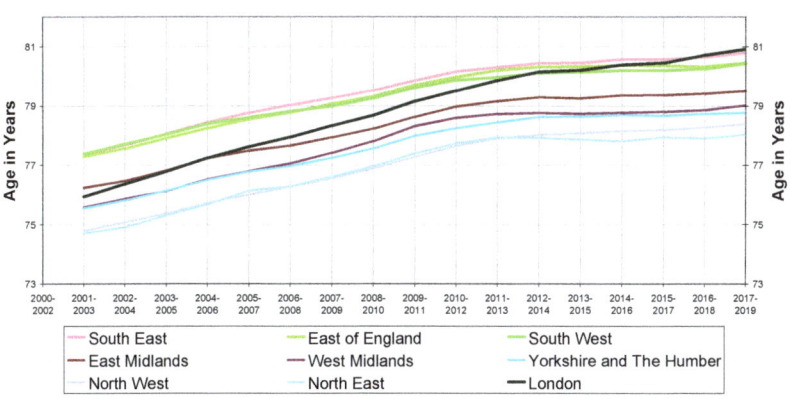

England Life Expectancy (ONS Life Tables, 2001-2003 to 2017-2019) - Males

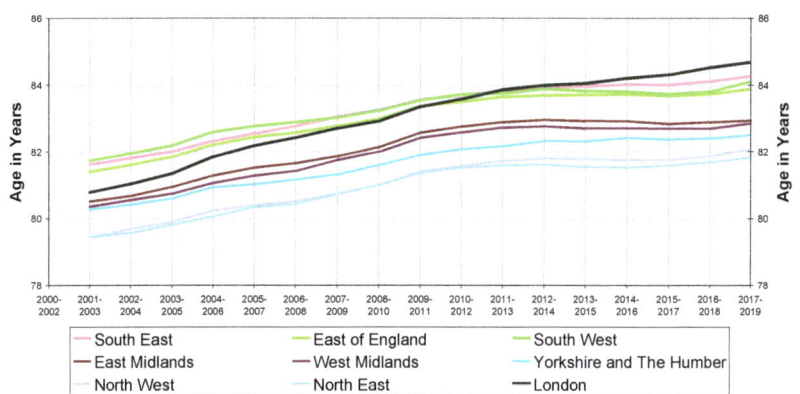

England Life Expectancy (ONS Life Tables, 2001-2003 to 2017-2019) - Females

English regions (2021 Imperial College London MSOA study)

Precisely because the slowing of the rate of increase of life expectancy for the UK and constituent nations from 2011 to 2018 has been observed and commented upon in the public discourse, a large team of thirteen health professionals and academics undertook a very detailed analysis of mortality and life expectancy outcomes for the English population, covering an eighteen year period from 2002 to 2019.

This study analysed life expectancy trends, in great detail to very small geographical areas known as *"middle-layer super output areas"* (MSOA), of which there are 6,791 defined for England and associated as sub-areas within English districts and in turn English regions.

It should be noted that in 2019 these small areas contained an average population of just under 8,300 people, almost 4,100 of whom were males, and almost 4,200 of whom were females. In addition, again for 2019, the average number of deaths per MSOA is calculated as 73.1, almost evenly split between males and females (for the first time in the 18 year period) at 36.5 per MSOA per sex. Though there is a notable trend towards such equal rates for the two sexes, based upon analysis of ONS published annual deaths for England, throughout these eighteen years.

The study findings by Rashid et al., published in October 2021 in the Lancet, as *"Life expectancy and risk of death in 6791 communities in England from 2002 to 2019: high-resolution spatiotemporal analysis of civil registration data"*, combined with their powerful geo-spatial analysis, identify the change in outcomes for males and females within MSOAs and highlight the concentrations of MSOAs that fared the worst during the period of the slowing of the rate of increase of life expectancy.

By undertaking a set of secondary analyses of the Imperial College London downloadable data, a useful confirmation of the regional concentrations of effects of annual change over time can be derived.

It is this secondary analysis that is strictly speaking *"incorrect"*, since it is not possible to re-weight this data by the true annual population estimates and deaths by sex per annum over the period. As such the precise resultant life expectancy years are wrong for each region and in fact consistently inflate the number of years of life expectancy for every region, for every year and for both sexes.

However the resulting annual trend patterns have proven to be very, very similar to the annual trend patterns published for England by the ONS, and even the *"consecutive 3 year"* trend patterns published by the ONS for English regions.

These consistent patterns are well demonstrated in the three charts on the opposite page, each of which is comparable to the equivalent three charts on the previous page. Visible in the results are the significant falls in 2015 and the out-performance of people in the London region against all other regions, as seen previously.

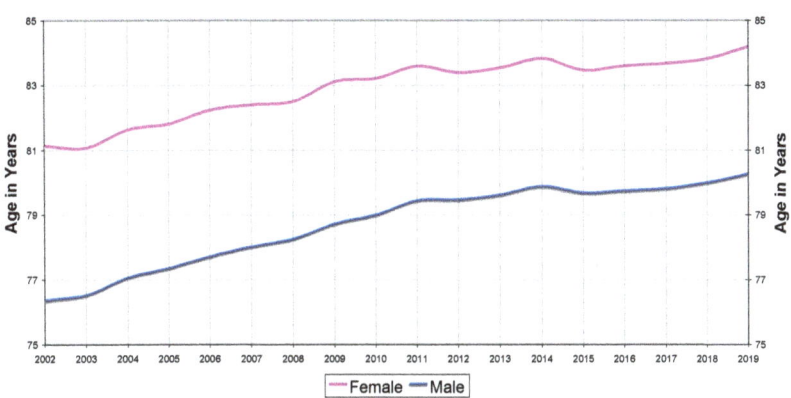

Crude Average Life Expectancy - England MSOA (middle layer super output areas)

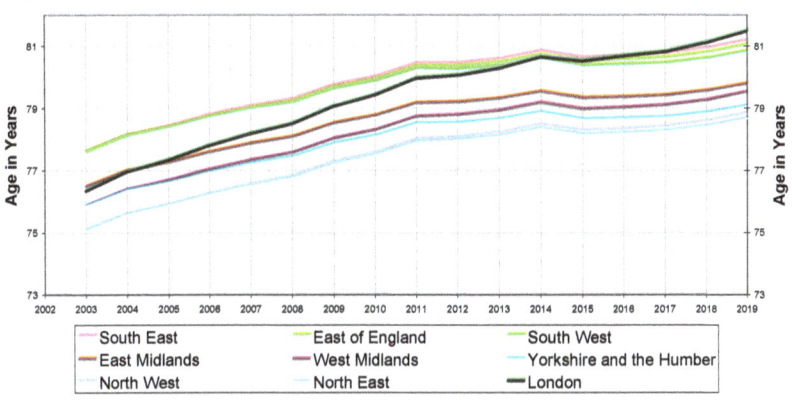

Crude Average Life Expectancy - Regions MSOA - Males

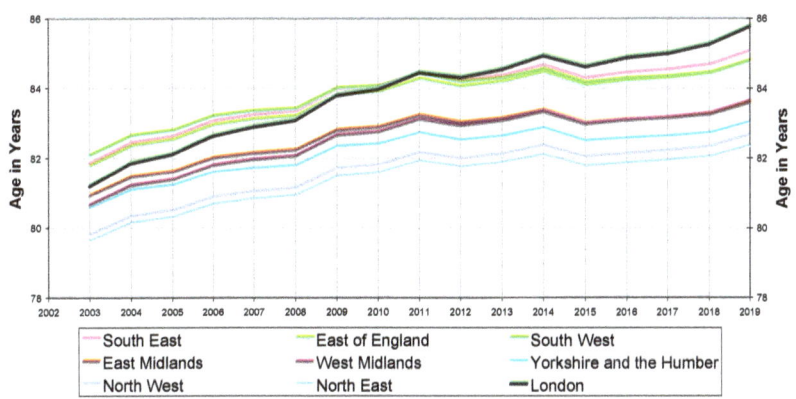

Crude Average Life Expectancy - Regions MSOA - Females

Annual changes (2021 Imperial College London MSOA study)

Accepting that the overall trends from this secondary analysis of the MSOA data from Imperial College London are at least reasonably comparable, it is possible to investigate these trends in relation to the annual change of outcome for males and females for England and the defined regions.

Again the precise gain or loss of years of life expectancy per annum is not necessarily always exact, since the un-weighted averages yield inflated years of life expectancy, but the trend does reveal differences and similarities over time.

In the chart at the top of the opposite page the overall annual changes for England from those un-weighted averages of all MSOAs are represented for females in the pink line and for males in the dark blue line.

This reveals three useful confirmatory trends.

In general the annual changes were more volatile for females than males throughout the period.

Also clearly visible is that in the fall/reduction in life expectancy outcomes in 2002-2003, 2011-2012 and 2014-2015 females consistently fared worse than males.

Also clear is that the annual changes are largely consistently lower in the right hand portion of the chart from 2011-2012 to 2017-2018, again only showing some sign of return to similar annual growth as the first decade in the rightmost annual change from 2018-2019.

Looking then at more detail for regions over this similar time period reveals that several striking patterns are visible for both males and females, represented in the charts in the middle and bottom of the opposite page respectively.

The first and most obvious is the consistent out-performance of annual change in life expectancy of the people of the London region, both males and females. This is revealed by the fact that the dark green lines, representing London, are consistently above the lines for all other regions throughout the study period from 2002 to 2019.

The second obvious pattern is that every region rises and falls for each year in concert, indicating that many aspects of the gains or losses of life expectancy are otherwise common for the populations of all regions, regardless of any particular differences or characteristics of those populations.

The third obvious pattern is that again, for all females in every region, annual changes were more volatile and loss of years of life expectancy greater for females in the same three annual changes as before, but particularly for the two worst years, marked as 2011-2012 and 2014-2015, with even London females experiencing an annual fall of years of life expectancy almost as great as people in all other regions.

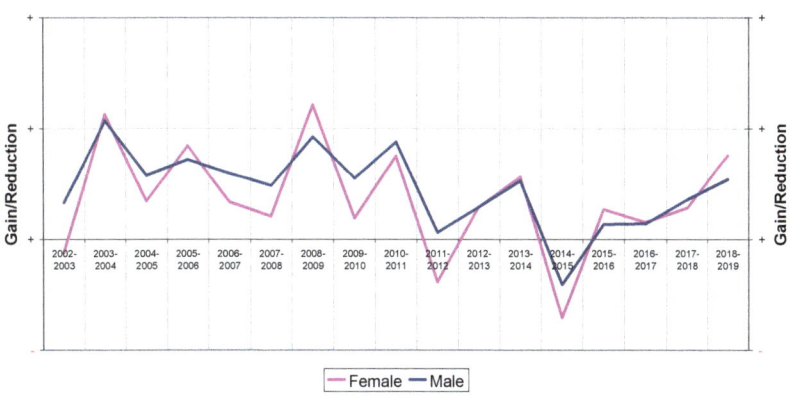

Crude annual gain/reduction of Life Expectancy for England - MSOA

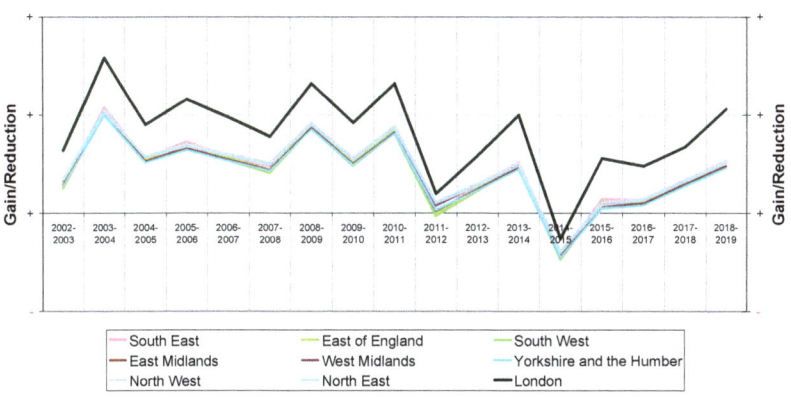

Crude annual gain/reduction of Life Expectancy for Regions MSOA - Males

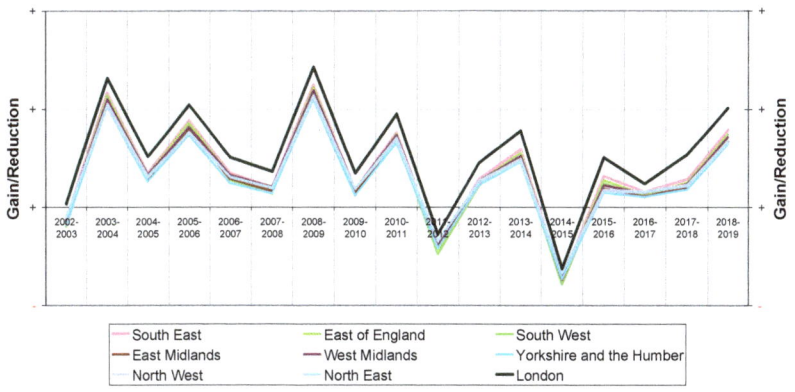

Crude annual gain/reduction of Life Expectancy for Regions MSOA - Females

England deciles sorted by change from 2011 to 2018 (2021 Imperial College London MSOA study)

Analysing the data for MSOAs for life expectancy outcome at birth by sex, for the years of gain or loss of that life expectancy between 2011 and 2018, allows us to return to a statistically more valid approach. This analysis ignores differences of population and deaths between MSOAs and treats each area as equivalent.

As such the total gain or loss of years of life expectancy, as calculated by the Imperial College analysis, is accumulated between 2011 and 2018, and is used to sort each MSOA in numerical order within sex.

By then dividing the 6,791 MSOAs into groups of 679 (or 680 for the last group) an analysis of the deciles (by 2011-2018 total outcome) of each MSOA can be produced for males and females.

The findings of the annual changes for each decile for males and females is presented in the two charts at the top and bottom of the opposite page respectively. It again reveals that in fact the annual change in gain or loss of years of life expectancy for each decile is almost perfectly consistent over the whole period, with only the 5th decile of females for the change between 2016 and 2017 showing a greater reduction, thereafter returning to the same relative change in the whole sequence.

This finding suggests unbroken annual consistency over the whole period for both males and females, but the analysis of these deciles by MSOA allows us to identify which regions have a greater or lesser share of their MSOAs within each decile. This is presented in the table below:

Decile	Yorkshire and the Humber	South West	East Midlands	East of England	North East	West Midlands	South East	North West	London
1	17.6%	16.3%	14.9%	11.7%	11.8%	8.0%	8.8%	7.0%	1.0%
2	14.2%	14.2%	13.4%	12.0%	10.7%	10.4%	9.3%	8.9%	1.8%
3	13.4%	13.3%	12.5%	10.5%	12.2%	10.7%	10.0%	10.3%	1.9%
4	10.9%	11.4%	12.0%	11.7%	9.3%	11.2%	11.1%	11.3%	2.8%
5	10.3%	9.5%	10.6%	11.5%	9.3%	11.5%	11.4%	12.2%	4.1%
6	8.6%	11.0%	11.1%	10.5%	9.1%	10.7%	11.6%	11.3%	6.0%
7	7.9%	9.8%	9.2%	9.0%	11.6%	12.2%	10.3%	11.3%	9.1%
8	8.8%	7.4%	7.9%	10.4%	12.2%	9.5%	11.2%	10.6%	11.2%
9	6.3%	5.5%	5.3%	8.3%	8.1%	11.5%	9.8%	11.5%	18.1%
10	2.0%	1.6%	3.0%	4.5%	5.7%	4.4%	6.4%	5.6%	43.9%
Bottom half	66.4%	64.7%	63.4%	57.3%	53.2%	51.8%	50.6%	49.7%	11.7%
Top half	33.6%	35.3%	36.6%	42.7%	46.8%	48.2%	49.4%	50.3%	88.3%

This analysis of MSOAs within deciles, based upon the loss or gain of life expectancy between 2011 and 2018, suggests that the people of the regions "Yorkshire and the Humber", "South West", "East Midlands" and "East of England" fared worst, in which a majority of their MSOAs fell in the bottom half of the dataset, whilst London fared dramatically better with almost 90% of its MSOAs falling in the top half of the dataset, and in fact almost 44% of their MSOAs falling in the top decile. These results support the statistical findings of the study team.

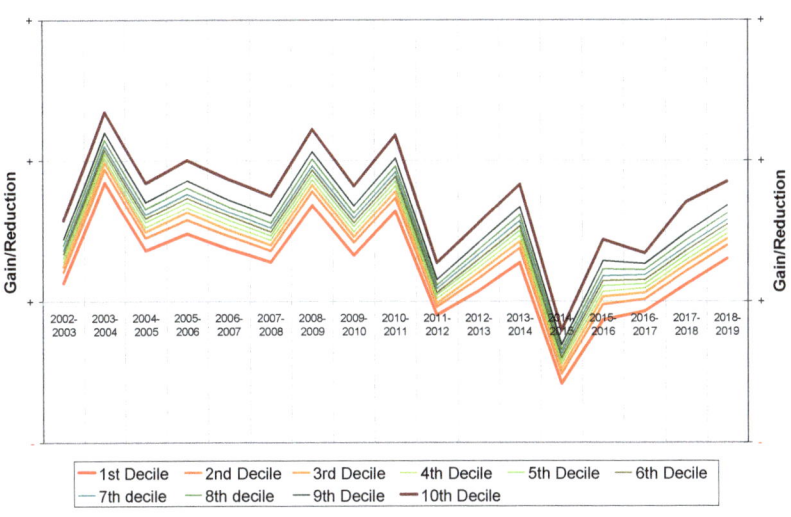

Crude annual gain/reduction of Life Expectancy for MSOA deciles - Males

Crude annual gain/reduction of Life Expectancy for MSOA deciles - Females

Life Expectancy by "deprivation deciles" (ONS)

Returning now to ONS data, they have provided a very useful analysis of life expectancy outcomes over the range of life's economic and social conditions, at least for most of the 21st century for the UK.

The divisions are expressed in terms of "deprivation deciles", being groupings of ten percent of each cohort of deaths in *"consecutive 3 year"* periods (to smooth the effects of annual changes), according to the relative socio-economic advantages and disadvantages (deprivation) of each ten percent group.

The ONS explain these groupings as: *"Deprivation deciles are based on the Index of Multiple Deprivation (IMD), which is the official measure of relative deprivation.*

"Decile 1 represents the most deprived and Decile 10 represents the least deprived."

These are not the same deciles as used in the previous analysis of the Imperial College London MSOA study, but are a very powerful analysis of socio-economic living conditions and subsequent life expectancy outcomes.

The two charts on the opposite page represent the *"consecutive 3 year"* life expectancy outcomes for the UK population for twelve *"consecutive 3 year"* periods, crucially incorporating the period of slowing of the improvement of life expectancy from 2011 to 2018.

Again these are split between males and females, with the patterns that emerge being very clear.

Firstly all decile groups of relative "deprivation" clearly show the presence of the effect of the slow down in the rate of improvement over the same time periods. However, now visible (as referred to previously), the trend for females tend to suggest an earlier and stronger slowing of the rate of improvement from 2010-2012, compared to males tending to exhibit a smaller reduction in the rate of improvement, gathering pace further from 2011-2013.

Very significant is that, whilst all deciles for both males and females exhibit at least the slowing of the rate of improvement, males in the lower half show only a slightly greater fall, and in fact tend to indicate little or no change, until a very small increase returns in the period 2017-2019.

However more striking is the loss of years of life expectancy for females in the first decile, from 2012-2014 to 2016-2018, with again a very small return to limited growth in the period 2017-2019.

This strongly tends to suggest that "deprivation" is a clear amplifying factor in determining life expectancy outcomes, and has noticeably fallen for the 1st decile of females during the period of slowing improvement for the UK as a whole. However the fact that all deciles of both sexes have experienced a slowing tends to suggest the cause is much more complex than the claims of the commonly held view in the public discourse.

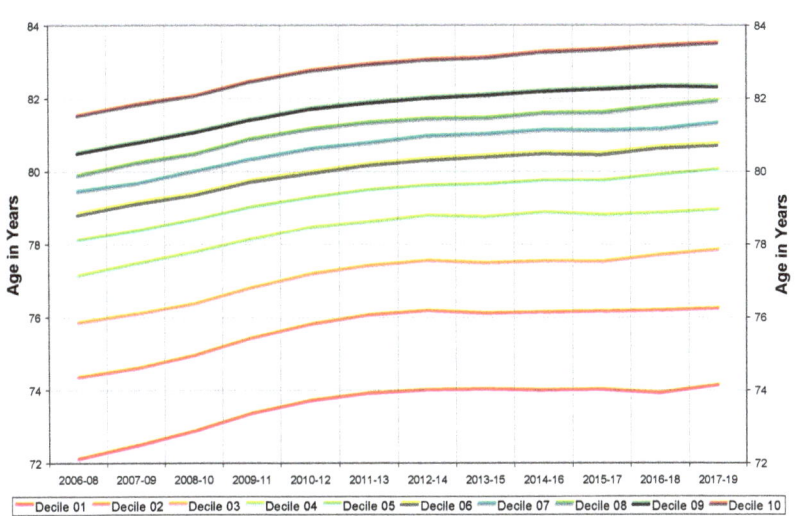

UK Life Expectancy by "deprivation" decile (ONS Life Tables) - Males

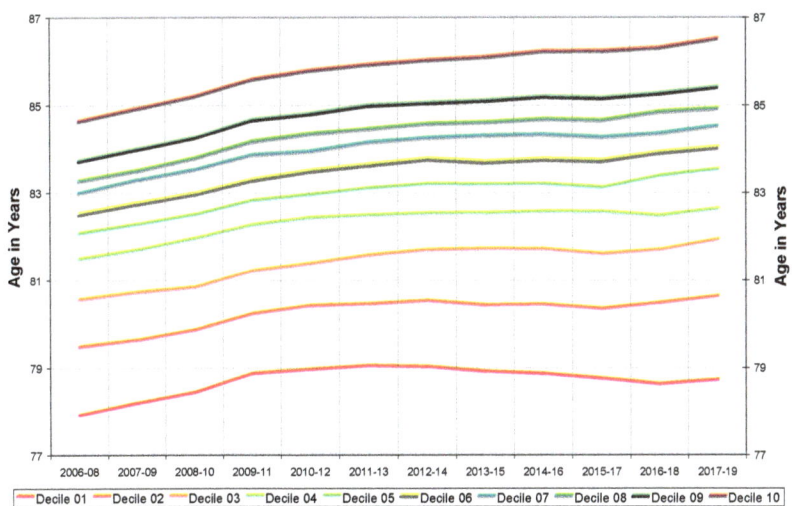

UK Life Expectancy by "deprivation" decile (ONS Life Tables) - Females

Life Expectancy since 1970 (World Bank, HMD, ONS)

At least on the basis of the analysis for life expectancy for the population of the UK as a whole, it is now very revealing to see if there are any comparable outcomes compared to other major developed countries over a similar time period.

The countries selected for comparisons are: *the USA, Canada, Australia, New Zealand, France, Germany, Spain, Netherlands, Norway and Sweden.*

The data source used, that offers an annual view of life expectancy for both males and females for these countries, is from the database of the World Bank. This extends from 1960 to 2019, for all these countries, of which the 50 years from 1970 to 2019 are used here.

Since we have established the compatibility of the single sex data lodged in the Human Mortality Database with the data for both sexes from the ONS, we continue to use that as the most representative picture of Life Expectancy for the UK.

The chart at the top of the opposite page presents the life expectancy outcomes for the ten countries mentioned against that for the UK (represented in the bold red line), all for the aforesaid period from 1970 to 2019.

At least from this data, the clear picture that is suggested from these data is that ten of the eleven countries, including the UK, exhibit varying degrees of the slowing of the rate of increase of life expectancy in most of the second decade of the 21st century; with only Sweden (represented in the light pink line) not showing any notable slowing trend.

Note an alternative data source that might have been used is from "Our World in Data", but this tends to show almost identical slowing to the World Bank data in the 8 years from 2011 to 2018, compared to the eight years from 2003 to 2010 for each country, though in a highly smoothed version, and is thus not an annual picture in the manner of the data from the World Bank, the Human Mortality Database and the ONS.

The chart in the middle of the opposite page extends the picture for the UK that collates the ONS annual data by sex and the combined picture for both sexes from the Human Mortality Database for the same 50 year period from 1970 to 2019, reiterating their similarity of trend.

Finally the chart at the bottom of the opposite page returns again to a representation of life expectancy outcome for the people of the UK by age range for the 50 years from 1970 to 2019.

The three charts again tend to support the notion that overall for the 50 year period, all of the eleven developed nations have found their population's life expectancy has improved, but clearly that of the USA has lagged behind the other ten since the 1990s.

Notably though, the slowing of the rate of improvement in life expectancy outcomes for most of the second decade of the 21st century is a near universal experience of the populations of ten of these countries.

Life Expectancy from World Bank/HMD/ONS (comparable selected countries)

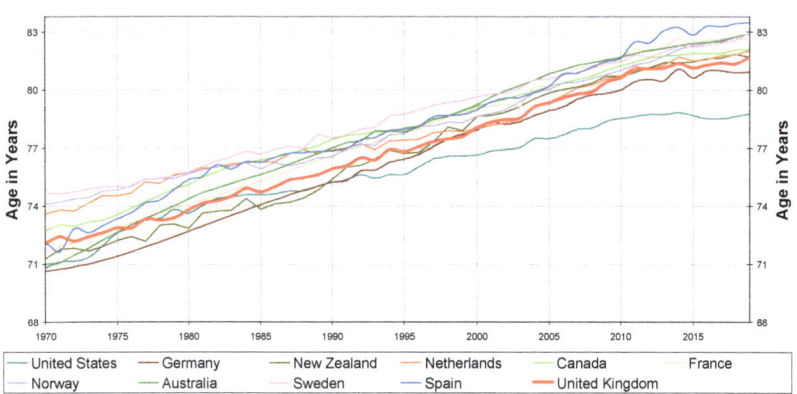

UK Life Expectancy (ONS Tables and Human Mortality Database)

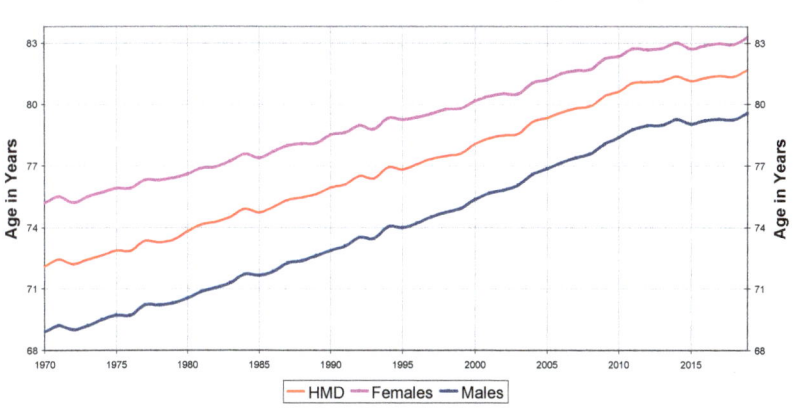

Life Expectancy at Decadal Age (ONS/Human Mortality Database)

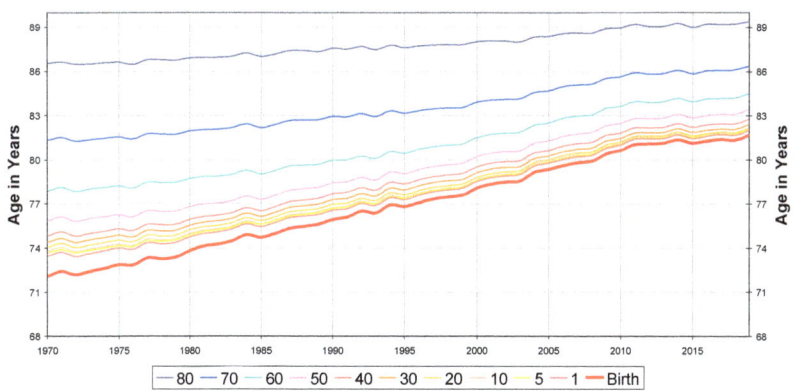

Is the 2008 economic crash a better explanation?

Not all countries in the group selected for comparison implemented policies of "*austerity*", and certainly not in the manner of that for the UK.

In addition we have seen that, most tellingly, all peoples of both sexes in all deprivation deciles in the UK experienced measurable slowing of their life expectancy outcomes in the near aftermath of the 2008 crash.

Plus all the peoples of both sexes from all constituent nations and English regions, and even for the broad age ranges from birth to age 80, all tended to exhibit the slowing of the rate of improvement over the same general period, and even some reduction in life expectancy outcomes for the least fortunate.

All findings are also re-iterated from the results of the secondary analyses of the Imperial College data for English people by MSOA.

It seems unavoidable to conclude that, as with the public discourses and the prevailing narratives previously discussed about;
- a house building "*shortage*",
- the prevalence of "*poverty*" (as normally conceived by most people),
- the "*pollution*" of the air (as caused by the majority of people's use of private motor vehicles),

that the claims that the slowing of the rate of improvement of life expectancy is the fault of the policy of "*austerity*", from June 2010 to October 2018, again seem to be somewhat exaggerated.

Once again the general tone of what appears to be ideological, and even partisan-political, claims, seem not to be well founded, at least as seen from the point of view of the best known facts, as derived from evidence, all available from all the most reliable sources.

Ten of the eleven countries all tend to exhibit similar and consistent slowing of life expectancy outcomes, though at varying rates, when comparing the 8 year period 2011-2018 to the 8 year period 2003-2010. In addition all other trends for the UK are repeated to different degrees from all analyses from all available data.

However, what is re-affirmed from these analyses is that the most significant contributor to improving life expectancy outcomes is prosperity, progress and economic well-being, as delivered slowly and falteringly, with many set-backs, for more than 300 years, from 1700 until the economic crash of 2008, being another of the set-backs.

Thus, lost in the public discourse, is the over-arching fact of 320 years of improvement of life expectancy outcomes, even in the 21st century.

Therefore the most important imperative is to re-focus attention back on the critically important driver of life expectancy (and also health), being prosperity and economic well-being.

As with the other narratives, pointing at the wrong "cause" guarantees that policies to address the problem will accordingly almost always fail.

Summary

"But it's in the nature of progress that it erases its tracks, and its champions fixate on the remaining injustices and forget how far we have come."

Steven Pinker:
Enlightenment Now,
2018

Findings from evidence

The journey, from the modern claims heard in the public discourse, as expressed throughout much of the broadcast and published media; plus increasingly the popular (self-expression) media, repeated over and over again by many prominent politicians; to the truth, found in the best known facts, derived from the actual evidence, produces a story of much greater relevance and power than any ideology or belief in unsubstantiated faith that any particular "imagined inexperience" can achieve.

Faith was and will always remain a major determinate of people's behaviour and ideas, but it was and equally will always remain a dangerous and distorting perspective on life's experiences when not based upon factual data from evidence and vital statistics.

Population

We have quantified the growth of the population of a set of small and insignificant islands to the north of the mainland continent of Europe. A set of islands repeatedly invaded and subjugated in the first millennium from the time of Christ; taking a further 700 years to find a new method of living and production of wealth; through the turbulence of the 16th century schism with the Roman Catholic church, the establishment of a local system of Protestant-like faith and gradually increasing self-belief, via a new reformation; in the 17th century accompanied by internal division and civil war, as well as continual internal constituent national division. From this long early development a new nation state emerged at the start of the 18th century, between 1688 and 1707.

Thereafter for over 300 years its population grew and spread around the world, along with its new language of English. It absorbed, developed and expanded an economic system, with the Dutch, that set in motion unprecedented social and economic progress for all humanity. All subsequently exported to and adopted by the world's great powers, those we variously call the "western", "developed" or "modern" powers.

We have seen that population grow from just 6.6 million people in 1700 to 67 million people in 2019 (as consistent with modern borders).

Notably when we look at the population of England and the UK in the middle of the 18th century and compare such with its major neighbours, the contrast is striking. In 1750 the English population is estimated to be just 5.8 million (7.6 million UK), whilst the French population is estimated to be 24.5 million, German 18.4 million, Italian 15.2 million and Spanish 11.3 million. Just a century later, England's population had increased to 16.5 million (22.1 million UK) (*288%* growth), French 35.9 million (*146%* growth), German 35 million (*190%* growth), Italian 23.7 million (*156%* growth) and Spanish 15.7 million (*139%* growth). These trends then accelerated further in the 170 years after the middle of the 19th century.

The Malthusian spectre of starvation, due to population growth outperforming productivity, had for the first time in history been overcome in a sustained way. All thanks to the development of the joint stock company, the new industrial methods of production, and international trade on a colossal scale; underpinned by the essential consistent and non-arbitrary rule of law; the slow development of strictly limited constitutional government, evolving into representational democracy; respecting property and the liberty of the individual.

We have seen the fall in death rates, the increase in birth rates, with a steady increase in life expectancy for all. Interestingly we have also seen that for almost the whole of the first three hundred years the English and British emigrated in good and steady numbers to found (in the earlier centuries) and establish strong new Anglo-phone colonies and subsequent new nation states, all imbued with these core principles; to the benefit of the populations throughout the nations and continents of the world.

Economy and State

We have seen that the economic system of these islands was transformed from an already unusually less agricultural basis, probably due to the trading nature of that early mercantile system, to a new evermore heavily industrialised method of producing goods, accompanied by evermore mechanised systems of agriculture. Powered by coal.

From these transformations, at first came hardship and gain in equal measures, accompanying large internal migration away from land-based labour and domicile to town and city-based labour and domicile. The modern access to, and interest in, historical family based records reveals, to the people and their ancestors native to these islands for these many centuries, this pattern of change over and over again.

Governments, both national and local, adapted their policies to offer some assistance, no matter how limited, to aid those in distress from these huge social and economic upheavals, and in turn, thanks to assiduous documentation, help us to discover evidence that illustrate these changes.

Thus, we have powerful measures, descriptions and evocations of the hardships of life, all substantiated by illustrative counts of people throughout the centuries living in the midst of these upheavals.

From these multiple sources, analysed by the foremost historians and academics, we have been able to build a solid picture of the real and sustained growth of the economy that, from a very slow start, gradually shared the benefits of the new "industrial revolution", as it gathered pace throughout the 18th and 19th century and into the 20th century.

We have also been able to see the huge economic consequences of ever greater expenditure on military systems and war. From the very outset of the new era, we saw King William III then Queen Anne and their General John Churchill, later ennobled as the Duke of Marlborough, in their wars against King Louis XIV of France. From those years onwards Great Britain continued to bring itself into great debt as the process of the growth of global trade, international expansion, and eventually direct continental conflicts erupted in the French Revolutionary and Napoleonic wars. Over a century later two similar conflicts with Germany erupted in the first half of the 20th century. All affordable, due to burgeoning wealth.

We have also been able to see the gradual awakening, amongst many of the powerful groups of people who were the direct beneficiaries of the new economy, of a perception of the need to move beyond the early ideological concepts of "Political Economy" and "laissez faire" government; this awakening, was particularly notable in the aftermath of the appalling numbers of deaths, extreme hardship and mass depopulation in Ireland following the great "potato famine" of the 1840s.

We have then been able to see the gradual introduction of new policies of education and the move away from the old "Poor Law" system of relief of distress, to a centralised approach to the nascent "Welfare State" from the early years of the 20th century.

Earnings and Incomes

Thanks to a multitude of disparate records, analysed again by the foremost academics of the last century and a half, who pieced together the soundest view of the earnings and incomes of the greatest range of people throughout the UK, we have seen a powerful picture of the gradual growth in the earnings of, particularly, working labourers.

For the earnings for labourers, at first we have seen the direct effects of the change of the economic system from a more agricultural pre-eminence to the new industrial pre-eminence over the first two centuries of our period of analysis. The shift of emphasis from agricultural work to the new work of the factories forced the previously mentioned migration to new and invariably over-crowded towns and cities. These changes gradually held back the earnings of agricultural labourers, but slowly increased the earnings of urban labourers over these centuries.

However, it is imperative to be under no illusion about the social and economic well-being of the agricultural labourers before the worst effects of these urbanisation changes are seen.

Rural life was never an idyll that was lost due to the "industrial revolution". The horrors of urban industrial life, so thoroughly described by Friedrich Engels in *"The Conditions of the Working Class in England"* (amply supported by the writings of Elizabeth Gaskell, Charles Dickens, Henry Mayhew, Andrew Mearns and countless others) do not mean that life for rural labourers in the preceding centuries was other than hard and short, living in dreadful accommodation with too little food and warmth.

Life expectancy simply did not rise for almost anyone until after the middle of the 18th century, particularly labourers and their families.

In addition, the growing wealth of the economy both needed and encouraged new non-labouring "white collar" roles in the economy, and so grew the group of people who became known as the "middle-classes" (so-called as they are supposed to sit socially and economically between the "upper-classes", generally the former land-owners and new major industrialists and the "lower-classes" or "working-classes" who earn their incomes from their own physical labour).

This group of people have become the largest and dominant social and economic grouping in society over the latter half of the period we have studied, and especially so since the gradual de-industrialisation of the economy since the end of The Second World War.

Also we have seen the growth in the value of, and broadening of, the receipt of state administered "social protection" for the least well off, from the early years of the 20th century, but again, particularly from the decades after the end of The Second World War.

These protections, of course, are never enough to satisfy everyone, and have become costly to fund and administer, but still mark a total contrast with the centuries before the 20th century, from when the real benefits of the new system started to become available to ever more people.

Income Inequality

Again thanks to several imperfect, but well understood, and correlated contemporary analyses of the distribution of incomes over the whole period we have studied, we have been able to gauge how the inequality of incomes have changed over these centuries.

From this we have seen that the data suggest a very small and probably almost imperceptible increase of inequality of income over the first century and half, almost certainly peaking in the period somewhere between the 1860s and 1880s, being the time of greatest accumulation of income by large industrialists.

This is mostly related to a move of greatest economic gain and wealth from the early landed "upper-classes" to the new industrial "upper-classes". Accompanied by the acquisition of estates by the latter from the declining families of the former.

All the data available then points to a general reduction of inequality, shocked into more extreme drops particularly by the effects of The Great War and The Second World War.

These findings apply to all of the best analyses of personal incomes, and are well documented from the work of Robert Dudley Baxter onwards, but especially by the detailed analysis of the Inland Revenue data from the period of the Liberal government in 1911 onwards, to the modern analysis known as the "Survey of Personal Incomes".

By also analysing the data from the detailed studies of household expenditure and earnings, undertaken to inform ever more beneficial government policies from the start of the 20th century, but especially after The Second World War, a similar pattern of reducing inequality has been found, at least until the end of the 1970s. This whole trend corresponds with the period of growing, and then almost universal acceptance, of what later became known as "*the post-war consensus*".

It is in the light of this period, that accompanied an economic adjustment that has become known as "de-industrialisation"; then the general social and economic disruptions of the decade of the 1970s, allied to the international "oil crisis", with its large and negative economic impact, that we have seen a new period of economic regeneration and greater freedom of commercial opportunity being unleashed by the Thatcher government of the 1980s. As with earlier shocks and transformations, this decade was one of significant regional disruption and some decline, some being still felt in some areas four decades later.

It is from this decade that we have seen a small increase of inequality of income until the early 1990s, after which it generally stabilised again with small increases to 2007, before the impact of the 2008 economic crash slightly reduced that inequality again for the subsequent decade.

The data analysed suggests continuing small changes each year, some of which are slightly greater than others, but none suggesting the levels of change and contortions present throughout previous centuries.

Cost of Living

Although data are not available to document the costs of all or even the majority of items typically purchased by most people on a weekly or monthly basis over the whole period, we have been able to track the price of the core staple of bread and its constituent grains (or as the English call it, corn) from 1700 onwards.

As with all other measures, as the economy and the population have become materially better off, so resources have increased to document and track more and more important items that have informed us of the cost of living for a typical or "average" household.

The foremost academic historians have built a well understood and reliable set of indices that support the analysis of these cost measures, and since the end of The Second World War, collected measures and indices have become more comprehensive and thorough, thanks to the ONS.

The findings from these data strongly support the overall qualitative impression of improving economic well-being for the overwhelming majority of people in the United Kingdom, as the real cost of living has improved, almost continuously over most of the 320 years of the study period.

Bread no longer constitutes a major share of typical household expenditure, and in fact its relative consumption per person has actually fallen compared to the 18th century, even this alone strongly suggests how much the cost of living has improved for almost everyone.

Expanding the analysis to other items we have seen that in most cases this improvement is also sustained for the more recent decades for such available data.

In the record we have seen the effects of the various wars and the "oil crisis" of the 1970s, but particularly significant for the modern era, we have repeatedly seen the effects of the 2008 economic crash.

This latter economic crash has shown itself to be sustained in the effect on both incomes and the living costs incurred, with only a very slow return at the end of the period studied, in 2019, to cost of living levels seen before the crash.

However other signals of worsening cost of living indicators in the 21st century are also available from the same data. These include very large increases in the "real" cost of housing, particularly if attempting to purchase a property of one's own; plus the "real" cost of household energy in the form of electricity and gas, particularly from the years 2000 and 2005 onwards respectively; plus the "real" cost of motor transport insurance, and to a lesser extent fuel, also show significant sustained increases from the middle of the first decade of the 21st century onwards.

Whilst food remained, on average, an ever deceasing share of the cost of living for most people, the improvement of material well-being of life in general in the second decade of the 21st century sadly does show a sustained lack of improvement, compared to improvements previously.

Housing

One of the very interesting findings that has emerged from the study of the vital statistics is the lack of strong supporting evidence for the narrative that a "shortage" of house building has led to an explosion of house prices relative to the incomes of prospective purchasers since the 1990s. The claim being that such a lack of new building has led to a shortage of purchasable housing that has thereby forced prices of those properties that have appeared on the market to rise accordingly in response to demand.

Historically we have found that there have been five notable periods of booms and four subsequent falls of house prices; the late 1940s in the immediate aftermath of The Second World War; the period of the early 1970s corresponding to the "Barber boom"; the period of late 1970s; the period of the late 1980s; then the fifth and now sustained period of hugely inflated house prices since the late 1990s. This last has shown no sign of house prices falling to previously calculated "affordable" levels in relation to incomes of households. This is true even in the aftermath of the 2008 crash, that itself was caused by these unsustainable house prices that preceded it.

Reviewing the five booms and four falls tells us: the first such boom is connected to the effects of economic disruption, loss of housing stock from the war itself and the subsequent shortage of labour and materials to begin rebuilding in the aftermath of war. This corrected itself after about a decade and allowed the rise of the home owning opportunity for the majority of people, at last, from the mid-1950s.

All of the next three booms and falls in house prices are all entirely connected to economic drivers, rather than availability or shortage of housing stock and the price booms are clearly stopped in each case due to high and rising interest rates that then subsequently fell, returning mortgage repayments to affordable levels at the reduced house prices.

The data suggest that the boom that began in the late 1990s again shows every sign of being economically and fiscally driven, but is then compounded by other policy effects of the government of those years.

Using the key macro data of population and housing counts, the resultant calculation of average economy-wide household occupancy rates suggest little apparent "shortage" of housing, viewed from the perspective of both long-term and medium-term trends since after The Second World War. Though slowing, falling occupancy rates do not halt until after the 2008 crash, in 2010, then rise slightly thereafter before returning to 2008 levels in 2019. This over-all macro calculation is also supported by the figures for the distribution of the size of households by the number of occupants from single person households and more.

Thus, since the decade from 1997 to 2007 was one of expansive and easily available credit, we see that this fuelled demand, including the new "buy-to-let" phenomenon; and the consequent surge in house prices was never checked by fiscal policy or market forces using interest rates as over the decades previously.

The imposition of the policy of mass immigration, introduced in 1997, gradually compounded the pressure on housing demand, but this tended to follow the start of the rise of house prices that began after the low point of 1995/1996, as the trend of easy credit availability that was prevalent from the mid-1990s onwards led the pressure.

The highest immigration numbers were felt from 2000 onwards, particularly after 2003 when the EU open borders policy was imposed, when thereafter annual estimates from Home Office/ONS "Long Term International Migration" analysis indicate over ¼ million people migrating into the UK per annum, net of those emigrating from the UK, for 15 years.

Thus the data strongly suggests easy availability of credit, and the behaviour it triggered internationally and in the UK, then caused the ultimate 2008 economic crash, "credit crunch" and collapse of house building.

Poverty

Using detailed and thorough data from over the centuries that describes household expenditure, receipt of "social protection" in its various forms, and, in the era from the early 20th century, actual surveys, a very strong pattern that represents a more consistent view of real poverty, distress and even destitution over the centuries has been found.

Taking a rational and evidence based view of these findings, that can be measured in any real sense, overwhelmingly supports the otherwise widespread qualitative view that real poverty in the UK has retreated compared to earlier centuries.

The primary driver of the retreat of real poverty is national economic productivity creating real tangible wealth that was slowly distributed to more and more people over the time period.

This gathered pace from the late 19th century as more enlightened perspectives, more akin to a modern sense of morality and justice, supplanted the morality of previous centuries.

It was this very shift of moral philosophy that started to express itself with the campaign to firstly abolish the slave trade, then abolish slavery itself, and even stamp it out internationally. It then extended wider and wider into the prevailing morality of the people of Britain, to look upon those subsisting on the meagre incomes, housing and food consumption who were called "the poor", and even worse the "destitute" and "paupers".

It was the very "industrial revolution", and the vast wealth that it created, that enabled the abolition of the ancient and abhorrent system of slavery, and then gradually shared the proceeds of that wealth with more and more people and created a new morality. All possible only thanks to increased productivity and wealth.

Again those lives of real poverty are painfully well documented in the writings of the aforesaid authors, including Engels, Gaskell, Dickens, Mayhew, Mearns and also the earlier writings about the rural poor by William Cobbett for example, and the early analysis by the Reverend David Davis and Sir Frederick Eden amongst many others. These emphatically describe real and debilitating poverty and destitution. Even the records kept by the Poor Law guardians throughout the UK, and England in particular, expose the depths and persistence of real poverty throughout those earlier centuries.

Looking at the best available analysis from the surveys from the start of the 20th century, alongside the studies of the greatest of the reformers and campaigners, Charles Booth and Seebohm Rowntree, the quantitative picture is strong and consistent. Looking then at the surveys after The Second World War, even including the work of the great campaigners Peter Townsend and Brian Abel-Smith, and particularly their own surveys akin to the Family Expenditure Survey, cannot avoid revealing the slow retreat of real poverty in the post-war decades.

Using the data in a consistent way from these detailed studies emphasises the fact of that retreat in every real sense, and also reveals the alternative "relative" patterns of inclusion and exclusion from economic gains that have become accepted in the modern public narrative as a representation of so-called "poverty".

Using the evidence, the data and these best known and understood facts, and by applying a more consistent approach, we have seen that real poverty, such that was described so well by the contemporaries of earlier centuries, has retreated even for all but the very least well served in modern Britain.

It might be argued that it is now, the thankfully much smaller numbers of those modern rough sleepers, compared to the very large numbers of "vagabonds", "tramps" and the "destitute" (as understood until the most recent years), who are the people left languishing in something akin to the same "real" state of poverty of the past.

This does not mean that poverty in any "real" sense, let alone the newly conceived "relative" sense, has been banished from the UK. It certainly has not. But it does afflict fewer people than ever before.

Using data based evidence is a much better way to identify, investigate and thereby attempt to understand the causes of such hardship, and only this way possibly to find ways to provide methods of assistance to help people to escape such difficult lives.

Air Quality

Although data based evidence of the state of air quality and pollutants, emitted by the processes that support our modern lives of well-being, health and freedom, is limited to just the last fifty years, it has revealed an overwhelmingly positive story of huge and consistent improvement.

Historically we know that cities in earlier centuries were always full of pollution of the air and water, with untreated sewage prevalent almost everywhere until the first modern attempts to clear all aspects of these pollutants in the middle of the 19th century.

The prime example of such pollution being the so-called "great stink" of 1858 and the subsequent work of, amongst others, Joseph Bazalgette. It is also useful to reflect upon an even earlier example revealed by the pioneering photography of William Henry Fox-Talbot who unwittingly captured the state of atmospheric pollution in London in 1844 when he photographed the construction of the new "Nelson's column" in Trafalgar Square in central London.

We are also aware of the so-called London "smog" of the 1950s and 1960s that were again evidence of significantly worse air quality and atmospheric pollution than at any time since data monitoring records have been kept from 1970.

By studying all of these published data and their analysis, they conclusively prove that for fifty years there has been continuous improvement of the air quality of the whole country, including all of the worst affected cities and even their worst roadside spots. All despite the continuous growth of the population; the ever greater ownership and use of motor transport; even despite the significant move to the use of diesel powered motor cars for private transport from the start of the 21st century. It is interesting to note that this latter was a classic example of a policy of governmental "persuasion" from the basis of incomplete and narrow ideology fixated on Carbon Dioxide emissions only.

Again we have seen that data provides evidence, and illustrates the best known facts of the improving air quality, in stark contrast to the public narrative of, what is in fact, imaginary "terrible" air quality from pollution, being most often blamed upon the vast majority of people who own and use private motor cars.

This contrast between reality, as exposed by the actual data, compared to the imaginary negative narrative is even revealed by the very large increase of life expectancy of the overwhelming majority of the people of London, as measured over the first two decades of the 21st century; corresponding to the very time in which the public narrative has become most shrill about "terrible" air quality harming people and foreshortening their lives.

Life Expectancy

Studying the greatest extent of historical data that provides the evidence of the start of the increase of life expectancy for the people of the UK from the middle of the 18th century, and then throughout most of these 320 years, re-emphasises the real progress achieved for the vast majority of people in that time.

The evidence reveals the interruptions from particularly The Great

War and The Second World War, the effects of the "Spanish Influenza" of 1918 and 1919, and shows recurring short term patterns of annual gain and loss that intersperse with the long term improvement.

We have seen that the relative life expectancy is generally higher for women than for men, though improving slowly for men in recent years. But particularly, the data has revealed the earlier terrible effects of infant mortality in which hygiene, dietary inadequacy and prevalence of disease killed very large numbers of new born and infant children for centuries.

In these data we have seen the gains that delivered real improvements from the time of the establishment of the National Health Service; that provided funded health care "free at the point of delivery", that made such a difference to the majority of people living in economic hardship, poverty and distress in earlier decades; already unimaginable to younger generations with no real knowledge of such a life.

The data has also revealed a consistent slowing of the rate of improvement in the second decade of the 21st century and that data has allowed us to reveal the variations of relative life expectancy and change of such over time for the UK's constituent nations and England's regions.

As previously mentioned, the one region in which the life expectancy outcomes of the people of that region have clearly not followed the same trend as the rest of the peoples of the UK is in London.

Looking at the data for life expectancy for the people of the UK grouped by the "deprivation deciles" the same trend of the slowing is evident for both males and females and in fact all deprivation deciles.

Thanks to the latest very detailed study from Imperial College London we see again the same patterns over the same period, though amply highlighting notable small districts experiencing the worst outcomes.

Again it is data that provides evidence that allows proper analysis of findings from the best known facts that can suggest meaningful solutions that can potentially be identified; and consequently rationally targeted actions and policies that might be attempted to address real issues for real people and help improve life expectancy outcomes for as many people as possible, in a cost effective way.

Real progress achieved

Collating and representing the story in the manner we have been able to do here, allows us to see the undeniable fact of real progress in every material aspect of life for the vast majority of the people of the United Kingdom for most of the last 320 years.

With faltering and slow gains that gathered momentum, accompanied by many set-backs including wars, from those of the 18th century, culminating in the French Revolutionary and Napoleonic Wars, that lasted from 1793 to 1815; then continuing smaller wars throughout the 19th century; and the huge and devastating conflicts of The Great War and The Second World War; terrible economic downturns such as the "the hungry

'40s", the "cotton famine", "the great depression" from 1929, the "oil crisis" and subsequent "IMF crisis" of the 1970s, the great economic upheaval of the 1980s that attempted to regenerate and revitalise the UK economy through profound restructuring, and more recently, the aftermath of the 2008 economic crash; we have been able to see that real progress by all measures has been made over these centuries.

From 1700 we have seen that for most of the these centuries, that population has grown, incomes have increased, income inequality fallen and largely settled at a sustainable level, social protection, education and health care have extended to help everyone in society, ownership of a home of one's own has extended to more people, "real" poverty has retreated, air quality has improved and people's general health and life expectancy has also improved for 300 years or so.

Real progress stalled

All of the these gains have noticeably slowed in the 21st century, in the wake of underlying issues from the mid-1990s, culminating in the 2008 economic crash and its persistent aftermath.

From these data we have seen that the very high population growth of the 21st century is mostly driven by policies of mass immigration introduced in 1997. Inevitably such a pace of immigration created immense social disruption and consequent loss of social cohesion. It is unsurprising that so many communities voted so overwhelmingly to leave the EU in the 2016 referendum on continuing membership.

We have seen that improvements of the GDP of the economy, share per person and the "real" incomes and earnings have stalled since 2008 and personal and household debt, corporate debt and national debt have all increased throughout the period since the start of the 21st century. The government response to implement a policy of "quantitative easing", or what was once formerly known as "printing money" has of course, delayed some of the worst immediate effects of the 2008 crash, but has also contributed to the building of pressure for a return to severe inflation. This of course has been accompanied by record low interest rates that in turn have allowed the huge debt levels to remain temporarily sustainable, but have further encouraged the acquisition of more debt and consequent unabated pressure on already inflated house prices.

We can see increased cost of living prevalent in the 21st century for the core items of housing, household energy and personal motor transport. Much of this was caused by the aforesaid policy choices of the decade before the economic crash, but another policy choice that emerged from the late 1990s was the new adoption of a "climate change" agenda that discouraged exploration for oil and gas, the ultimate moratorium on extraction of shale gas in 2019 and the hugely expensive diversion of tax payer funded subsidies to so-called "renewable energy", such as the grossly inefficient solar power generation (achieving only an 11% load-factor, and contributing only 0.7% of the UK's energy in 2019 and requiring enormous land areas that produce tiny amounts of power per square kilometre); the only slightly less inefficient on-shore wind turbine power generation (load factors of 25% and also requiring huge land areas); at least off-shore wind turbine power generation has the potential to be slightly more efficient (currently managing 40% load factors). It is worth noting that all wind power generation only contributed 3.5% of the UK's energy in 2019, evenly split between on-shore and off-shore generation.

All such "renewable" generation sources require continued huge tax-payer subsidies, thereby encouraging their adherents to make claims that they are "cheap" energy sources compared to coal, oil, gas and nuclear energy. Note also that they are entirely unreliable for much of the time and are yet to be supported by any affordable or practical method of storing excess power that may be later recovered when needed.

We have seen that the house price crisis, and the failure of the government and the Bank of England to attempt any fiscal control in the late 1990s, led directly to the reduced ability of first time buyers to buy a home of their own from the mid-1990s onwards, and the fall in the share of households who were owner occupiers from 2002. All leading directly to the 2008 economic crash and making housing more expensive for younger families throughout the 21st century.

We have also seen a measurable return to slightly greater levels of hardship in the first decile of surveyed household expenditure from the late-1990s onwards, despite a very slow and limited recovery in other measures, at least returning at the end of the second decade of the 21st century, to levels seen on the eve of the 2008 crash.

Interestingly whilst air quality continues to improve, there is some slowing of the rate of improvement in the aftermath of the 2008 economic crash, perhaps correlated with the need for more people to keep older motor cars running for longer, due to household budgets being squeezed by the cost of living increases in the wake of the crash, and the energy policy choices governments have imposed on people. The increasing average age of registered motor cars since the 2008 economic crash is evident in the data from the Department for Transport.

We have even seen the slowing of the rate of improvement of life expectancy in most of the second decade of the 21st century, again correlating very closely with the aftermath of the 2008 economic crash.

Evidence contra ideology

Evidence, data and the best known facts present us with truth. It seems that economic and affordable technical progress overwhelmingly underpin real life-enhancing well-being for people. This well-being can only be achieved if governments, commentators and therefore people are presented with these best known facts and appreciate the findings from that evidence, in preference to fixated ideology and prejudice.

Historically we have seen the effects of fixated ideology, that passed moral judgements on the majority of people who were genuinely in real poverty, many in extreme poverty and even real destitution.

We have seen direct effects in their most severe case in the ideological fixation with "laissez faire" policies in the terrible outcome following the potato famine in Ireland in the 1840s. We have seen the corruption of thinking and ideology in the era of colonialism in which some colonists began to believe in some inherent superiority of purpose and judgement and even morality again. We have seen the ultimate adherence to that inflated sense of self-belief and superiority in which multiple great powers allowed themselves to engage in a war of destruction, The Great War, not seen before, that itself and its aftermath ended up in the even greater devastation of The Second World War.

From the emergence of new secular faith based ideologies of the 19th century, new political movements emerged and took hold in the 20th century that resulted in deaths on a colossal scale, especially for the peoples of the countries in which these ideologies seized power in Russia, Italy, Germany, Japan and China and several other smaller countries throughout the later 20th and even still the 21st century.

Even in the "western", "developed" or "modern" powers there has been a growth of counter-factual based ideologies gradually dominating the public discourse over the past 20 or more years in which we see the meaning of words strangely changed to suit a narrative of that ideology.

Poverty was the first word to undergo such a radical change of meaning, harnessing the emotion attached to the word for many hundreds of years, using it to justify focussing on something more in keeping with an ideology than historical facts and the trends from the evidence.

The narrative of lack of house building also carries overtones of the "need" for greater state controlled and directed activity.

The claims of greater and greater income inequality and possible negative effects and in turn some imagined effect on increasing poverty fails to be supported by the evidence.

The repeated claims of "poor" or "terrible" air quality and particularly such caused by the greater and greater access for the majority of people to private motor transport turns out to be simply counter-factual, when one studies the evidence.

In the midst of these claims we are also told that the possible, even probable, cause of the slowing of the rate of improvement of life expectancy is caused by a harsh government policy of "austerity", yet again the evidence does not seem to support such a claim.

In every case the evidence turns out to be contra to the disparate collection of ideologies of groups of people who seem to allow themselves to be driven by "superior" causes; in every case in complete opposition to the unprecedented reality of three centuries of real progress for the people of the UK and the whole of humanity.

Afterword

"Sunt lacrimae rerum et mentem mortalia tangunt."

"There are tears shed for things even
here and mortality touches the heart."

Virgil (Publius Vergilius Maro):
Aeneid bk. I, l. 603,
29-19 B.C.

The arrival of a new pandemic

Unexpectedly, at the very end of 2019, a new virus was announced that formed the basis for the creation of a pandemic, that threatened to be of a magnitude previously seen a century earlier, the "Spanish Influenza" of 1918 to 1919.

In a bizarre twist, this pandemic caused governments around the world to react in an entirely unprecedented and incongruous way, not seen in "western", "developed" or "modern" powers before.

The justification offered, was to save lives and protect health services. What appears not to have been considered was the probable non-health consequences of such restrictions and the severe impacts that would follow in damage to the economy and people's livelihoods. This latter is still emerging, but data for the mortality outcomes is now available.

Population and deaths 1970-2021

Coincidentally, having been researching the history of the UK and constituent nations, including the population and mortality counts and rates, including by age ranges, I was provided with a ready source of comparative data for the two years that followed after the intended end point of the study.

Thus it has proven an interesting afterword to the analysis of the population and mortality effects visible for the previous centuries to compare these to the outcomes of the worst two years of the recent pandemic.

The start point of the population is shown, from the data published by the ONS for England and Wales by quinquennial age ranges, in the chart at the top of the next page, from 1970, at least up to the year 2021. The year 2021 was a census year and at the time of completion of this work in 2023, estimates for that year, or enumerated data from the census, have now been published. Colourising quinquennial age ranges in a consistent manner from yellows for the youngest, via shades of orange and pale pinks to light greens and blues to the darkest blues for the oldest age ranges, reveals the patterns and trends clearly.

The chart in the middle of the next page illustrates the numbers of annual deaths for the same years, including to the year 2021, again from data published by the ONS, and again divided and colourised into the same quinquennial age ranges.

This reveals the numerical outcomes for 52 years for people in England and Wales, and on the right end of the chart the jump in the number of deaths in 2020 and drop in 2021 can be clearly seen.

Also visible in the chart is the strong preponderance of the deaths in the age ranges from the 55-59 years age range and above, with ever larger jumps for each higher quinquennial range compared to the previous years. This is revealed by the overwhelming preponderance of mostly darker blues. Thus already we can see a strong signal in the data suggesting that the Covid-19 disease was especially severe for older age cohorts, particularly for those over the age of 60 or so.

The chart at the bottom of the page then shows the crude death rate and the "Age Standardised Mortality Rate", each per thousand population. Both of these calculations factor for the size of the population, and thereby cater for the growth of the population over time and therefore the generally expected increase in the number of deaths.

The crude death rate in the violet line shows the steady fall, followed by a small increased rate in the time of the second decade of the 21st century (discussed in the ninth chapter **Life Expectancy**), then reveals the large jump in 2020 and small drop in 2021. The age standardised mortality rate in the green line factors for the ageing of the population and reveals a strong fall until the levelling in the same decade of the 21st century followed by the jump of 2020 and small drop in 2021.

Population by age range for England & Wales (ONS/Human Mortality Database)

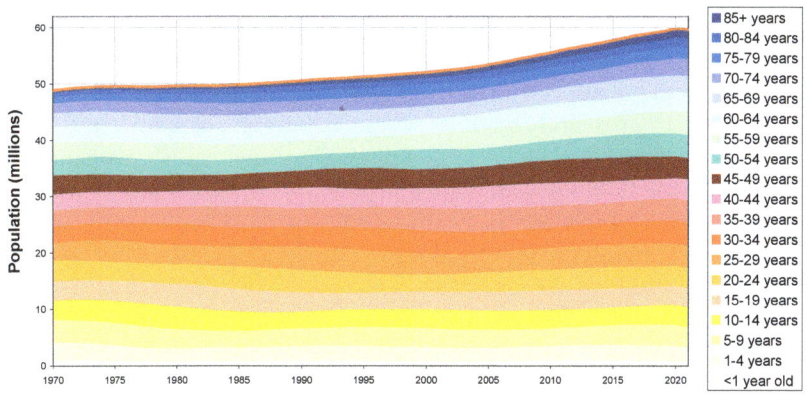

Annual deaths by age range for England & Wales (ONS/Human Mortality Database)

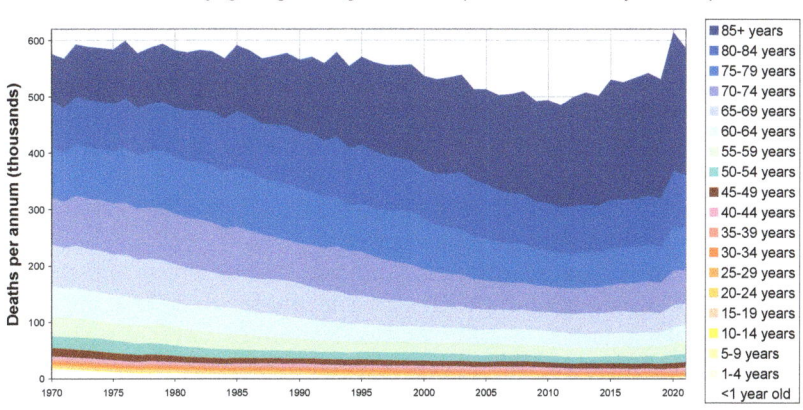

Death Rates ("crude and Asmr) per thousand population for England & Wales

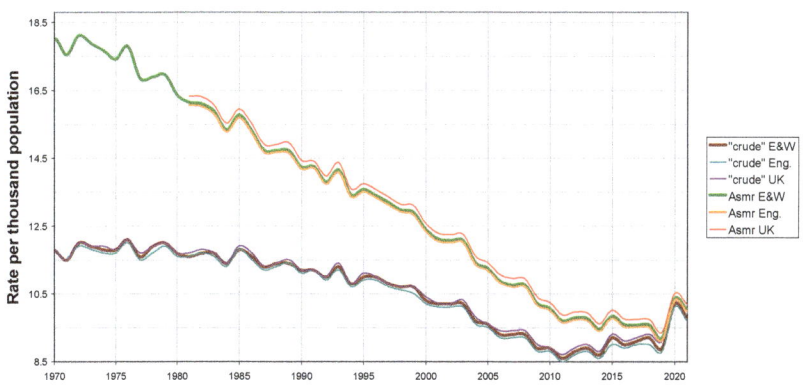

217

Covid diagnosis and deaths 2020-2021

The government's Covid-19 dashboard published the recorded data for the whole period, for diagnosed cases and deaths "within 28 days of a positive diagnosis", including by age range for England. Note that data for Covid-19 on the death certificate was not readily available by age range at the time of early research, but now analysed, though not shown here.

By correlating this data for England with the weekly ONS published all-cause mortality data for England and Wales, including colourised data for quinquennial age ranges, several strong patterns emerge.

The first and most overwhelming pattern is the significant under-reporting of diagnosed cases and deaths "within 28 days of a Covid-19 diagnosis", during what has been called the first wave, centred on April 2020, that petered out towards the end of June 2020.

In the chart at the top of the opposite page we see the number of daily cases reported for England, both categorised by quinquennial age and also the total as the green line overlaid on the chart.

The overwhelming impression of colour for age ranges is one of the preponderance of yellow and orange with tiny levels for the pink, being the age ranges up to approximately the mid-40s.

The overall breakdown of ages by a commonly used break point in the data reported up to 31st December 2021, informs us that 81.4% of the population was in the age range up to 64 years of age, whilst 18.6% of the population were aged 65 and over. The diagnosed cases however indicated that 91.5% who were diagnosed as having Covid-19 were aged up to 64 years and 8.5% aged 65 and over.

The first significant pointer to the real and serious effects of the Covid-19 infections can be seen in the chart in the middle of the next page, that represents the number of daily deaths "within 28 days of a Covid-19 diagnosis". In this chart the overwhelming impression is clearly of the preponderance of blues, representing those aged 60 years and over.

The data for the whole period in turn informs us that, on the raw basis of the testing outcomes, 11.5% of those who died "within 28 days of a Covid-19 diagnosis" were aged up to 64 years, whilst 88.5% were aged 65 and over.

This age-related effect has proven to be largely consistent throughout the whole period of the various waves of Covid-19 in England, but was also noted by Max Roser, in an article published on 4th March 2020 at "Our World in Data", that explained that this was the likely outcome of the age impact of the then new virus, based upon the analysis of the data from the first wave of the virus in China; from where the virus emanated.

In the chart at the bottom of next page, we present the ONS data for all-cause mortality by age range for England and Wales for 2020 and 2021. This clearly suggests the significant under-recording of Covid-19 related deaths in the spring of 2020, revealed by the very large peak of all-cause mortality for that period from April to May 2020.

Daily Cases of diagnosed Coronavirus for England by age range

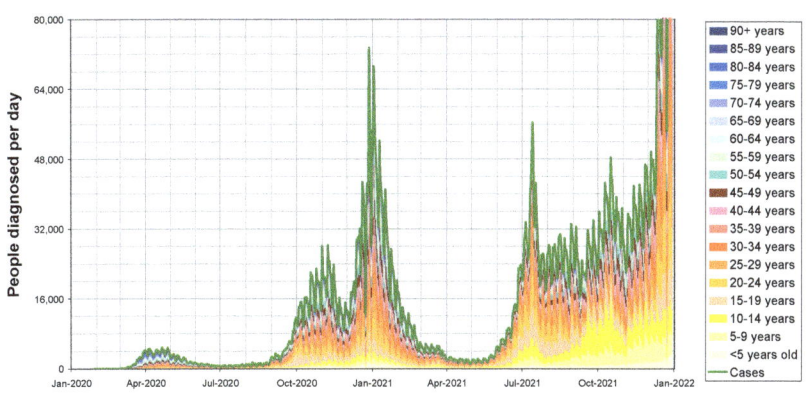

Daily Deaths (within 28 Days of Coronavirus diagnosis) for England by age range

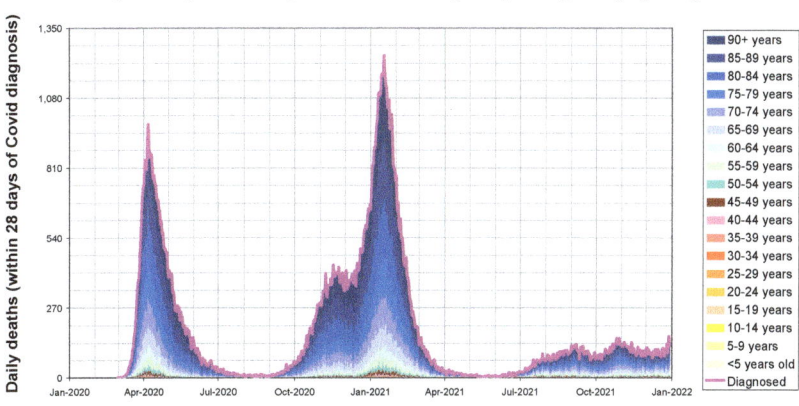

Weekly Deaths in England and Wales by age range

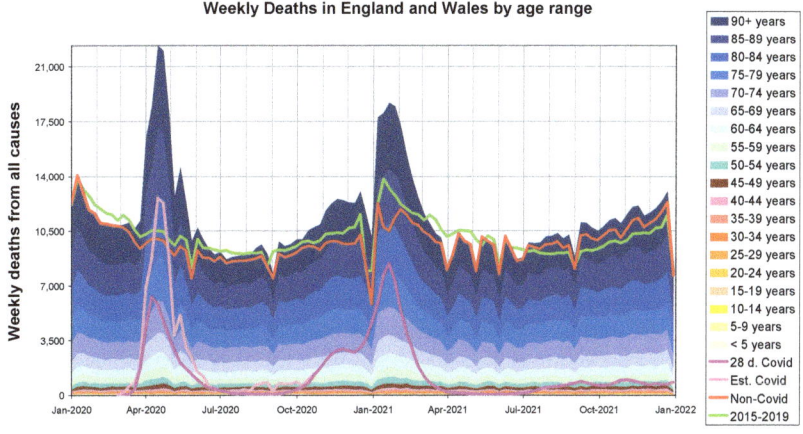

Notably the all-cause mortality outcomes by the same age distributions quoted previously; for those aged up to aged 64 yields 15.6% of deaths in 2020-2021 and 15.4% for the period 2015-2019, whilst for those aged 65 and over yields 84.4% for 2020-2021 compared to 84.6% for 2015-2019.

As noted, from these data it is very clear that true Covid-19 mortality is not fully captured from diagnosed cases and subsequent deaths during the first wave in Spring 2020. This is made clear by the magnitude of the all-cause peak at that time, compared with the lower peak during the winter 2020-2021 wave. This latter being after the testing capacity had caught up in the autumn of 2020 with the need for diagnosis.

Comparing the two major waves of deaths "within 28 days etc." to the all-cause mortality waves for the same period and the percent of positive tests strongly suggests as many as 40,000 Covid-19 related deaths are actually un-diagnosed in terms of the simplistic "within 28 days etc.".

In addition the other major finding is that when comparing the "all-cause" mortality counts for 2020 and 2021 to the 5 year average from 2015 to 2019, the excess deaths for England and Wales are approximately 130,000, though interestingly the deaths "within 28 days of a Covid-19 diagnosis" from the dashboard are approximately 136,000, a ratio repeated for the whole of the UK.

These data therefore strongly confirm that Covid-19 was a virulent disease that was able to prey on the vulnerable, through age and co-morbidity, but it turns out was not a serious disease for the younger cohorts and those without co-morbidity conditions; being essentially responsible for the untimely deaths of 0.22% of the UK's population.

Age shares of diagnosis and deaths

The shares of the same total recorded figures, again by quinquennial age ranges, in the chart at the top of the next page, re-emphasises the previously discussed age distributions for diagnosed cases. Again the general impression offered by the consistent colourisation is of the younger age ranges being more prevalent in the numbers diagnosed.

However another pointer from the data emerges in the greater share of the older age ranges in the very early figures reported for April and May 2020 in particular. From all other data and the findings here discussed, this is almost certainly a consequence of the older age ranges being more severely affected by the virus and therefore coming forward for testing and receiving attention within the scope of the limited testing capabilities available in the spring of 2020.

In the chart in the middle of the opposite page, again we see deaths "within 28 days etc." and when such daily death counts are high, indicated by the higher peaks of the overlaid pink line, we see a very consistent distribution of deaths, overwhelmingly affecting the older age ranges, as represented in the various blue blocks, and is notably also the case in the first wave despite testing and diagnosis being so limited.

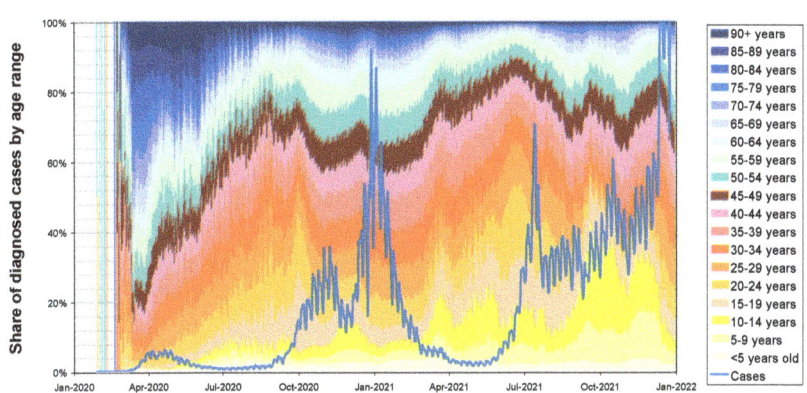

Daily Cases of diagnosed Coronavirus for England by age range (share)

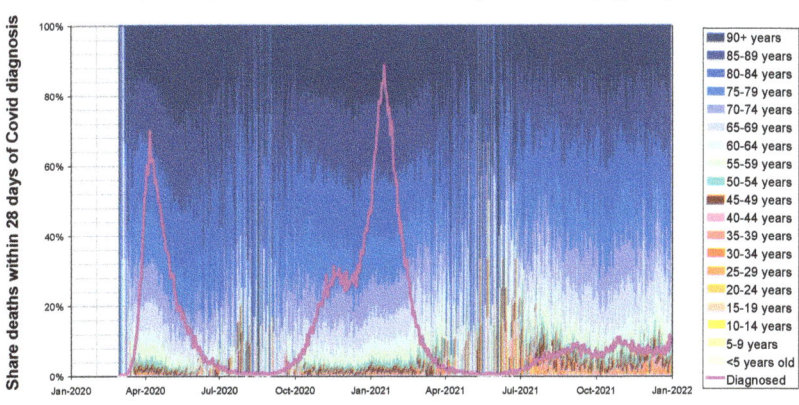

Daily deaths (within 28 Days of Coronavirus diagnosis) share by age range

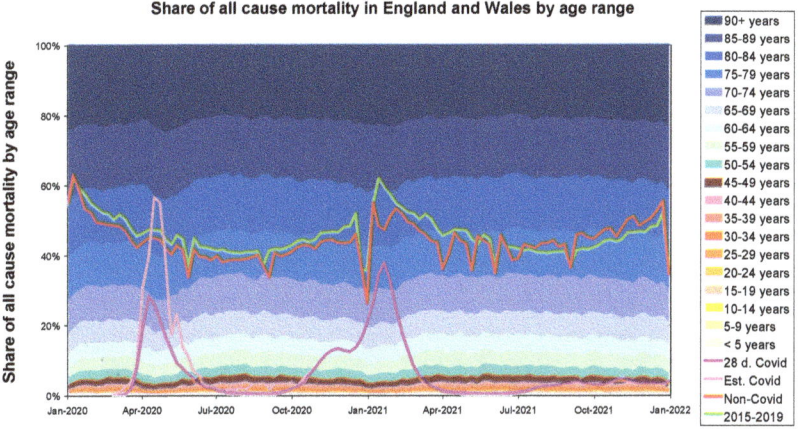

Share of all cause mortality in England and Wales by age range

221

In the chart at the bottom of the previous page, we then represent the total weekly deaths for England and Wales, regardless of cause, as shares of total deaths, by the same colourised quinquennial age ranges. The real effects are fully revealed as the age distributions of deaths by all causes turn out to be almost identical to the age distributions of deaths "within 28 days etc.".

In fact there is even a notable repeated marker in the data that when the Covid-19 waves are at their most severe in spring 2020 and winter 2020-2021, the ages of those dying, regardless of cause, are in fact higher than during periods of less severe waves.

This is then reflected in the calculations of the average age at death related to the Covid-19 disease being 82.5 years, whilst the average age at death not related to Covid-19 was 81.5 years.

Analysis of death rates 2020-2021

A further view of the under-reporting of real Covid-19 related deaths is offered in the chart at the top of the next page. Total excess deaths are presented in the red line, whilst deaths "within 28 days etc." are presented in the bright pink line. By applying the simple numerical relationship between excess deaths and "diagnosed" death for the winter 2020-2021 to the earlier spring 2020 wave, results in the dashed pink line and yields the previously mentioned missed diagnosis of Covid-19 related death count of possibly up to 40,000 people.

The chart in the middle of the next page represents an analysis of the whole period in measured rates of cases (mid-blue), hospitalisation (orange) and subsequent deaths (bright pink), all smoothed to 7 day rolling averages.

The chart reveals the four primary waves of the four primary variants; the first, "original" wave in the spring of 2020; followed by the Kent/Alpha variant in the winter of 2020-2021; then the Indian/Delta variant from July 2021 until the end of November 2021; and then South African/Omicron variant from late November 2021 to the period shown at the end of December 2021.

Note that the hospitalisation rates plotted on the right axis, with death rates, are correlated to match the case rates plotted on the left axis. By doing this the four patterns of apparent severity are revealed. Again we can see the underreporting of cases in the first wave, in relation to those admitted to hospital. The two then match closely during the Kent/Alpha wave, once testing capacity was able to keep up with case rates. After this we see hospitalisation and death rates have fallen dramatically, relative to case rates for firstly the Indian/Delta variant and even more so the South African/Omicron variant. This was firstly the result of the natural reducing virulence of the virus, particularly the South African/Omicron variant, despite it being a more contagious variant, but also the widespread use of the new vaccines from the very end of December 2020.

Estimated undiagnosed Covid-19 related deaths (39,700) for England & Wales

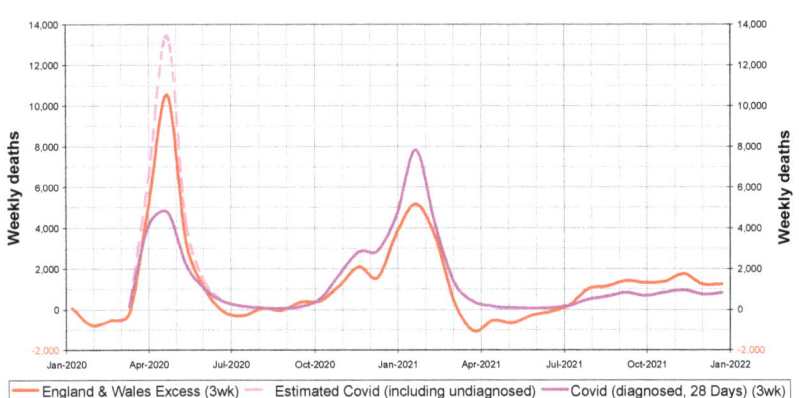

Analysis of daily reported UK cases, UK hospitalisations and UK deaths

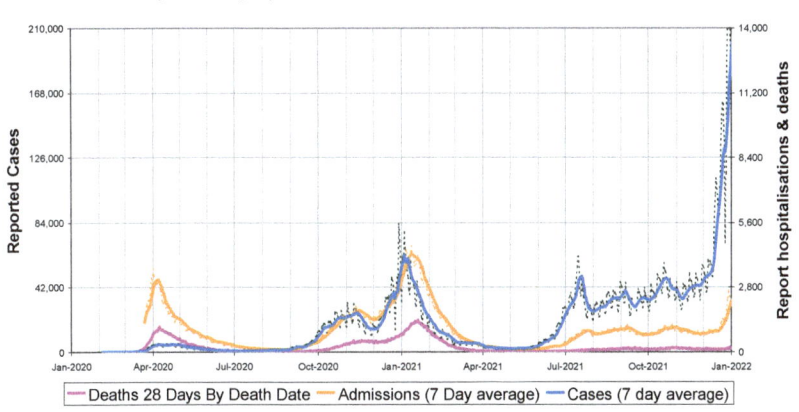

2020-2021 Selected Country, Excess mortality P-scores - OWID/WMD

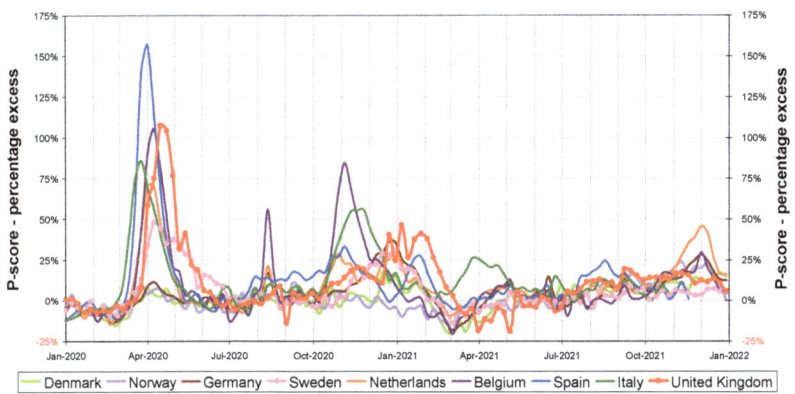

The chart at the bottom of the previous page presents data from "Our World in Data", reporting excess deaths for the UK and eight selected "modern", "developed" and comparable European nation states.

These data are expressed as a percentage change compared to each nation's expected outcome from their own historical data for 2015-2019 for the equivalent each week, and reveals the same waves for almost every nation at least at similar times of the year.

Most severely impacted amongst the nine nations, at least for the whole two calendar year period are Italy, Spain, the UK, Belgium and the Netherlands. The overall excess death effect for Sweden and Germany was barely half that of the UK, though compared to their near neighbours of Norway and Denmark, Sweden did fare notably worse.

Sweden did however experience a significant death toll amongst the people living in care homes, as did the UK. This was unquestionably a grave failure of basic rigour throughout government and management during the first wave in both countries.

Notable though is that the Swedish government is renowned for not having imposed significant and draconian restrictions upon its populace.

"Spanish flu" and Covid 2020-2021

A simple comparative analysis is now possible between the "Spanish Influenza" of 1918-1919 and the Covid-19 pandemic of 2020-2021 for England and Wales.

Whilst of course there are many social, economic and health differences between the two eras, it does remain useful to reflect upon the different outcomes from the different diseases and also different government reactions to the two pandemics.

In the chart at the top of the next page are the annual deaths registered for males for England and Wales from 1900 to 2021, whilst the chart in the middle of the next page are the annual deaths for females for England and Wales for the same years.

Clearly the terrible deaths tolls of The Great War and The Second World War, particularly prevalent for younger males, can be seen in the top chart. This sadly overwhelmingly masks the death toll from the "Spanish Influenza" as it so closely over-laps with the death toll of the final year of The Great War, until the armistice of 11th November 1918.

The more useful representation of the effects of that earlier pandemic can be seen in the middle chart for females, who at that time were not combatants. As such this shows the toll of pandemic deaths were significantly mostly amongst the young, represented in the spike of yellows and oranges in 1918; whilst the Covid-19 spikes of 2020 and 2021 are clearly amongst the older age cohorts. Also notable is the relative magnitude of the two pandemic spikes compared to the years before and after their presence. This is re-emphasised in the chart at the bottom of the page, in which death rates by age cohorts are presented.

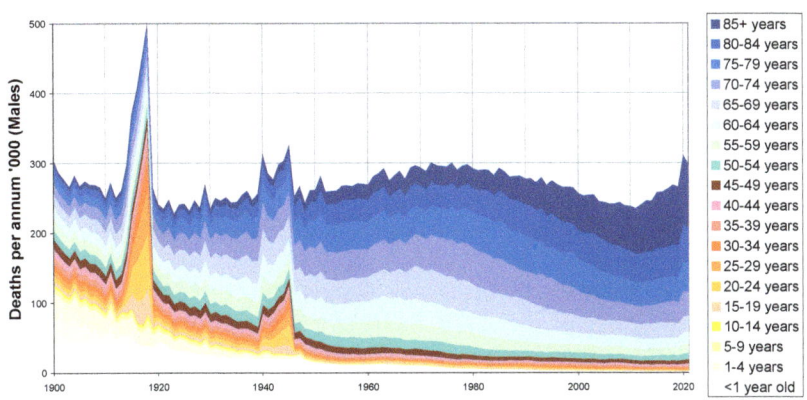

Male deaths by age range for England & Wales (ONS/Human Mortality Database)

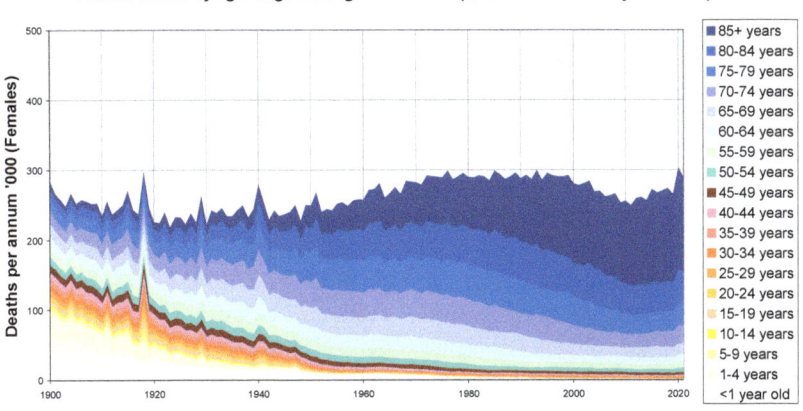

Female deaths by age range for England & Wales (ONS/Human Mortality Database)

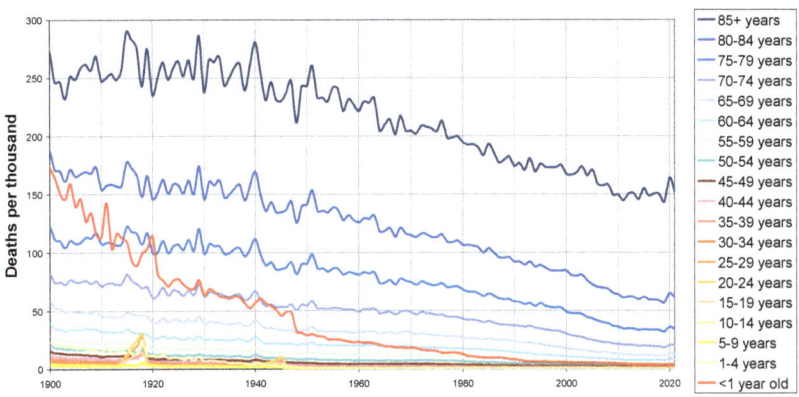

Death rates per thousand population by age range for England & Wales

This shows the death rate amongst infants in the later years of The Great War in the red line; for Covid-19 this suggests a notable death rate jump for those same old age cohorts in 2020 and slight fall in 2021 in the blue lines compared to the second decade of the 21st century.

It is worth reflecting on the fact that, when calculating the relative effects and factoring for the size of the population between the two pandemics, in simple, "crude" numerical terms, the excess death toll of the "Spanish Influenza" pandemic for the populations of England and Wales was twice that of the Covid-19 pandemic. Note again that this does not cater for other social, economic or health factors prevalent during the two eras.

One suggestion made by Professor Sunetra Gupta of Oxford University about the virulence of the 1918 influenza outbreak upon the younger members of the world's population, is the long period since a serious influenza outbreak had previously occurred, perhaps almost 30 years since the major influenza outbreak in the 1890s.

The data for the period for the greatest prevalence of the Covid-19 pandemic, at least for the UK, and generally supported by outcomes for most of the other "modern", "developed" nations, all confirm that Covid-19 was a contagious coronavirus, but that it was a virulent disease only for the aged and otherwise those with co-morbidities, and in fact seems a relatively weak disease for the majority of the healthy and the young.

We see that those aged under 20 years constitute 23.6% of the population of England, contributed 25.2% of diagnosed cases of Covid-19, yet only contributed 3% of hospital admissions, and thankfully fewer than 0.1% of the deaths "within 28 days etc.". Although not as overwhelmingly strong, we see a similar pattern for those aged 20 to 64, who constitute 58% of the population of England, contributed 66% of the diagnosed cases and 38% of hospital admissions, but thankfully only 11% of the deaths "within 28 days etc.".

From this outcome it appears that the authors and signatories of "The Great Barrington Declaration" seem to be vindicated in their proposal for strongly targeted protection for the most vulnerable, whilst not imposing broader restrictions that were always going to result in severe economic and social damage. This was almost universally vilified and ignored by most "modern", "developed" governments around the world, excepting Sweden.

Whilst the economic impacts are now haunting everyone since the later months of 2021, the medium and long term effects cannot yet be known, though look potentially disastrous at present. The whole episode looks like a repeat of the failed policies of successive governments from the mid-1990s; housing policy, energy policy, monetary policy etc. etc.; all amplified immeasurably for the vast majority of people, who placed their trust in and funded these governments, thanks to pandemic panic.

References

"You will find it a very good practice
always to verify your references, sir!"

Martin Joseph Routh (1755-1854):
quoted in –
John W. Burgon:
The Lives of Twelve Good Men, Vol. 1,
1888

Foreword

pp. 5-6   Onions, C. T. (Ed.), (1932/1983) 'The Shorter Oxford
            English Dictionary...', p. 531, p. 1057, pp. 1628-1629, pp.
            1643-1644, p. 2447

            Also: Johnson, S., (1755/1758/1818) 'A Dictionary of the
            English Language', (1758) - p. 501, p. 652, p. 681: (1818) -
            p. 108, p. 799, pp. 917-918

            Also: Oxford Dictionary - Lexico

            Also: internet search for definitions of poverty etc.

p. 7   Onions, C. T. (Ed.), (1932/1983) 'The Shorter Oxford
            English Dictionary...', p. 1981, p. 1622

Population

pp. 23-27   Hinde, Professor A., (2003) 'England's Population - A History...', pp. 22-37

Also: Wrigley, Professor Sir E. A. and Dr. R. S. Schofield, (1982/1989) 'The Population History of England, 1541-1871...', Table A3.1 - pp. 528-529, Table A2.3 – pp. 496-502, pp. 588-596

Also: MeasuringWorth, see UK GDP, "Historic Series" and "Consistent Series" population

Also: Bank of England - "Millennium Database", Version 3.1 - Tables A2 and A18

Also: Kyd, James G. (Ed.), (1952) 'Scottish Population Statistics...', Introduction – ix-xxxiii

Also: ONS - Population estimates

Also: Vision of Britain - Census

Also: internet search for population density by country

pp. 28-32   Wrigley, Professor Sir E. A. and Dr. R. S. Schofield, (1982/1989) 'The Population History of England, 1541-1871...', Table A3.1 - pp. 528-529, Table A2.3 – pp. 496-502, pp. 588-596

Also: ONS - Vital statistics, births, deaths and marriages, 'Vital statistics in the UK: births, deaths and marriages (annual data)' – see latest version

Also: Human Mortality Database

pp. 32-35   Wrigley, Professor Sir E. A. and Dr. R. S. Schofield, (1982/1989) 'The Population History of England, 1541-1871...', Table A3.1 - pp. 528-529

Also: Human Mortality Database

Also: ONS - Population estimates

pp. 36-37   Our World in Data - Life expectancy

Also: Human Mortality Database

Also: ONS - National life tables

pp. 38-40   Wrigley, Professor Sir E. A. and Dr. R. S. Schofield, (1982/1989) 'The Population History of England, 1541-1871...', Table A3.1 - pp. 528-529

Also: Human Mortality Database

Also: ONS - Population and migration, 'Long term international migration'

Also: ONS - Population, 'Our population - Where are we?'

Economy and state

pp. 41-44   MeasuringWorth, see UK GDP, "Consistent Series" population plus GDP and GDP deflator (Clarke)

Also: Office for Budget Responsibility - Data banks

Also: Bank of England - "Millennium Database", Version 3.1 - Tables A7, A8 and A9 (Feinstein)

pp. 44-46   Bank of England - "Millennium Database", Version 3.1 - Tables A3, A4, A7, A8, A9, A11, A12, A13, A14, A16 and A53

Also: Mitchell, B. R. and Deane, Professor P. M., (1962) 'Abstract of Historical Statistics', National Income and Expenditure 1., p. 366 (from Deane and Cole, 1962)

Also: Allen, Professor R. C., (2016) 'Revising England's Social Tables Once Again', Table 11, p. 28 and Table 15, p. 32

Also: Crafts, Professor N. F. R. and Harley, Professor C. K., (1992) 'Output Growth and the British Industrial Revolution...', Table A3.1, pp. 725-727

Also: Broadberry, Professor S. N. et al., (2015) 'British Economic Growth, 1270-1870', Appendix 5.3, pp. 226-244

pp. 46-50   MeasuringWorth, see UK GDP

Also: Bank of England - "Millennium Database", Version 3.1 - Table A29

Also: Office for Budget Responsibility - Data banks

Also: Christopher Chantrill - UK Public Revenue

Also: Christopher Chantrill - UK Public Spending

pp. 50-51   Bank of England - "Millennium Database", Version 3.1 - Tables A49, A50 and A51

Also: Feinstein, Professor C. H., (1972) 'National Income Expenditure and Output of the United Kingdom 1855-1965', Table 57, pp. T125-T127, Table 58, p. T128, Table 59, pp. T129-T130

pp. 50-54   Bank of England - "Millennium Database", Version 3.1 - Table A9

Also: Office for Budget Responsibility - Data banks

Also: Mitchell, B. R., (1988) 'British Historical Statistics', Chapter XI, Public Finance 1, pp. 575-577, Public Finance 2, pp. 578-580, Public Finance 3, pp. 581-586, Public Finance 4, pp. 587-595

	Also: Christopher Chantrill - UK Public Revenue
	Also: Christopher Chantrill - UK Public Spending
	Also: Office for Budget Responsibility - Data banks
pp. 54-56	Mitchell, B. R., (1988) 'British Historical Statistics', Chapter XI, Public Finance 9, p. 605, Public Finance 12, pp. 612-618
	Also: Christopher Chantrill - UK Public Spending
	Also: HM Treasury - Public expenditure statistical analysis
pp. 56-58	Lindert, Professor P. H. and Williamson, Professor J. G., (1983) 'Reinterpreting Britain's Social Tables', D. Table, p. 101
	Also: Boyer, Professor G. R., (2019) 'The Winding Road to the Welfare State...', Table 2.A.1, p.74 and Table 3.3, p. 87
	Also: Department for Work and Pensions - Statistics
	Also: UK Government - Stat-Xplore
pp. 58-60	Bank of England - "Millennium Database", Version 3.1 - Table A57
	Also: ONS - National balance sheet

Earnings and incomes

pp. 61-64	Bank of England - "Millennium Database", Version 3.1 - Table A47
	Also: Clark, Professor G., (2011) 'Average Earnings and Retail Prices, UK, 1209-2010', Table 2, pp. 22-23
	Also: Lyle, M. A., (2007) 'Regional agricultural wage variations in early nineteenth-century England', Table 1., p. 98
	Also: Department of Employment and Productivity, (1971) 'British Labour Statistics, Historical Abstract 1886-1968', Table 7, p. 38
	Also: Mitchell, B. R., (1988) 'British Historical Statistics', Chapter XI, Labour Force 28, p. 163
	Also: Wilson, A. Fox, (1903) 'Agricultural Wages in England and Wales...', p. 280 and Appendix II, pp. 331-332
	Also: Wages through history - A. Wilson Fox agricultural wages
pp. 64-67	Bank of England - "Millennium Database", Version 3.1 - Table A47

Also: Clark, Professor G., (2011) 'Average Earnings and Retail Prices, UK, 1209-2010', Table 2, pp. 22-23

Also: Department of Employment and Productivity, (1971) 'British Labour Statistics, Historical Abstract 1886-1968', Table 7, p. 38

Also: MeasuringWorth, see UK average nominal earnings

Also: Feinstein, Professor C. H., (1998) 'Pessimism Perpetuated Real Wages & Standard of Living...', Appendix Table 1, pp. 652-653

Also: ONS - Inflation and price indices

pp. 66-68   ONS - Labour force survey, earnings and working hours

pp. 68-70   ONS - Average equivalised household disposable income

Also: Institute for Fiscal Studies - Living standards, poverty and inequality in the UK

Also: UK Data Service, see study 7916, Gazeley and Newell

pp. 70-74   Boyer, Professor G. R., (2019) 'The Winding Road to the Welfare State...', Table 2.A.1, p.74 and Table 3.3, p. 87

Also: Department for Work and Pensions - Statistics

Also: UK Government - Stat-Xplore

Also: MeasuringWorth, see UK average nominal earnings

Also: Office for Budget Responsibility - Welfare spending by age (Chart 3.2)

Also: Office for Budget Responsibility - Welfare spending by age (Removed)

Also: Bowley, Professor Sir A. L., (1937) 'Wages and Income in the United Kingdom Since 1860'

Income inequality

pp. 75-86   Lindert, Professor P. H. and Williamson, Professor J. G., (1983) 'Reinterpreting Britain's Social Tables', Table 2, pp. 98-99

Also: ONS - Income and wealth

Also: Institute for Fiscal Studies - Living standards, poverty and inequality in the UK

pp. 78-86   Chalmers, G., (1782/1804) 'An Estimate of the Comparative Strength of Great Britain', see Appendix C3, appendix page 29, King, G. (1696), 'Natural and Political Observations and Conclusions Upon the State and...'

Also: Massie, J., (1756) 'Calculations of Taxes for a Family of Each Rank, Degree or Class: for One Year'

Also: Mathias, P., (1957) 'The Social Structure in the Eighteenth Century: A Calculation by Joseph Massie'

Also: Colquhoun, P., (1806) 'A Treatise on Indigence'

Also: Colquhoun, P., (1815) 'Treatise on the Wealth Power and Resources of the British Empire'

Also: Smee, W. R., (1846) 'THE INCOME TAX: Its Extension at the Present Rate Proposed to all Classes'

Also: Baxter, R. D., (1868) 'National Income. The United Kingdom'

Also: Baxter, R. D., (1869) 'The Taxation of the United Kingdom'

Also: Lindert, Professor P. H. and Williamson, Professor J. G., (1982) 'Revising England's Social Tables 1688-1812'

Also: Lindert, Professor P. H. and Williamson, Professor J. G., (1983) 'Reinterpreting Britain's Social Tables'

Also: Mitchell, B. R., (1988) 'British Historical Statistics', Chapter XI, Labour Force 1, p. 102

Also: Lindert, Professor P. H. - Downloads

Also: Allen, Professor R. C., (2016) 'Revising England's Social Tables Once Again'

Also: Allen, Professor R. C., (2018) 'Class structure and inequality during the industrial revolution...'

Also: HMRC - Survey of personal incomes, Table 3.1a

pp. 86-90   UK Data Service, see study 7916, Gazeley and Newell, Ministry of Labour and National Service FES 1953/54

Also: UK Data Service, see study 3054, ONS (OPCS), FES 1977

Also: UK Data Service, see study 6118, ONS, EFS 2007

Also: UK Data Service, see study 8686, ONS, LCFS 2018/19

Also: UK Data Service, see study 3300, IFS, FES/HBAI 1961 – 1993/94

Also: UK Data Service, see study 8583, IFS, FES/EFS/LCFS 1968 – 2017/18

Also: Institute for Fiscal Studies - Living standards, poverty and inequality in the UK

Cost of living

pp. 91-93   MeasuringWorth, see UK RPI and earnings

Also: ONS - Inflation and price indices, see RPI and CPI

Also: Bank of England - "Millennium Database", Version 3.1 - Tables A47, see "Consumer Price indices", see column D, E and CB

pp. 94-95   MeasuringWorth, see UK RPI and earnings

Also: ONS - Labour force survey, earnings and working hours

Also: Mitchell, B. R., (1988) 'British Historical Statistics', Chapter XIV, Prices 22, pp. 769-770

Also: ONS - Retail Prices Index: average price of selected food items: 1914 to 2004

Also: ONS - Inflation and price indices, see "Ave price - Bread: white loaf, sliced, 800g"

pp. 96-97   As before

Also: Clark, Professor G., (1999) 'Housing Rents, Housing Quality, and Living Standards...', Table 3, p. 12

pp. 98-99   As before

Also: MeasuringWorth, see UK GDP, "Consistent Series" and "Historic Series" population

Also: Bank of England - "Millennium Database", Version 3.1 - Tables A57

Also: ONS - Gross disposable household income, see "Households (S.14): Disposable income, gross (B.6g)"

pp. 100-101   As before

Also: ONS - Retail Prices Index: average price of selected food items: 1914 to 2004

Also: ONS - Inflation and price indices, see "Ave price - Bread: white loaf, sliced, 800g"; "Ave price – Cheese"; "Ave price – Milk"

pp. 102-103   Department for Transport - Vehicle statistics

Also: Holmans, Dr. A., (2005) 'Historical Statistics of Housing in Britain', p. 43, p385

Also: Ministry of Housing, Communities and Local Government – Housing, see Live tables 101, 102, 106, 107 and 108 (discontinued)

Also: Chartered Institute of Housing, UK Housing Review, Table 17a

Also: Historical car prices from internet searches

pp. 104-108   As before Earnings and incomes

Also: ONS - Retail Prices Index: average price of selected food items: 1914 to 2004

Also: ONS - Inflation and price indices, see individual item ONS indexes and values

Also: OECD - Housing prices, rental cost index

Also: Housing mortgage repayment costs, see next chapter

Housing

pp. 109-111   Davenant, C., (1695) 'An Essay of the Ways and Means of Supplying the War'

Also: Chalmers, G., (1782/1804) 'An Estimate of the Comparative Strength of Great Britain', see Appendix C3, appendix page 29, King, G. (1696), 'Natural and Political Observations and Conclusions Upon the State and...'

Also: Mathias, P., (1957) 'The Social Structure in the Eighteenth Century: A Calculation by Joseph Massie'

Also: Colquhoun, P., (1806) 'A Treatise on Indigence'

Also: Colquhoun, P., (1815) 'Treatise on the Wealth Power and Resources of the British Empire'

Also: Wrigley, Professor Sir E. A. and Dr. R. S. Schofield, (1982/1989) 'The Population History of England, 1541-1871...', Table A3.1 - pp. 528-529, Table A2.3 – pp. 496-502, pp. 588-596

Also: MeasuringWorth, see UK GDP, "Consistent Series" population

Also: ONS - Population estimates

Also: Vision of Britain - Census

Also: Holmans, Dr. A., (2005) 'Historical Statistics of Housing in Britain', p. 43, p385

Also: Ministry of Housing, Communities and Local Government – Housing, see Live tables 101, 102, 106, 107 and 108 (discontinued)

Also: Chartered Institute of Housing, UK Housing Review, Table 17a

pp. 112-113	As above
	Also: Holmans, Dr. A., (2005) 'Historical Statistics of Housing in Britain', p. 18
	Also: NOMIS – Official census and labour market statistics, see 2001 and 2011 census analysis tables QS406EW
	Also: ONS - Labour force survey, see workbook tablesregionaltable52020fandh.xls
pp. 114-115	Piddington, Nicol, Garrett and Custard, (2020) 'The Housing Stock of The United Kingdom' BRE Trust, see pp. 14-19
	Also: Ministry of Housing, Communities and Local Government - Housing
	Also: Ministry of Housing, Communities and Local Government - English housing survey, see table DA1101
pp. 116-117	Mitchell, B. R., (1988) 'British Historical Statistics', Chapter VII, Building 4, 5, 5a, 6, 7 pp. 389-393
	Also: Holmans, Dr. A., (2005) 'Historical Statistics of Housing in Britain', pp. 23-59
	Also: ONS - House building, UK house build tables 3a, 3b, 3c, 3d and 3e
	Also: Ministry of Housing, Communities and Local Government - House building, see live tables 208 and 209 (discontinued)
pp. 118-119	As above
	Also: Ministry of Housing, Communities and Local Government - House building, see live table 244
pp. 120-127	Bank of England - "Millennium Database", Version 3.1 - Tables A32
	Also: Nationwide - Housing historic data
	Also: Halifax - House price data
	Also: MeasuringWorth, see UK average nominal earnings
	Also: ONS - Labour force survey, earnings and working hours
	Also: Bank of England - "Millennium Database", Version 3.1 - Tables A31
	Also: Building Societies Association - Mortgage interest rates
pp. 128-134	Ministry of Housing, Communities and Local Government - House building, see live table 102

Also: ONS – Housing, see current UK dwelling dataset workbook, table 2

Also: Ministry of Housing, Communities and Local Government – Housing, see live table 104

Also: Ministry of Housing, Communities and Local Government - English housing survey, see table FA1211

Also: Hicks and Allen, (1999) 'A Century of Change: Trends in UK statistics since 1900', pp. 12-13

Also: Holmans, Dr. A., (2005) 'Historical Statistics of Housing in Britain', pp. 124-146 (note p. 130, paragraph 16)

Also: Alvaredo, F., Atkinson, A. B., Morelli, S., (2018) 'Top wealth shares in the UK over more than a century'

Poverty

pp. 135-137   Baxter, R. D., (1868) 'National Income. The United Kingdom'

Also: Baxter, R. D., (1869) 'The Taxation of the United Kingdom'

Also: Lindert, Professor P. H. and Williamson, Professor J. G., (1982) 'Revising England's Social Tables 1688-1812'

Also: Lindert, Professor P. H. and Williamson, Professor J. G., (1983) 'Reinterpreting Britain's Social Tables'

Also: Mitchell, B. R., (1988) 'British Historical Statistics', Chapter XI, Labour Force 1, p. 102

Also: Lindert, Professor P. H. - Downloads

Also: Allen, Professor R. C., (2016) 'Revising England's Social Tables Once Again'

Also: Allen, Professor R. C., (2018) 'Class structure and inequality during the industrial revolution...'

Also: HMRC - Survey of personal incomes, Table 3.1a

pp. 138-143   UK Data Service, see study 7916, Gazeley and Newell, Ministry of Labour and National Service FES 1953/54

Also: UK Data Service, see study 3054, ONS (OPCS), FES 1977

Also: UK Data Service, see study 6118, ONS, EFS 2007

Also: UK Data Service, see study 8686, ONS, LCFS 2018/19

Also: UK Data Service, see study 3300, IFS, FES/HBAI 1961 – 1993/94

Also: UK Data Service, see study 8583, IFS, FES/EFS/LCFS 1968 – 2017/18

Also: Institute for Fiscal Studies - Living standards, poverty and inequality in the UK

pp. 144-158   Vanderlint, J., (1734) 'Money Answers all Things', see pp. 77-78

Also: Clark, Professor G., (2001) 'Farm Wages and Living Standards in the Industrial Revolution England, 1670-1850'

Also: Clark, Professor G., (2005) 'The Condition of the Working Class in England, 1209–2004'

Also: Massie, J., (1758) 'A Plan for the Establishment of Charity Houses', see p. 105

Also: Davies, Rev. D., (1795) 'The Case of Labourers in Husbandry, Stated and Considered'

Also: Eden, Sir F. M. (Bart.), (1797) 'The State of the Poor, or An History of the Labouring Classes in England (Three volumes)'

Also: Horrell, Professor S., (1996) 'Home Demand and British Industrialisation'

Also: Gazeley, Professor I. and Verdon, Professor N., (2014) ''The first poverty line? Davies and Eden's...'

Also: Booth, C., (1892) 'Life and Labour of the People in London'

Also: Rowntree, B. Seebohm, (1901) 'Poverty: A Study of Town Life'

Also: Griffin, E., (2018) 'Diets, Hunger and Living Standards During the British Industrial Revolution'

Also: Anon., (1823/1828) 'A New System of Practical Domestic Economy'

Also: Inglis, B., (1971) 'Poverty and the Industrial Revolution'

Also: Chadwick, D., (1860) 'On the Rate of Wages in Manchester and Salford, and the Manufacturing Districts of Lancashire, 1839-59'

Also: Knowles, J. (Ed.), (1888) 'The Nineteenth Century. A Monthly Review. Volume XXIII'

Also: Boyer, Professor G. R., (2019) 'The Winding Road to the Welfare State...', see analysis of Rowntree, Bowley

Also: UK Data Service, see studies 7916, 3042, 3045, 3053, 3054, 2647, 3963, 6118, 8459, 8686, 3300, 8583, 1671

Also: ONS - Percentage of households with durable goods, see table A45 and A46

Also: Department of Employment and Productivity, (1971) 'British Labour Statistics, Historical Abstract 1886-1968', see page 394, tables 195 and 195

Also: Department of Employment, (1978) 'British Labour Statistics, Year Book 1976', see page 308, tables 137 and 138

Also: Fitzpatrick, S. et al., (2016) 'Destitution in the UK'

Also: Fitzpatrick, S. et al., (2018) 'Destitution in the UK 2018'

Air Quality

pp. 159-169   DEFRA - Air Quality and Emissions Statistics

Also: DEFRA - Air Pollution in the UK

Also: National Atmospheric Emissions Inventory - Data

Also: WHO, (2006) 'WHO Air quality guidelines for...'

Also: UK Government – Air Quality Standards Regulation 2010

Also: Ayres, Professor J. G. (Chair) and Hurley J. F. (Chair), (2010) 'The Mortality Effects of Long-Term Exposure to...'

pp. 170-177   As above

London Air Quality (Imperial College London) - Data

Also: London Average Air Quality Levels (King's College London)

pp. 178-180   London Congestion Zone - Camera captures

Also: Department for Transport - Coronavirus transport use

Life Expectancy

pp. 181-183   Our World in Data - Life expectancy

Also: Human Mortality Database

pp. 184-189   ONS - Life expectancy

Afterword

Bibliography, Selected Reading and Internet Data

"For out of old fields, as men saith,
Cometh all this new corn from year to year;
And out of old books, in good faith,
Cometh all this new science that men learn."

Geoffrey Chaucer:
Parliament of Foules,
1381-1382

Bibliography and Selected Reading

Adelino, N, Schoar, A and Severino, F	(2013) 'Credit Supply and House Prices: Evidence from Mortgage Market Segmentation' National Bureau of Economic Research Working Paper 17832
Adler, Professor M.	(2017) 'Extreme Poverty in the Midst of Unprecedented Affluence - Summary' University of Edinburgh
Adler, Professor M.	(2017) 'Extreme Poverty in the Midst of Unprecedented Affluence' University of Edinburgh
Adler, Professor M.	(2018) 'Cruel, Inhuman or Degrading Treatment? Benefit Sanctions in the UK' Palgrave Macmillan ISBN: 978-3-319-90355-2
Ainsworth, R. B.	(1949) 'Earnings and Working Hours of Manual Wage-Earners the United Kingdom in October, 1938' Wiley DOI: 10.2307/2984178

241

Akhtar, Galaiya and Reynolds	(2014) 'Residential mortgages: a comparison of the Bank of England's published statistical and regulatory data collections' Bank of England
Allen, Professor R. C.	(1994) 'Real Incomes in the English Speaking World, 1879-1913 (from Labour Market Evolution)' Routledge ISBN: 978-0-415-10865-2
Allen, Professor R. C.	(2007) 'Pessimism Preserved: Real Wages in the British Industrial Revolution' University of Oxford Working Paper 314
Allen, Professor R. C.	(2009) 'Engels' pause: Technical change, capital accumulation, and inequality in the British Industrial Revolution' Science Direct DOI: 10.1016/j.eeh.2009.04.004
Allen, Professor R. C.	(2009) 'The British Industrial Revolution in Global Perspective' Cambridge University Press ISBN: 978-0-521-68785-0
Allen, Professor R. C.	(2016) 'Revising England's Social Tables Once Again' University of Oxford Discussion Paper Number: 146
Allen, Professor R. C.	(2018) 'Class structure and inequality during the industrial revolution: lessons from England's social tables, 1688–1867' Wiley DOI: 10.1111/ehr.12661
Alvaredo, F., Atkinson, A. B., Morelli, S.	(2018) 'Top wealth shares in the UK over more than a century' Science Direct DOI: 10.1016/j.jpubeco.2018.02.008
Anon.	(1823/1828) 'A New System of Practical Domestic Economy'
Arkell, T.	(2006) 'Illuminations and Distortions, Gregory King's Scheme Calculated for the Year 1688' Wiley DOI: 10.1111/j.1468-0289.2005.00330.x
Armstrong, W. A.	(1981) 'The Influence of Demographic Factors on the Position of the Agricultural Labourer in England and Wales, c1750-1914' British Agricultural History Society The Agricultural History Review, Vol. 29, No. 2 (1981), pp. 71-82
Ashworth, H.	(1842) 'Statistics of the Present Depression of Trade in Bolton' Wiley DOI: 10.2307/2337951
Atkinson, Professor A. B.	(1997) 'Distribution of Income and Wealth in Britain over the Twentieth Century (from Twentieth Century British Social Trends)' Springer ISBN: 978-0-333-72149-0
Atkinson, Professor A. B.	(2002) 'Top Incomes in the United Kingdom over the Twentieth Century' University of Oxford Discussion Paper No 43
Atkinson, Professor A. B.	(2005) 'Top Incomes in the United Kingdom over the Twentieth Century' Wiley DOI: 10.1111/j.1467-985X.2005.00351.x
Atkinson, Professor A. B.	(2007) 'The Distribution of Top Incomes in the United Kingdom 1908–2000 (from Top Incomes over the 20th Century)' Oxford University Press ISBN: 978-0-199-28688-1
Atkinson, Professor A. B.	(2013) 'Wealth and Inheritance in Britain from 1896 to the Present' London School of Economics CASE/178
Atkinson, Professor A. B.	(2016) 'Pareto and the upper tail of the income distribution in the UK: 1799 to the present' London School of Economics CASE papers (198)
Atkinson, Professor A. B. and Jenkins, S. P.	(2019) 'A different perspective on the evolution of UK income inequality' London School of Economics Working Paper 01-19

Atkinson, Professor A. B., Piketty, T. and Saez, E.
(2011) 'Top Incomes in the Long Run of History' American Economic Association DOI: 10.1257/jel.49.1.3

Ayres, Professor J. G. (Chair) and Hurley J. F. (Chair)
(2010) 'The Mortality Effects of Long-Term Exposure to Particulate Air Pollution in the United Kingdom' COMEAP ISBN: 978-0-85951-685-3

Banks, J. and Johnson, P.
(1998) 'How Reliable is the Family Expenditure Survey' Institute for Fiscal Studies ISBN: 978-1-873357-70-2

Baxter, R. D.
(1868) 'National Income. The United Kingdom' MacMillan and Co.

Baxter, R. D.
(1869) 'The Taxation of the United Kingdom' MacMillan and Co.

Belfield et al.
(2017) 'Two decades of income inequality in Britain: the role of wages, household earnings and redistribution' The Institute for Fiscal Studies Working Paper W17/01

Belfield, Chandler and Joyce
(2015) 'Housing: Trends in Prices, Costs and Tenure' Institute for Fiscal Studies ISBN: 978-1-909463-79-0

Berry, Harrison, Ryland & de Weymarn
(2007) 'Interpreting movements in broad money' Bank of England BofE Quarterly Bulletin

Block, F. and Somers, M.
(2003) 'In the shadow of Speenhamland Social Policy and the Old Poor Law' Sage Publications DOI: 10.1177/0032329203252272

Bogdanor, Professor V. B.
(2016) 'The IMF Crisis, 1976: Transcript' Gresham College, Oxford

Bolton
(2019) 'Student Loan Statistics' House of Commons Library Briefing Paper 1079

Booth, C.
(1892) 'Life and Labour of the People in London' MacMillan and Co.

Booth, C.
(1904) 'Life and Labour of the People in London' MacMillan and Co.

Bosanquet, S. R.
(1841) 'The Rights of the Poor and Christian Alms Giving Vindicated'

Boulter, Thorpe, Harrison and Allen
(2005) 'Road vehicle non-exhaust particulate matter: final report on emission modelling' TRL Limited

Bourquin and Waters
(2019) 'The effect of taxes and benefits on UK inequality' The Institute for Fiscal Studies Briefing Note No 249

Bourquin, Cribb, Waters and Xu
(2019) 'Living standards, poverty and inequality in the UK: 2019' The Institute for Fiscal Studies ISBN: 978-1-912-80527-3

Bowley, Professor Sir A. L.
(1900) 'Wages in the United Kingdom in the Nineteenth Century' Cambridge University Press

Bowley, Professor Sir A. L.
(1920) 'The Change in the distribution of National Income 1880-1913' Clarenden Press (Oxford)

Bowley, Professor Sir A. L.
(1937) 'Wages and Income in the United Kingdom Since 1860' Cambridge University Press ISBN: 978-1-316-50960-9

Boyer, Professor G. R.
(2019) 'The Winding Road to the Welfare State - Economic Insecurity & Social Welfare Policy in Britain' Princeton University Press ISBN: 978-0-691-17873-8

Boyer, Professor G. R. and Hatton, Professor T. J.
(1994) 'Regional Labour Market Integration in England and Wales, 1850-1913 (from Labour Market Evolution)' Routledge ISBN: 978-0-415-10865-2

Boyer, Professor G. R. and Hatton, Professor T. J.
(2002) 'New Estimates of British Unemployment, 1870-1913' Cambridge University Press DOI: 10.1017/S0022050702001031

Bradshaw, Professor J.	(2001) 'Methodologies to Measure Poverty: More Than One is Best!' University of York
Brewer, Goodman and Leicester	(2006) 'Household spending in Britain What can it teach us about poverty?' Joseph Rowntree Foundation ISBN: 978-1-861-34855-5
Brewer, Sibieta and Wren-Lewis	(2008) 'Racing away? Income inequality and the evolution of high incomes' The Institute for Fiscal Studies Briefing Note No 76
Broadberry, Professor S. N. et al.	(2015) 'British Economic Growth, 1270-1870' Cambridge University Press ISBN: 978-1-107-67649-7
Broadberry, Professor S. N. and Burhop, Professor C.	(2009) 'Real wages and labour productivity in Britain and Germany, 1871-1938: a unified approach to the international comparison of living standards' Max Planck Society DOI: 10.1017/S0022050710000331
Broadberry, Professor S. N. et al.	(2011) 'British Economic Growth and the Business Cycle 1700-1850' Broadberry et al. AnnualGDP10a
Broadberry, Professor S. N. et al.	(2011) 'British Economic Growth, 1270-1870: An Output Based Approach' Broadberry et al. BritishGDPLongRun16a.docx
Broadberry, Professor S. N. et al.	(2011) 'The Sectoral Distribution of the Labour Force and Labour Productivity of Britain, 1381-1951' Broadberry et al. SectoralSharesGB10b
Brundage, Professor A.	(2002) 'The English Poor Laws, 1700-1930' Palgrave Macmillan ISBN: 978-0-333-68271-8
BSA	(2014) 'Extract from BSA Yearbook 2013/14 - Interest Rates' Building Societies Association
Bunn and Rostom	(2014) 'Household debt and spending' Bank of England BofE Quarterly Bulletin
Burkhauser, Professor R. V. et al.	(2018) 'Top incomes and inequality in the UK: reconciling estimates from household survey and tax return data' Oxford University Press DOI: 10.1093/oep/gpx041
Burrell, Older, Watmough, Ripley and Hopkins	(2018/2020) 'The financial lives of consumers across the UK' Financial Conduct Authority
Carrington and Madsen	(2010) 'House Prices, Credit and Willingness to Lend' Monash University JEL: E44; E51
Chadwick, D.	(1849) 'Poor Rates Principle of Rating Letter to the Mayor of Salford'
Chadwick, D.	(1860) 'On the Rate of Wages in Manchester and Salford, and the Manufacturing Districts of Lancashire, 1839-59' Wiley DOI: 10.2307/2338478
Chalmers, G.	(1782/1804) 'An Estimate of the Comparative Strength of Great Britain'
Chapman, L. (revised)	(1977/1988) 'Roget's International Thesaurus - Fourth Edition' Harper Collins ISBN: 978-0-004-33176-1
Clark, Professor G.	(1999) 'Housing Rents, Housing Quality, and Living Standards in England and Wales, 1640-1909' University of California Davis
Clark, Professor G.	(2001) 'Farm Wages and Living Standards in the Industrial Revolution England, 1670-1850' University of California Davis
Clark, Professor G.	(2001) 'Land Rental Values and the Agrarian Economy - England and Wales 1500-1912' University of California Davis

Clark, Professor G.   (2002) 'The Agricultural Revolution and the Industrial Revolution, 1500-1912' University of California Davis

Clark, Professor G.   (2003) 'The Price History of English Agriculture, 1209-1914' University of California Davis

Clark, Professor G.   (2005) 'The Condition of the Working Class in England, 1209–2004' The University of Chicago Press DOI: 10.1086/498123

Clark, Professor G.   (2007) 'The Long March of History Farm Labourers Wages in England, 1208-1850' University of California Davis

Clark, Professor G.   (2011) 'Average Earnings and Retail Prices, UK, 1209-2010' University of California Davis

Clark, Professor G.   (2014) 'The Industrial Revolution' University of California Davis

Clark, Professor G.   (2018) 'Average Earnings and Retail Prices, UK, 1209-2017' University of California Davis

Clark, Professor G.   (2020) 'What Were British Earnings and Prices Then? A Question-and-Answer Guide' MeasuringWorth

Cobbett, W.   (1830/2001) 'Rural Rides' Penguin Classics ISBN: 978-0-140-43579-4

Colquhoun, P.   (1806) 'A Treatise on Indigence'

Colquhoun, P.   (1815) 'Treatise on the Wealth, Power and Resources of the British Empire'

Corlett, A. et al.   (2019) 'The Living Standards Audit 2019' Resolution Foundation

Corlett, A. and Judge, L.   (2017) 'HOME AFFRONT: Housing across the generations' Resolution Foundation

Coulson, R. L.   (2017) 'Clarifying Income Distribution' Policy Exchange ID report mon-2347

Crafts, Professor N. F. R.   (1985) 'British Economic Growth during the Industrial Revolution' Oxford University Press ISBN: 978-0-198-73067-5

Crafts, Professor N. F. R.   (1995) 'Recent research on the national accounts of the UK, 1700–1939' Routledge DOI: 10.1080/03585522.1995.10415893

Crafts, Professor N. F. R.   (1997) 'Some Dimensions of the Quality of Life during the British Industrial Revolution' London School of Economics ISBN: 978-0-85328-387-7

Crafts, Professor N. F. R.   (2020) 'Slow Real Wage Growth during the Industrial Revolution: Productivity Paradox or Pro-Rich Growth?' CAGE Working paper no. 474

Crafts, Professor N. F. R. and Harley, Professor C. K.   (1992) 'Output Growth and the British Industrial Revolution: A Restatement of the Crafts-Harley View' Wiley DOI: 10.2307/2597415

Crafts, Professor N. F. R. and Harley, Professor C. K.   (2002) 'Precocious British Industrialization: A General Equilibrium Perspective (from British Exceptionalism)' Cambridge University Press ISBN: 978-0-511-52383-0

Crafts, Professor N. F. R. and Mills, Professor T. C.   (2017) 'Six centuries of British economic growth: a time-series perspective' Oxford University Press DOI: 10.1093/ereh/hew020

Crafts, Professor N. F. R. and Mills, Professor T. C.   (2020) 'The Race between Population and Technology: Real Wages in the First Industrial Revolution' University of Warwick ISSN: 2059-4283

Crafts, Professor N. F. R., Gazeley and Newell (Ed.)	(2007) 'Work and Pay in Twentieth-Century Britain' Oxford University Press ISBN: 978-0-199-21266-8
Cribb, J. et al.	(2017) 'Living standards, poverty and inequality in the UK: 2017' Institute for Fiscal Studies ISBN: 978-1-911102-56-4
Darton, D. and Streilitz, J. (Ed.)	(2003) 'Tackling UK poverty and disadvantage in the twenty-first century' Joseph Rowntree Foundation ISBN: 978-1-85935-090-9
Davenant, C.	(1695) 'An Essay of the Ways and Means of Supplying the War'
Davies, Rev. D.	(1795) 'The Case of Labourers in Husbandry, Stated and Considered'
Deane, Professor P. M.	(1979) 'The First Industrial Revolution' Cambridge University Press ISBN: 978-0-521-29609-0
Deane, Professor P. M. and Cole, Professor W. A.	(1962/1969) 'British Economic Growth 1688-1959 (Second Edition)' Cambridge University Press 978-0-521-09569-7
DEFRA	(2019) 'Defra National Statistics Release: Air quality statistics in the UK 1987 to 2018' DEFRA
DEFRA	(2020) 'Air Pollution in the UK 2019' DEFRA
DEFRA	(2020) 'Air Pollution in the UK 2019: Compliance Assessment Summary' DEFRA
DEFRA	(2022) 'Air quality statistics in the UK - https://www.gov.uk/government/statistics/air-quality-statistics' DEFRA
Department of Employment	(1978) 'British Labour Statistics, Year Book 1976' Her Majesty's Stationery Office SBN 11 360695 8
Department of Employment and Productivity	(1971) 'British Labour Statistics, Historical Abstract 1886-1968' Her Majesty's Stationery Office
Devine	(2020) 'Poverty in the UK: Statistics' House of Commons Library Briefing Paper 7096
Devine	(2021) 'Income inequality in the UK' House of Commons Library Briefing Paper 7484
Devlin, S.	(2016) 'Agricultural labour in the UK' Food Research Collaboration ISBN: 978-1-903-95717-2
Dorling, D. et al.	(2007) 'Poverty, wealth and place in Britain, 1968 to 2005' Joseph Rowntree Foundation ISBN: 978-1-86134-995-8
Eden, Sir F. M. (Bart.)	(1797) 'The State of the Poor, or An History of the Labouring Classes in England (Three volumes)'
Emmerson and Leicester	(2002) 'A survey of the UK benefit system' The Institute for Fiscal Studies Briefing Note No 13
Engels, F.	(1845/1969) 'The Conditions of the Working Class in England - From Personal Observations and Authentic Sources' Panther Books Limited ISBN: 978-0-586-02880-3
English Housing Survey	(2020) 'English Housing Survey: Headline Report, 2019-20' Ministry of Housing, Communities and Local Government
Favara and Imbs	(2012) 'Credit Supply and the Price of Housing' HEC Lausanne
Feinstein, Professor C. H.	(1972) 'National Income Expenditure and Output of the United Kingdom 1855-1965' Cambridge University Press ISBN: 978-0-521-07230-1

Feinstein, Professor C. H.	(1988) 'The Rise and Fall of the Williamson Curve' Cambridge University Press DOI: 10.1017/S0022050700005969
Feinstein, Professor C. H.	(1990) 'New estimates of average earnings in the United Kingdom, 1880-1913' Wiley DOI: 10.1111/j.1468-0289.1990.tb00547.x
Feinstein, Professor C. H.	(1995) 'Changes in nominal wages, the cost of living and real wages in the United Kingdom over two centuries' Edward Elgar Publishing ISBN: 978-1-85278-971-9
Feinstein, Professor C. H.	(1996) 'Conjectures and Contrivances - Economic Growth and the Standard of Living in Britain during the Industrial Revolution' Oxford University Press Pubs. Id. 1167895
Feinstein, Professor C. H.	(1998) 'Pessimism Perpetuated Real Wages & Standard of Living in Britain during & after the Industrial Revolution' Cambridge University Press DOI: 10.1017/S0022050700021100
Ferragina, E. , Tomlinson, M. and Walker, R.	(2013) 'Poverty, Participation And Choice, The Legacy Of Peter Townsend' Joseph Rowntree Foundation ISBN: 978-1-85935-976-1
Fitzpatrick, S. et al.	(2016) 'Destitution in the UK' Joseph Rowntree Foundation ISBN: 978-1-91078-356-6
Fitzpatrick, S. et al.	(2018) 'Destitution in the UK 2018' Joseph Rowntree Foundation ISBN 978-1-911581-35-2
Floud, Professor Sir R., Humphries and Johnson (Ed.)	(2014) 'The Cambridge Economic History of Modern Britain Volume I, 1700-1870' Cambridge University Press ISBN: 978-1-107-63143-4
Floud, Professor Sir R., Humphries and Johnson (Ed.)	(2014) 'The Cambridge Economic History of Modern Britain Volume II, 1870 to the Present' Cambridge University Press ISBN: 978-1-107-68673-1
Floud, Professor Sir R., Wachter and Gregory	(1990) 'Height, health and history - Nutritional status in the United Kingdom, 1750-1980' Cambridge University Press ISBN: 978-0-521-02998-8
Foreman-Peck, Professor J. (Ed.)	(1991) 'New perspectives on the late Victorian economy - Essays in quantitative economic history, 1860-1914' Cambridge University Press ISBN: 978-0-521-89085-3
Freeman, M. D.	(1999) 'Social Investigation in Rural England, 1870-1914' Mark David Freeman PhD Thesis
Freud, Baron D.	(2021) 'Clashing Agendas - Inside the Welfare Trap' Nine Elms Books Limited ISBN: 978-1-910-53352-9
Gazeley, Professor I.	(1989) 'The Cost of Living for Urban Workers in late Victorian and Edwardian Britain' Wiley DOI: 10.1111/j.1468-0289.1989.tb00494.x
Gazeley, Professor I. and Newell, Professor A.	(2007) 'Poverty in Britain in 1904' University of Sussex PRUS Working Paper no. 38
Gazeley, Professor I. and Newell, Professor A.	(2009) 'No Place to Live, Urban Overcrowding in Edwardian Britain' IZA Discussion Paper 4209
Gazeley, Professor I. and Newell, Professor A.	(2009) 'The End of Destitution' IZA Discussion Paper 4295
Gazeley, Professor I. and Newell, Professor A.	(2011) 'The end of destitution: evidence from urban British working households 1904–37' Oxford University Press DOI: 10.1093/oep/gpr032

Gazeley, Professor I. and Verdon, Professor N.	(2014) 'The first poverty line? Davies and Eden's investigation of rural poverty in late 18th century England' Science Direct DOI: 10.1016/j.eeh.2012.09.001
Gazeley, Professor I. et al.	(2017) 'The poor and the poorest, 50 years on: evidence from British Household Expenditure surveys of the 1950s and 1960s' Wiley DOI: 10.1111/rssa.12202
Gazeley, Professor I. et al.	(2017) 'What Really Happened to British Inequality in the Early 20th Century? Evidence from National Household Expenditure Surveys 1890-1961' IZA DP No. 11071
Gazeley, Professor I.	(2003) 'Poverty in Britain, 1900-1965' Palgrave Macmillan ISBN: 979-0-333-71619-1
Giles, C. and Webb, S	(1993) 'Poverty Statistics: a Guide for the Perplexed' Institute for Fiscal Studies ISBN: 978-1-873357-24-9
Gillie, A.	(1996) 'The origin of the poverty line' Wiley DOI: 10.2307/2597970
Gillie, A.	(2008) 'Identifying the Poor in the 1870s and 1880s' Wiley DOI: 10.1111/j.1468-0289.2007.00395.x
Glennerster H. et al.	(2004) 'One hundred years of poverty and policy' Joseph Rowntree Foundation ISBN: 978-1-85935-222-7
Gordon, D. and Pantazis, C	(1997) 'Breadline Britain in the 1990s' Routledge DOI: 10.4324/9780429460173
Grannum, C	(2006) 'Policy briefing: Home ownership' Shelter ISBN: 978-1-903595-63-0
Grant and Williams - Kantar Public	(2017) 'The FCA's Financial Lives Survey 2017 - Technical Report' Kantar Public
Gregory, I. N., Dorling, D. and Southall, H. R.	(2001) 'A century of inequality in England and Wales using standardized geographical units' Royal Geographical society DOI: 10.1111/1475-4762.00033
Gregory, Mclaughlin, Mullender and Sundararajah	(2016) 'New solutions to air pollution challenges in the UK' Imperial College London
Griffin, E.	(2018) 'Diets, Hunger and Living Standards During the British Industrial Revolution' Oxford University Press DOI: 10.1093/pastj/gtx061
Grigoratos and Martini	(2014) 'Non-exhaust traffic related emissions. Brake and tyre wear PM' EU Commission - JRC Report EUR 26648 EN
Harari	(2018) 'Household debt: statistics and impact on economy' House of Commons Library Briefing Paper 7584
Harley, Professor C. K.	(1982) 'British Industrialization Before 1841: Evidence of Slower Growth During the Industrial Revolution' Cambridge University Press DOI: 10.1017/S0022050700027431
Harley, Professor C. K.	(2019) 'The Industrial Revolution in General Equilibrium' University of Oxford Working Paper 170
Harley, Professor C. K. and Crafts, Professor N. F. R.	(2000) 'Simulating the Two Views of the British Industrial Revolution' Cambridge University Press ISSN: 0022-0507
Hatton, Professor T. J., Bailey, R. E.	(2000) 'Seebohm Rowntree and the post-war poverty puzzle' Wiley DOI: 10.1111/1468-0289.00169

Hatton, Professor T. J., Boyer and Bailey	(1994) 'The union wage effect in late nineteenth century Britain' Wiley DOI: 10.2307/2555032
Hatton, Professor T. J., Boyer and Bailey	(2005) 'Unemployment and the UK Labour Market Before, During and After the Golden Age' Cambridge University Press DOI: 10.1017/S1361491604001376
Hick, Dr. R.	(2013) 'On 'Consistent' Poverty' London School of Economics CASE/167
Hicks and Allen	(1999) 'A Century of Change: Trends in UK statistics since 1900' House of Commons Library ISSN: 1368-8456
Hills, Ryland (BofE) and Dimsdale (Oxford)	(2010) 'The UK recession in context — what do three centuries of data tell us?' Bank of England BofE Research and analysis
Hinde, Professor A.	(2003) 'England's Population - A History Since the Domesday Survey' Hodder Education ISBN: 978-0-340-78190-8
HM Treasury	(2019) 'Public Expenditure Statistical Analyses 2019' HM Treasury CP 143
HM Treasury	(2020) 'Public Expenditure Statistical Analyses 2020' HM Treasury CP 276
HM Treasury	(2021) 'Public Expenditure Statistical Analyses 2021' HM Treasury CP 507
Hobsbawm, Professor E. J. E. and George Rudé	(1969) 'Captain Swing' Penguin University Books ISBN: 978-0-140-60013-2
Holgate CBE, Professor S. (Working Party Chair) et al.	(2016) 'Every breath we take: The lifelong impact of air pollution. Report of a working party' Royal College of Physicians ISBN: 978-1-86016-568-9
Holmans, Dr. A.	(2005) 'Historical Statistics of Housing in Britain' University of Cambridge ISBN: 978-1-86190-218-2
Holmans, Dr. A.	(2014) 'Housing need and effective demand in England: A look at "the bigger picture"' University of Cambridge
Holmans, Dr. A.	(2014) 'new estimates of housing demand and need in england, 2011 to 2031' Town & Country Planning Tomorrow Series Paper 16
Holmes, G. S.	(1977) 'King and the Social Structure of Pre-Industrial England' Cambridge University Press DOI: 10.2307/3679187
Hood and Keiller	(2016) 'A survey of the UK benefit system' The Institute for Fiscal Studies Briefing Note No 13
Hopkins et al.	(2018) 'Financial Lives Survey 2017 - Weighted Data Tables User Guide' Financial Conduct Authority
Horrell, Professor S.	(1996) 'Home Demand and British Industrialisation' Cambridge University Press DOI: 10.1017/S0022050700016946
Horrell, S., Humphries, J. and Weisdorf, J.	(2019) 'Family standards of living over the long run, England 1280-1850' University of Warwick Working Paper 419
Howard, Beevers and Dajnak	(2015) 'UP IN THE AIR How to Solve London's Air Quality Crisis: Part 2' Capital City Foundation
Howard, R.	(2015) 'UP IN THE AIR How to Solve London's Air Quality Crisis: Part 1' Capital City Foundation

Hume, Professor R. D.	(2015) 'The Value of Money in Eighteenth-Century England: Incomes, Prices, Buying Power— and Some Problems in Cultural Economics' Henry E. Huntington Library and Art Gallery DOI: 10.1525/hlq.2014.77.4.373
Humphries, Professor J.	(2012) 'Childhood and child labour in the British industrial revolution' Wiley DOI: 10.1111/j.1468-0289.2012.00651.x
Inglis, B.	(1971) 'Poverty and the Industrial Revolution' Panther Books Limited ISBN: 978-0-586-03792-8
Jefferys, J. B. and Walters D.	(1952) 'National Income and Expenditure of the United Kingdom, 1870-1952' Wiley DOI: 10.1111/j.1475-4991.1955.tb01075.x
Jenkins, Professor S. P.	(1999) 'Trends in the UK Income Distribution' Institute for Social and Economic Research
Jenkins, Professor S. P. and Micklewright, Professor J.	(2007) 'New Directions in the Analysis of Inequality and Poverty' Institute for Social and Economic Research ISER Working Paper 2007-11
Jin, W. et al.	(2011) 'Poverty and Inequality in the UK: 2011' Institute for Fiscal Studies ISBN: 978-1-903274-84-2
Johnson, S.	(1755/1758/1818) 'A Dictionary of the English Language'
Jones, F. et al.	(2008) 'The distribution of household income 1977 to 2006/07' Office for National Statistics Economic & Labour Market Review, Vol 2, No 12, pp. 18-31
Jones, F. et al.	(2009) 'The redistribution of household income 1977 to 2006/07' Office for National Statistics Economic & Labour Market Review, Vol. 3, No 1, pp. 31-43
Joyce and Xu	(2019) 'Inequalities in the twenty-first century, Introducing the IFS Deaton Review' The Institute for Fiscal Studies ISBN: 978-1-912-80521-1
Joyce, Mitchell and Norris Keiller	(2017) 'The cost of housing for low-income renters' Institute for Fiscal Studies ISBN: 978-1-911102-66-3
Justiniano, Primiceri, and Tambalotti	(2017) 'Credit Supply and the Housing Boom' Federal Reserve Bank etc. css6-7
Keep	(2020) 'The budget deficit: a short guide' House of Commons Library Briefing Paper 06167
Kelly, M. and O'Grada, C.	(2016) 'Adam Smith, Watch Prices, and the Industrial Revolution' Oxford University Press DOI: 10.1093/qje/qjw026
Kelly, M., O'Grada, C. and Mokyr, J.	(2013) 'Precocious Albion: a New Interpretation of the British Industrial Revolution' University College Dublin WP13/11
Kennedy	(2004) 'Poverty: Measures and Targets' House of Commons Library RP04-23
Kennedy, L. and Solar, P. M.	(2012) 'Markets and Price Fluctuations in England and Ireland, 1785-1913' Taylor Francis ISBN: 978-1-315-85237-9
Keohane and Broughton	(2013) 'The Politics of Housing' National Housing Federation
Kitson, Professor M. and Michie OBE, Professor J.	(2014) 'The De-industrial Revolution - The Rise and Fall of UK Manufacturing, 1870-2010' University of Cambridge Working Paper No. 459
Knowles, J. (Ed.)	(1888) 'The Nineteenth Century. A Monthly Review. Volume XXIII' Keegan Paul

Kyd, James G. (Ed.)	(1952) 'Scottish Population Statistics - Including Webster's Analysis of Population 1755' University of Edinburgh
Laybourn-Langton, Quilter-Pinner and Ho	(2016) 'LETHAL & ILLEGAL Solving London's Air Pollution Crisis' IPPR
Lindert, Professor P. H.	(1986) 'Unequal English Wealth since 1670' The University of Chicago Press DOI: 10.1086/261427
Lindert, Professor P. H.	(1998) 'Three Centuries Of Inequality In Britain And America' University of California Davis Working Paper Series 97-09
Lindert, Professor P. H.	(2000) 'When did inequality rise in Britain and America?' Elsevier Science Inc. DOI: 10.1016/S0926-6437(99)00012-8
Lindert, Professor P. H. and Williamson, Professor J. G.	(1982) 'Revising England's Social Tables 1688-1812' Academic Press, Inc. DOI: 10.1016/0014-4983(82)90009-2
Lindert, Professor P. H. and Williamson, Professor J. G.	(1983) 'English Workers' Living Standards During the Industrial Revolution' Wiley DOI: 10.2307/2598895
Lindert, Professor P. H. and Williamson, Professor J. G.	(1983) 'Reinterpreting Britain's Social Tables' Academic Press, Inc. DOI: 10.1016/0014-4983(83)90044-X
Long et al. (Shelter commissioners)	(2018) 'A vision for social housing' Shelter
Lupton et al.	(2009) 'Growing up in social housing in Britain' Joseph Rowntree Foundation
Lyle, M. A.	(2007) 'Regional agricultural wage variations in early nineteenth-century England' British Agricultural History Society The Agricultural History Review, Vol. 55, No. 1 (2007), pp. 95-106
Lyons, Murphy, Snelling and Green	(2017) 'What More Can Be Done To Build The Homes We Need?' IPPR
Malthus, Rev. T. R.	(1798) 'An Essay on the Principle of Population' Oxford University Press ISBN: 978-0-192-84747-8
Marner, Dr. B.	(2016) 'Deriving Background Concentrations of NOx and NO2' Air Quality Consultants
Marner, Dr. B.	(2016) 'Emissions of Nitrogen Oxides from Modern Diesel Vehicles' Air Quality Consultants
Massie, J.	(1756) 'Calculations of Taxes for a Family of Each Rank, Degree or Class: for One Year'
Massie, J.	(1758) 'A Plan for the Establishment of Charity Houses'
Mathias, P.	(1957) 'The Social Structure in the Eighteenth Century: A Calculation by Joseph Massie' Wiley DOI: 10.2307/2600060
Mayhew, H.	(1851/1987) 'London Labour and the London Poor' Wordsworth Classics ISBN: 978-1-840-22619-5
Mayor of London (GLA)	(2019) 'PM2.5 in London: Roadmap to meeting World Health Organization guidelines by 2030' Greater London Authority
McCloskey, Professor D. N.	(2014) 'Measured, unmeasured, mismeasured, and unjustified pessimism: a review essay of Thomas Piketty's Capital in the twenty-first century' EJPE Erasmus Journal for Philosophy and Economics, Volume 7, Issue 2, Autumn 2014, pp. 73-115

McDonald and Whitehead	(2015) 'new estimates of housing demand and need in England, 2012 to 2037' Town & Country Planning Tomorrow Series Paper 17
McGuinness and Harari	(2019) 'Income inequality in the UK' House of Commons Library Briefing Paper 7484
McLeay, Radia and Thomas	(2014) 'Money creation in the modern economy' Bank of England BofE Quarterly Bulletin
McLeay, Radia and Thomas	(2014) 'Money in the modern economy: an introduction' Bank of England BofE Quarterly Bulletin
Mearns, Rev. A.	(1883) 'The Bitter Cry of Outcast London'
Meen, Professor G.	(2018) 'How should housing affordability be measured?' UK Collaborative Centre for Housing Evidence R2018_02_01
Miles and Monro	(2019) 'UK house prices and three decades of decline in the risk free real interest rate' Bank of England Staff Working Paper No. 837
Ministry of Labour	(1940) 'The Ministry of Labour Gazette' Her Majesty's Stationery Office Vol. 48, No. 12
Ministry of Labour	(1941) 'The Ministry of Labour Gazette' Her Majesty's Stationery Office Vol. 49, No. 1
Ministry of Labour	(1941) 'The Ministry of Labour Gazette' Her Majesty's Stationery Office Vol. 49, No. 2
Mitchell, B. R.	(1988) 'British Historical Statistics' Cambridge University Press ISBN: 978-1-107-40244-7
Mitchell, B. R. and Deane, Professor P. M.	(1962) 'Abstract of Historical Statistics' Cambridge University Press ISBN: 978-0-521-05738-8
Mokyr, Professor J. (Ed.)	(1999) 'The British Industrial Revolution - An Economic Perspective' Westview Press ISBN: 978-8-813-33389-2
Monks, Professor P. et al.	(2019) 'Non-Exhaust Emissions from Road Traffic' Air Quality Expert Group PB14581
Mulheirn, I.	(2019) 'Tackling the UK housing crisis: is supply the answer?' UK Collaborative Centre for Housing Evidence
Neild, W.	(1842) 'Comparative Statement of the Income and Expenditure of Certain Families of the Working Class in Manchester and Dukinfield, in the Years 1836 and 1841' Wiley DOI: 10.2307/2337693
Nesteling, H. P. H.	(1993) 'English population statistics for the first half of the Nineteenth Century : a new answer to old questions' Societe de Demographie Historique DOI: 10.3406/adh.1993.1840
Niemietz, Dr. K.	(2011) 'A New Understanding of Poverty - Poverty Measurement and Policy Implications' The Institute of Economic Affairs ISBN: 978-0-255-36638-0
Niemietz, Dr. K.	(2012) 'Redefining the Poverty Debate - Why a War on Markets is No Substitute for a War on Poverty' The Institute of Economic Affairs ISBN: 978-0-255-36652-6
O'Donoghue (ONS), Goulding (ONS) & Allen (HofC Lib.)	(2004) 'Consumer Price Inflation since 1750' Office for National Statistics Economic Trend 604

Officer, Professor L. H.	(2007) 'What Were the U.K. Earnings Rate and Consumer Price Index Then? A Data Study' University of Illinois at Chicago
Officer, Professor L. H.	(2007) 'What Were the UK Earnings and Prices Then? A Question-and-Answer Guide' MeasuringWorth
Onions, C. T. (Ed.), Little, Fowler and Coulson	(1932/1983) 'The Shorter Oxford English Dictionary on Historical Principles (2 volumes)' Guild Publishing CN 5647
ONS	(2014) 'UK Wages Over the Past Four Decades' Office for National Statistics
ONS	(2021) 'A guide to sources of data on income and earnings' Office for National Statistics
ONS	(2021) 'Average household income, UK: financial year 2020' Office for National Statistics
Orr, J. et al.	(2021) 'Regional differences in short stature in England between 2006 and 2019: A cross-sectional analysis from the National Child Measurement Programme' PLOS Medicine DOI: 10.1371/journal.pmed.1003760
Ortiz-Ospina, Esteban and Hannah Ritchie	(2018) 'What's happening to life expectancy in Britain?' Our World in Data
Palma, N.	(2016) 'Book review of Broadberry, Campbell, Klein, Overton, and van Leeuwen, British Economic Growth, 1270-1870' Maddison-Project Working Paper WP-5
Patriquin, Professor L.	(2007) 'Agrarian Capitalism and Poor Relief in England, 1500–1860' Palgrave Macmillan ISBN: 978-0-230-59138-7
Perkin, Professor H.	(1969/2002) 'The Origins of Modern English Society' Routledge ISBN: 978-0-415-29880-2
Perkin, Professor H.	(1989/2002) 'The Rise of the Professional Society - England Since 1880' Routledge ISBN: 978-0-415-30178-5
Perkin, Professor H.	(1996) 'The Third Revolution - Professional Elites in the Modern World' Routledge ISBN: 978-0-415-14338-1
Phaup, H.	(2015) 'Historical sources of mortgage interest rate statistics' Bank of England
Piddington, Nicol, Garrett and Custard	(2020) 'The Housing Stock of The United Kingdom' BRE Trust PEN02 20
Pinker, Professor S. A.	(2018) 'Enlightenment Now' Allen Lane ISBN: 978-0-241-00431-9
Platt, L.	(2003) 'Putting Childhood Poverty on the Agenda: The Relationship Between Research and Policy in Britain 1800-1950' Young Lives
Polanyi, K.	(1944/2001) 'The Great Transformation: The Political and Economic Origins of Our Time' Beacon Press ISBN: 978-0-8070-5643-x
Pope and Waters	(2016) 'A survey of the UK tax system' The Institute for Fiscal Studies Briefing Note No 09
Raleigh, Veena (Senior Fellow, King's Fund)	(2021) 'What is happening to life expectancy in England' The Kings Fund
Rashid, T. et al.	(2021) 'Life expectancy and risk of death in 6791 communities in England from 2002 to 2019' The Lancet DOI: 10.1016/S2468-2667(21)00205-X

Ravallion, Professor M.   (2013) 'The Idea of Anti-Poverty Policy' National Bureau of Economic Research Working Paper 19210

Ravallion, Professor M.   (2016) 'The Economics of Poverty - History, Measurement and Policy' Oxford University Press ISBN: 978-0-190-21276-6

Ravallion, Professor M.   (2020) 'On the Origins of the Idea of Ending Poverty' National Bureau of Economic Research Working Paper 27808

Razzell, P. E.   (2016) 'Mortality, Marriage and Population Growth in England, 1550-1850' Caliban Books ISBN: 978-0-904573-19-0

Razzell, P. E.   (2018) 'Population Growth and the Increase of Socio-Economic Inequality in England, 1550-1850' Razzell, P.

Registrar General   (1904) 'Census of England and Wales, 1901, General Report with Appendices' Her Majesty's Stationery Office

Ridley, Dr. Viscount M. W.   (2011) 'The Rational Optimist' 4th Estate (Harper Collins) ISBN: 978-0-007-26712-5

Roantree and Shaw   (2017) 'What a difference a day makes: inequality and the tax and benefit system from a long-run perspective' Springer DOI: 10.1007/s10888-017-9362-x

Roser, Max   (2020) 'The Spanish flu (1918-20): The global impact of the largest influenza pandemic in history' Our World in Data

Rosling, Dr., H., Rosling and Ronnlund   (2018) 'Factfulness' Sceptre (Hodder & Stoughton) ISBN: 978-1-473-63746-7

Rowntree, B. Seebohm   (1901) 'Poverty: A Study of Town Life' MacMillan and Co. ISBN 978-1-86134-202-0

Samaras, Professor Z. et al.   (2013) 'Transport related Air Pollution and Health impacts – Integrated Methodologies for Assessing Particulate Matter' TRANSPHORM

Scott, Professor P. M. and Walker, Professor J. T.   (2014) 'Demonstrating Distinction at 'the Lowest Edge of the Black-coated Class': The Family Expenditures of Edwardian Railway Clerks' Henley Business School Discussion Paper Number: IBH-2014-04

Scott, Professor P. M. and Walker, Professor J. T.   (2020) 'The Comfortable, the Rich, and the Super-Rich. What Really Happened to Top British Incomes during the First Half of the Twentieth Century?' Cambridge University Press DOI: 10.1017/S0022050719000767

Scott, Professor P. M., Walker, J. T. and Miskell, P. M.   (2014) 'British Working-class Household Composition, Labour Supply and Commercial Leisure Participation during the 1930s' Henley Business School Discussion Paper Number: IBH-2014-03

Sen, Professor A. K.   (1982) 'Poor, Relatively Speaking' The Economic and Social Research Institute ISBN: 978-0-7070-0055-6

Shaw-Taylor, Dr. L.   (2009) 'The Occupational Structure of England 1750-1871 Some Preliminary Results' University of Cambridge

Shaw-Taylor, Dr. L. and Wrigley, E. A.   (2006) 'The Occupational Structure of England c.1750-1871: A Preliminary Report' University of Cambridge

Shaw-Taylor, Dr. L. et al.   (2010) 'The Occupational structure of England and Wales c.1817-1881' University of Cambridge

Shaw-Taylor, Dr. L. et al.   (2010) 'The Occupational structure of England c.1710 to c.1871 Work in progress' University of Cambridge

Smee, W. R.	(1846) 'THE INCOME TAX: Its Extension at the Present Rate Proposed to all Classes'
Snell, Professor K. D. M.	(1985) 'Annals of the Labouring Poor - Social Change in Agrarian England, 1660-1900' Cambridge University Press ISBN: 978-0-521-33558-4
Solomou, Professor S. and Ryland Thomas	(2019) 'Feinstein Fulfilled: Updated Estimates of UK GDP 1841-1920' ESCOE (NIESR) and ONS ISSN: 2631-3588
Spiegelhalter OBE, Professor Sir D. J.	(2017) 'Does air pollution kill 40,000 people each year in the UK?' Winton Centre
Spiegelhalter OBE, Professor Sir D. J.	(2019) 'The Art of Statistics - Learning from Data' Pelican (Penguin Books) ISBN: 978-0-241-25876-7
Starling, B. and Bradbury, D.	(2020) 'The Official History of Britain - Our story in numbers as told by the Office for National Statistics' Harper Collins ISBN: 978-0-008-41219-7
Stroud, P. (Chair)	(2019) 'Equivalisation In Poverty Measures: Can We Do Better?' Social Metrics Commission ISBN: 978-1-911125-52-5
The Intergenerational Commission	(2018) 'A New Generational Contract' Resolution Foundation ISBN: 978-1-999-72011-7
The Trussell Trust	(2019) 'The State of Hunger' The Trussell Trust
Thomas	(2015) 'Analysis of Long-run Historical Data at the Bank of England' Bank of England BofE Archival Worksop
Thompson et al.	(2012) 'Olympic Britain: Social and economic change since the 1908 and 1948 London Games' House of Commons Library
Thompson, E. P.	(1963) 'The Making of the English Working Class' Vintage Books ISBN: 978-0-394-70322-0
Timmers and Achten	(2016) 'Non-exhaust PM emissions from electric vehicles - 134 (2016) 10e17' Atmospheric Environment DOI: 10.1016/j.atmosenv.2016.03.017
Townsend, Professor P.	(1954) 'Measuring Poverty' Wiley DOI: 10.2307/587651
Townsend, Professor P.	(1966) 'Poverty, socialism and Labour in power' Fabian Society Fabian Tract 371
Townsend, Professor P.	(1979) 'Poverty in the United Kingdom' Penguin Books ISBN: 978-0-140-22139-8
Townsend, Professor P.	(2010) 'The meaning of poverty' Wiley DOI: 10.1111/j.1468-4446.2009.01241.x
Turner, C. and NHBC	(2015) 'Homes through the decades' NHBC Foundation ISBN: 978-0-9930691-3-0
Twigger, R.	(1999) 'Inflation: the Value of the Pound 1750-1998' House of Commons Library Research Paper 99/20
UK Statistics Authority	(2019) 'Statistics on air quality and emissions of air pollutants' UK Statistics Authority Assessment Report 344
Vamplew, W.	(1980) 'A Grain of Truth The Nineteenth-Century Corn Averages' British Agricultural History Society The Agricultural History Review, Vol. 28, No. 1 (1980), pp. 1-17 (17 pages)

van de Ven, Dr. J.	(2011) 'Expenditure and Disposable Income Trends of UK Households: Evidence from Micro-Data' National Institute of Economic and Social Research DOI: 10.1177/002795011121800105
Vanderlint, J.	(1734) 'Money Answers all Things'
Voth, H-J.	(2003) 'Living Standards During the Industrial Revolution: An Economist's Guide' American Economic Association DOI: 10.1257/000282803321947083
Watts, Fitzpatrick, Bramley and Watkins	(2014) 'Welfare Sanctions and Conditionality in the UK' Joseph Rowntree Foundation ISBN: 978-1-909-58646-8
Welshman, J.	(2006/2013) 'Underclass: A History of the Excluded Since 1880' Bloomsbury ISBN: 978-1-4725-0498-2
WHO	(2006) 'WHO Air quality guidelines for particulate matter, Ozone, Nitrogen Dioxide and Sulphur Dioxide' World Health Organisation
Williamson, Professor J. G.	(1984) 'Why Was British Growth So Slow During the Industrial Revolution' Cambridge University Press DOI: 10.1017/S0022050700032320
Williamson, Professor J. G.	(1985) 'Did British Capitalism Breed Inequality?' Routledge ISBN: 978-1-138-86489-4
Wilson	(2019) 'Under-occupying social housing: Housing Benefit entitlement' House of Commons Library Briefing Paper 06272
Wilson and Barton	(2018) 'Tackling the under-supply of housing in England' House of Commons Library Briefing Paper 07671
Wilson and Barton	(2020) 'Overcrowded housing (England)' House of Commons Library Briefing Paper 1013
Wilson Fox, A.	(1903) 'Agricultural Wages in England and Wales during the Last Fifty Years' Wiley DOI: 10.2307/2339234
Wilson, W	(2019) 'Stimulating housing supply - Government initiatives (England)' House of Commons Library Briefing Paper 06416
Wolff, J. et al.	(2015) 'A Philosophical Review of Poverty' Joseph Rowntree Foundation ISBN: 978-1-90958-659-8
Wrigley, Professor Sir E. A. and Dr. R. S. Schofield	(1982/1989) 'The Population History of England, 1541-1871, A reconstruction' Cambridge University Press ISBN: 978-0-521-35688-6
Wrigley, Professor Sir E. A. and Dr. R. S. Schofield	(1997) 'English Population History from Family Reconstitution, 1580-1837' Cambridge University Press ISBN: 978-0-521-59015-0
Zmolek, M. A.	(2019) 'The Dark World of Reverend Malthus' University of Nebraska Omaha ISSN: 2476-0269

Internet Data

Bank of England - "Millennium Database"	https://www.bankofengland.co.uk/statistics/research-datasets
BRE Trust - UK Housing Stock Report	https://files.bregroup.com/bretrust/The-Housing-Stock-of-the-United-Kingdom_Report_BRE-Trust.pdf
Building Societies Association - Mortgage interest rates	https://www.bsa.org.uk/BSA/files/f8/f86888ee-716c-4f95-9c63-1dfa26d86742.xlsx
Building Societies Association - Mortgages and housing	https://www.bsa.org.uk/statistics/mortgages-housing
Chartered Institute of Housing	https://www.ukhousingreview.org.uk/ukhr21/compendium.html
Christopher Chantrill - UK Public Revenue	https://ukpublicrevenue.co.uk/
Christopher Chantrill - UK Public Spending	https://ukpublicspending.co.uk/
Clark, Professor G. - Downloads	http://faculty.econ.ucdavis.edu/faculty/gclark/data.html
DEFRA - Air Pollution in the UK	https://uk-air.defra.gov.uk/library/annualreport/
DEFRA - Air Quality and Emissions Statistics	https://www.gov.uk/government/collections/air-quality-and-emissions-statistics
DEFRA - UK Air Information Resource - Data	https://uk-air.defra.gov.uk/data/
Department for Transport - Coronavirus transport use	https://www.gov.uk/government/statistics/transport-use-during-the-coronavirus-covid-19-pandemic
Department for Transport - Vehicle statistics	https://www.gov.uk/government/collections/vehicles-statistics
Department for Work and Pensions - Statistics	https://www.gov.uk/government/collections/dwp-statistical-summaries
Drax Electric Insights	https://electricinsights.co.uk/#/homepage?&_k=o6odgj
Economic Statistics Centre of Excellence	https://www.escoe.ac.uk
Economic Statistics Centre of Excellence - Documents	https://www.escoe.ac.uk/research/historical-data/etarticles/
Economic Statistics Centre of Excellence - Historical data	https://www.escoe.ac.uk/research/historical-data/
Halifax - House price data	https://www.halifax.co.uk/media-centre/house-price-index.html
HM Treasury - Country and regional analysis	https://www.gov.uk/government/collections/country-and-regional-analysis

HM Treasury - Public expenditure statistical analysis	https://www.gov.uk/government/collections/public-expenditure-statistical-analyses-pesa
HMRC - Survey of personal incomes	https://www.gov.uk/government/collections/personal-incomes-statistics
Human Mortality Database	https://www.mortality.org/
Institute for Fiscal Studies - Living standards, poverty and inequality in the UK	https://ifs.org.uk/tools_and_resources/incomes_in_uk
Lindert, Professor P. H. - Downloads	https://gpih.ucdavis.edu/files/
London Air Quality (Imperial College London) - Data	https://www.londonair.org.uk/london/asp/datadownload.asp
London Average Air Quality Levels (Kings College London)	https://data.london.gov.uk/dataset/london-average-air-quality-levels
London Congestion Zone - Camera captures	https://data.london.gov.uk/dataset/vehicles-entering-c-charge-zone-month
Measuring Worth	https://www.measuringworth.com/
Ministry of Housing, Communities and Local Government - English housing survey	https://www.gov.uk/government/collections/english-housing-survey
Ministry of Housing, Communities and Local Government - House building	https://www.gov.uk/government/statistical-data-sets/live-tables-on-house-building
Ministry of Housing, Communities and Local Government - Housing	https://www.gov.uk/government/statistical-data-sets/live-tables-on-dwelling-stock-including-vacants
National Atmospheric Emissions Inventory - Data	https://naei.beis.gov.uk/data/
National Infrastructure Commission - Historic Energy Dataset	https://nic.org.uk/data/all-data/historic-energy/
Nationwide - Housing historic data	https://www.nationwidehousepriceindex.co.uk/resources/
NHS - National child measurement programme	https://digital.nhs.uk/data-and-information/publications/statistical/national-child-measurement-programme
NHS - Workforce statistics	https://digital.nhs.uk/data-and-information/publications/statistical/nhs-workforce-statistics
NOMIS - Official census and labour market statistics	https://www.nomisweb.co.uk/
OECD - Housing prices	https://data.oecd.org/price/housing-prices.htm

Office for Budget Responsibility	https://obr.uk/
Office for Budget Responsibility - Data banks	https://obr.uk/data/
Office for Budget Responsibility - Welfare spending by age (Chart 3.2)	https://obr.uk/docs/dlm_uploads/Welfare-Trends-Report.pdf
Office for Budget Responsibility - Welfare spending by age (Removed)	https://obr.uk/forecasts-in-depth/brief-guides-and-explainers/an-obr-guide-to-welfare-spending/
Ofgem - Electricity prices	https://www.ofgem.gov.uk/data-portal/breakdown-electricity-bill
Ofgem - Energy bills explained	https://www.ofgem.gov.uk/publications-and-updates/infographic-bills-prices-and-profits
Ofgem - Gas prices	https://www.ofgem.gov.uk/data-portal/breakdown-gas-bill
ONS - Average equivalised household disposable income	https://www.ons.gov.uk/peoplepopulationandcommunity/personalandhouseholdfinances/expenditure/datasets/detailedhouseholdexpenditurebyequivaliseddisposableincomedecilegroupoecdmodifiedscaleuktable31e
ONS - Deaths by single year of age	https://www.ons.gov.uk/peoplepopulationandcommunity/birthsdeathsandmarriages/deaths/datasets/deathregistrationssummarytablesenglandandwalesdeathsbysingleyearofagetables
ONS - Deaths registered weekly in England and Wales, provisional	https://www.ons.gov.uk/peoplepopulationandcommunity/birthsdeathsandmarriages/deaths/datasets/weeklyprovisionalfiguresondeathsregisteredinenglandandwales
ONS - Environmental accounts	https://www.ons.gov.uk/economy/environmentalaccounts
ONS - GDP	https://www.ons.gov.uk/economy/grossdomesticproductgdp
ONS - Gross disposable household income	https://www.ons.gov.uk/economy/regionalaccounts/grossdisposablehouseholdincome
ONS - Health inequalities	https://www.ons.gov.uk/peoplepopulationandcommunity/healthandsocialcare/healthinequalities
ONS - House building	https://www.ons.gov.uk/peoplepopulationandcommunity/housing/datasets/ukhousebuildingpermanentdwellingsstartedandcompleted
ONS - Housing	https://www.ons.gov.uk/peoplepopulationandcommunity/housing/datasets/dwellingstockbytenureuk
ONS - Income and wealth	https://www.ons.gov.uk/peoplepopulationandcommunity/personalandhouseholdfinances/incomeandwealth
ONS - Inflation and price indices	https://www.ons.gov.uk/economy/inflationandpriceindices
ONS - Labour force survey, earnings and working hours	https://www.ons.gov.uk/employmentandlabourmarket/peopleinwork/earningsandworkinghours

ONS - Life expectancy	https://www.ons.gov.uk/peoplepopulationandcommunity/health andsocialcare/healthandlifeexpectancies/datasets/lifeexpectancy estimatesallagesuk
ONS - National balance sheet	https://www.ons.gov.uk/economy/nationalaccounts/uksectoracc ounts/datasets/thenationalbalancesheetestimates/current
ONS - National life tables	https://www.ons.gov.uk/peoplepopulationandcommunity/births deathsandmarriages/lifeexpectancies/datasets/nationallifetables unitedkingdomreferencetables
ONS - Percentage of households with durable goods	https://www.ons.gov.uk/file?uri=/peoplepopulationandcommuni ty/personalandhouseholdfinances/expenditure/datasets/percent ageofhouseholdswithdurablegoodsuktablea45/1970tofinancialye arending2018/a45201718rerun.xls
ONS - Population and migration	https://www.ons.gov.uk/peoplepopulationandcommunity/popul ationandmigration
ONS - Population estimates	https://www.ons.gov.uk/peoplepopulationandcommunity/popul ationandmigration/populationestimates
ONS - Population, Our population - Where are we?	https://www.ons.gov.uk/peoplepopulationandcommunity/popul ationandmigration/populationestimates/articles/ourpopulationw herearewehowdidwegetherewhereareswegoing/2020-03-27
ONS - Retail Prices Index: average price of selected food items: 1914 to 2004	https://www.ons.gov.uk/file?uri=/economy/inflationandpriceind ices/methodologies/consumerpricesindexcpiandretailpricesindex rpibasketofgoodsandservices/rpiaverageprices19142004tcm771 68515tcm77420253.xls
ONS - UK Families and households	https://www.ons.gov.uk/peoplepopulationandcommunity/births deathsandmarriages/families/datasets/familiesandhouseholdsfa miliesandhouseholds
ONS - Vital statistics, births, deaths and marriages	https://www.ons.gov.uk/peoplepopulationandcommunity/popul ationandmigration/populationestimates/datasets/vitalstatisticsp opulationandhealthreferencetables
ONS - Workbook 4 - Expenditure by Household Characteristics	https://www.ons.gov.uk/file?uri=/peoplepopulationandcommuni ty/personalandhouseholdfinances/expenditure/datasets/familys pendingworkbook4expenditurebyhouseholdcharacteristic/2020/ familyspendingworkbook4expenditurebyhouseholdcharacteristic s.xlsx
Our World in Data	https://ourworldindata.org/
Our World in Data - CO2 and GHG emissions	https://github.com/owid/co2-data
Our World in Data - Coronavirus pandemic (Covid-19)	https://ourworldindata.org/coronavirus
Our World in Data - Excess mortality during the Coronavirus pandemic (COVID-19)	https://ourworldindata.org/excess-mortality-covid
Our World in Data - Excess mortality P-scores	https://ourworldindata.org/grapher/excess-mortality-p-scores-average-baseline
Our World in Data - Life expectancy	https://ourworldindata.org/life-expectancy

Oxford Dictionary - Lexico	https://www.lexico.com/en
Peter Lindert - Data-garden	https://psychology.ucdavis.edu/people/fzlinder/peter-linderts-webpage/data-garden
Rashid et al (Imperial College) - Life expectancy and risk of death in 6791 communities in England	https://globalenvhealth.org/download/24423/
Renewable Energy Foundation	https://www.ref.org.uk
UK Data Service	https://beta.ukdataservice.ac.uk/
UK Government – Air Quality Standards Regulation 2010	https://www.legislation.gov.uk/uksi/2010/1001/made
UK Government - Coronavirus dashboard	https://coronavirus.data.gov.uk/
UK Government - Stat-Xplore	https://stat-xplore.dwp.gov.uk/webapi/jsf/login.xhtml
UK Government BEIS - Annual January prices of road fuels and petroleum products	https://www.gov.uk/government/statistical-data-sets/oil-and-petroleum-products-annual-statistics
UK Government BEIS - Crude oil and petroleum: production, imports and exports	https://www.gov.uk/government/statistical-data-sets/crude-oil-and-petroleum-production-imports-and-exports
UK Government BEIS - Digest of UK Energy Statistics (DUKES)	https://www.gov.uk/government/collections/digest-of-uk-energy-statistics-dukes
UK Government BEIS - Energy Consumption in the UK	https://www.gov.uk/government/statistics/energy-consumption-in-the-uk
UK Government BEIS - Historical coal data: coal production, availability and consumption	https://www.gov.uk/government/statistical-data-sets/historical-coal-data-coal-production-availability-and-consumption
UK Government BEIS - Historical electricity data	https://www.gov.uk/government/statistical-data-sets/historical-electricity-data
UK Government BEIS - Historical gas data: gas production and consumption and fuel input	https://www.gov.uk/government/statistical-data-sets/historical-gas-data-gas-production-and-consumption-and-fuel-input
Vision of Britain - Census	https://www.visionofbritain.org.uk/census/
Wages through history - A. Wilson Fox agricultural wages	https://historyofwages.blogspot.com/2011/02/agricultural-labourers-wages-1850-1914.html
World Bank - Life expectancy	https://data.worldbank.org/indicator/SP.DYN.LE00.IN

Worldometers - Covid-19   https://www.worldometers.info/coronavirus/
Coronavirus Pandemic

Index

Milton Keynes UK
Ingram Content Group UK Ltd.
UKHW022223180823
427047UK00001B/9